# Introduction to Parallel Programming

Traditionally computers have been machines that operate processes in parallel. Even the earliest computers were made from parts that worked together, collaboratively and simultaneously. Processors today consist of more than a billion transistors, many of which are active simultaneously while executing a program. In modern computer science, there exists no truly sequential computing system. While sequential programming can still be used due to the parallelization built into the compilers and the hardware, for most demanding problems, parallel programming is rapidly becoming essential. This is most evident in modern application domains like scientific computation, data science, machine intelligence, etc. As a result, parallel programming is increasingly being offered as an elective course in undergraduate computer science and engineering programmes. This book intends to introduce a beginner to the gamut of parallel programming and will be useful for undergraduate students of computer science and engineering. It should also be a handy reference for the practitioner.

**Subodh Kumar** is Professor in the Department of Computer Science and Engineering at the Indian Institute of Technology, Delhi. He has headed the High Performance Computing group of the institute, and taught several courses on computer graphics, data structures and algorithms, design practices in computer science, and parallel programming. His research interests include rendering algorithms, virtual reality, geometry processing, human machine interface, visualization, large scale parallel computation, and high performance computing.

# Introduction to Parallel Programming

Subodh Kumar

# CAMBRIDGE
## UNIVERSITY PRESS

Shaftesbury Road, Cambridge CB2 8EA, United Kingdom

One Liberty Plaza, 20th Floor, New York, NY 10006, USA

477 Williamstown Road, Port Melbourne, VIC 3207, Australia

314–321, 3rd Floor, Plot 3, Splendor Forum, Jasola District Centre, New Delhi – 110025, India

103 Penang Road, #05–06/07, Visioncrest Commercial, Singapore 238467

Cambridge University Press is part of Cambridge University Press & Assessment, a department of the University of Cambridge.

We share the University's mission to contribute to society through the pursuit of education, learning and research at the highest international levels of excellence.

www.cambridge.org
Information on this title: www.cambridge.org/9781009069533

First published 2022

*A catalogue record for this publication is available from the British Library*

*Library of Congress Cataloging-in-Publication data*
Names: Kumar, Subodh (Computer scientist), author.
Title: Introduction to parallel programming / Subodh Kumar.
Description: Cambridge, United Kingdom ; New York, NY, USA : Cambridge
    University Press, 2022. | Includes bibliographical references and index.
Identifiers: LCCN 2021061754 (print) | LCCN 2021061755 (ebook) |
    ISBN 9781009069533 (paperback) | ISBN 9781009071314 (ebook)
Subjects: LCSH: Parallel programming (Computer science) | BISAC: COMPUTERS / General
Classification: LCC QA76.642 .K86 2022 (print) | LCC QA76.642 (ebook) | DDC 005.2/75–dc23/eng/20220112
LC record available at https://lccn.loc.gov/2021061754
LC ebook record available at https://lccn.loc.gov/2021061755

ISBN    978-1-009-06953-3    Paperback

*To Smita and Avi*

# Contents

# Figures

# Introduction

Lessons in programming often start with a definition of the term *algorithm*. Webster's dictionary defines algorithm as "a step-by-step procedure for solving a problem." Not only does this definition lend itself naturally to an imperative programming style, but it often also leads to a focus on sequential programming. However, the truth is that program execution is hardly ever in a step-by-step fashion, even if it may sometimes appear to be so. This nonsequentiality can be due to multiple instructions being in flight simultaneously, that is, the instructions are in various stages of their executions at the same time. This is true even when a program is presented as a linear sequence of instructions, and its correctness depends on their execution in that exact sequence. This is also true when the program is "parallel" instead, that is, the order among instructions is not necessarily specified.

In this book, we focus on this parallel programming, where instructions are neither specified nor expected to be in a single sequence. Further, the execution of these programs is also in a parallel context, where potentially several thousand instructions, or even more, execute at any given time.

## Concurrency and Parallelism

Sometimes the terms "concurrent" and "parallel" are informally used interchangeably, but it is important to recognize the distinction. Parallelism may be defined as performing two activities at the same time. These activities may be related in some manner or not. Usually, these activities are not instantaneous: each takes a finite time. Two related activities are said to be concurrent if there is no predetermined order between them – they may or may not overlap in time when they do occur. We will see that in certain situations, concurrency is not desirable, and a relative order is imposed. When such an order is enforced on two activities, they clearly cannot be executed in parallel.

Although our focus in this book is on parallel programming, concurrency must often be managed in a parallel program, and we discuss practical aspects of concurrency as well.

## Why Study Parallel Programming

Natural processes are inherently parallel, whether they be molecular and nuclear behavior, weather and geological phenomena, or biological and genetic manifestation. By no means does that imply that their simulation and computation must be parallel. It should be possible to compute them in an artificial order. However, these computations can be highly complex. For example, nanosecond-long molecular dynamics simulation of barely a million atoms can take more than $10^{17}$ steps. Highly detailed week-long weather modeling requires even more orders of magnitude. Modern CPUs are barely able to complete a few billion sequential steps in a second. Many useful computations then would literally take a lifetime.

Concomitantly, computers are parallel. Indeed, even the earliest computers were made from parts that worked together, collaboratively and simultaneously. The earliest "programs" required many knobs to be turned together or in sequence to achieve the desired outcome. That has not changed: processors today consist of more than a billion transistors, many of which are active simultaneously while executing a program.

Indeed, one might rather ask: if all executions are parallel, why do we study sequential programming at all?

The human brain is sometimes described as a massive parallel computer. This expression is not surprising considering that the human brain comprises an estimated hundred billion neurons connected in a complex network. A large number of them can simultaneously fire, meaning they collect signals from other neurons and produce new signals. However, our ability to clearly understand or explain the logic embedded in this process is limited, and computer architecture of the day makes no attempt to mimic it. Indeed, even before the term "algorithm" came into usage, the proofs and procedures presented by the likes of Pythagoras and Aristotle were sequences of steps. That ostensibly remained the case with the Turing machine. One might hence conclude that even though we may actually think, reason, or solve in parallel, we are at most ease describing processes in a sequential manner. That also means that sequential programming is easier to learn. That is why, in spite of relying on performance improvement tools like pipelined execution, speculative execution, and out-of-order execution, processor architecture is designed to guarantee results consistent with in-order execution of a sequence of program instructions. On the other hand, power constraints and physical limits of transistor signaling speed have resulted in a cap on how fast an instruction can be executed.

Once we conclude that physics limits the time taken for each step, we can solve increasingly complex problems in a limited time only if we either increase the complexity of each step or take many steps at the same time. Increasing the complexity of instructions too much can lead to expensive hardware and loss of generality. That leaves the option of executing many instructions in parallel. However, making their results consistent with a sequential ordering without suffering a significant reduction in instruction throughput becomes quite challenging with increasing parallelism. In this sense, the sequential nature of instructions is a handicap. On the other hand, it is often possible to express a procedure or algorithm in a nonsequential or loosely sequential manner, allowing significantly more parallelism. Expressing and implementing such algorithms in an efficient manner is the subject of this book.

Take, for example, the problem of moving a large number of boxes from point A to point B. If there is a speed limit, a single van may be too slow. To complete the task quicker, one may then use multiple vans (assuming multiple drivers are available) or larger vans. Note, however, that larger vans can be quite inefficient for small jobs, and it may be strategic for the moving company to invest primarily in medium-sized vans. Thus the main problem is to employ resources effectively to deploy the available vans. Of course, one must also account for constraints like bottlenecks (checkpoints, fixed lanes, and bridges, where only one or two vans may pass at a time) and labor zones (restriction on where a particular driver is allowed to drive).

## What Is in This Book

Having extolled the virtues of parallel programming, I must add that parallel programming can be an intricate exercise. Many an application developer will just be able to use parallel libraries and frameworks to speed up the time-consuming parts. In most cases, they do not care to delve deep into the trenches of parallel programming. This book is not intended for them. Rather, it is for the developers of those libraries and frameworks, and for ab initio programmers.

In particular, this book is designed to support the first course in parallel programming. Its intended audiences include sophomore and junior-level computer science majors and majors allied with computer science. It assumes that the reader is well versed with the basic concepts of data structures and algorithms. Knowledge of a C-like language is assumed, as are elementary algorithm analysis and proof techniques. While brevity is a stated goal of this book, it also tries to be relatively self-contained. It introduces prerequisite concepts that are usually taught in courses like computer architecture and operating systems. Hence, even those students who have not yet taken those courses should be able to follow. Students with a background in those topics may skip the corresponding sections in Chapters 1 and 4. Even though this book strives to keep the discussion informal, formalism is sometimes necessary for precision. Such description is augmented with ample figures for easier understanding. This should particularly help readers who are not interested in becoming parallel programmers per se, but want to get an overview of one or two core concepts.

This book starts by introducing hardware and software architecture, performance metrics, and programming paradigms and solution design before it delves into practical programming tools in Chapter 6. That chapter is really where actual programming begins. Pedagogic principles dictate that the preliminaries be understood before actual programming. However, for many, Chapter 6 would come too late in the book, and studying the earlier scaffolding only "on paper" may become dull. Even beginners may choose to jump ahead to Chapter 6 and start to write programs "in parallel" with mastering the earlier chapters.

In this book, we briefly discuss standard CPU- and GPU-based parallel computational and memory architecture. We also discuss prevalent software architecture and programming models that allow the specification and management of unordered instructions. Popular parallel programming platforms are described. The book covers parallel program design principles as well as techniques for algorithm design. We also examine the issues related to decomposing a problem into parallel tasks and executing these tasks by allocating them to computational components like processors or memory transfer engines. Note that parallel data transfer (through memory, files, or network) are important aspects of parallel programs, and we study them. We cover synchronization required between task-doers so that they may correctly inter-operate.

The questions listed at the beginning of each chapter and some sections indicate their learning objectives. Exercises at the end of each chapter are vital to reaching those objectives. They not only review the concepts introduced in the chapter, but also spur thinking beyond them.

# CHAPTER 1

# An Introduction to Parallel Computer Architecture

This chapter is not designed for a detailed study of computer architecture. Rather, it is a cursory review of concepts that are useful for understanding the performance issues in parallel programs. Readers may well need to refer to a more detailed treatise on architecture to delve deeper into some of the concepts.[1]

## 1.1 Parallel Organization

There are two distinct facets of parallel architecture: the structure of the processors, that is, the hardware architecture, and the

*Question*: What are execution engines and how are instructions executed?

structure of the programs, that is, the software architecture. The hardware architecture has three major components:

1. Computation engine: it carries out program instructions.
2. Memory system: it provides ways to store values and recall them later.
3. Network: it forms the connections among processors and memory.

An understanding of the organization of each architecture and their interaction with each other is important to write efficient parallel programs. This chapter is an introduction to this topic. Some of these hardware architecture details can be hidden from application programs by well-designed programming frameworks and compilers. Nonetheless, a better understanding of these generally leads to more efficient programs. One must similarly

---

[1] Hennessy and Patterson, *Computer Architecture*.
   Duato et al., *Interconnection Networks*.

understand the components of the program along with the programming environment. In other words, a programmer must ask:

1. How do the multiple processing units operate and interact with each other?
2. How is the program organized so it can start and control all processing units? How is it split into cooperating parts and how do parts merge? How do parts cooperate with other parts (or programs)?

One way to view the organization of hardware as well as software is as graphs (see Sections 1.6 and 2.3). Vertices in these graphs represent processors or program components, and edges represent network connection or program communication. Often, implementation simplicity, higher performance, and cost-effectiveness can be achieved with restrictions on the structure of these graphs. The hardware and software architectures are, in principle, independent of each other. In practice, however, certain software organizations are more suited to certain hardware organizations. We will discuss these graphs and their relationship starting in section 2.3.

Another way to categorize the hardware organization was proposed by Flynn[2] and is based on the relationship between the instructions different processors execute at a time. This is popularly known as Flynn's taxonomy.

## SISD: Single Instruction, Single Data

A processor executes program instructions, operating on some input to produce some output. An SISD processor is a serial processor. A single sequence – or stream – of instructions operates on a single stream of operands, producing a single output stream. Note that it does not preclude an instruction operating on multiple operands, meaning a small number of operands may be processed at each step. For example, two input numbers may be added to produce one sum. We treat such an operand set as a single item in a stream of operands. Similarly, the results of the operation form a single output stream.

## SIMD: Single Instruction, Multiple Data

A SIMD (often pronounced sim.dee) processor indicates multiple simultaneous operations of a kind. It describes an architecture with a single stream of operations but multiple streams of operands. At each step, one operation in the stream is repeated on operands from all data-streams simultaneously. For each data-stream, an output is produced. This presumes the availability of multiple execution units performing the operation on multiple streams in parallel. For example, each pair in eight pairs of numbers may be added

---

[2] Flynn, "Some computer organizations."

and eight sums produced. Thus, there are as many output streams as input streams. Such operations are sometimes referred to as vector operations. (Usually, the number of data-streams is limited by the number of execution units available, but also see SIMT [single instruction, multiple threads] in the summary at the end of the chapter.)

## MIMD: Multiple Instruction, Multiple Data

MIMD refers to a general form of parallelism, where multiple independent operations are performed by a number of processors, each processing operands from its own stream. Each processor produces its own stream of output as well. Since the processors remain effectively independent of other processors in MIMD architecture, there is no requirement that the processors execute their steps simultaneously or remain in synchrony.

## MISD: Multiple Instruction, Single Data

The only other possible category in this taxonomy has multiple processors, each with a separate instruction stream. All operate simultaneously on the same operand from a single data-stream. This is a rather specialized situation, and a general study of this category is not common. (Sometimes, the same data-stream is processed by different processors, either for redundancy, or with differing objectives. For example, in an aircraft, one instruction stream may be analyzing data for anomaly, while another uses it to control pitch, and yet another simply encodes and records the data.) These can often be studied as multiple SISD programs.

Modern parallel computers are generally designed with a mix of SIMD and MIMD architectures. SIMD provides high efficiency at a lower cost because only a single instruction stream needs to be managed, but when vector operations are not required, meaning there is an insufficient number of data-streams available, the execution engines can be underutilized.

Another useful taxonomy is based on memory connectivity (see Figure 1.1). Memory[3] contains addressable *words*, or data items. Given an address, it can fetch the word or overwrite it. If all processors are connected to the same memory, we call it a shared-memory system or *shared-memory architecture*. These CPU–memory connections need not be direct point-to-point, but could be via one or more intermediate routers. Thus, some parts of memory may be accessed directly, while others are accessed through intermediaries. This makes for nonuniform access to different parts of memory and is called NUMA[4] memory architecture.

[4] *Defined*: NUMA = Non-Uniform Memory Access

---

[3] Memory includes the storage as well as its controlling hardware, that is, memory controller.

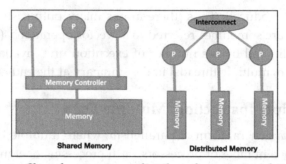

**Figure 1.1** Shared-memory vs. distributed-memory architecture

The alternative is *distributed-memory architecture*, in which different processors have access to their own separate memory. While it may be possible to access the memory of other processors as well, such access must be made through instructions executed on that remote processor. In contrast, even for NUMA-style shared-memory organization, a processor can communicate with all the shared memory by executing only its own instructions and does not need a cooperating processor to execute instructions on its behalf.

## 1.2  System Architecture

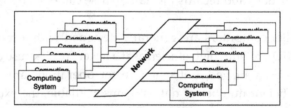

**Figure 1.2** Parallel computing cluster

Highly parallel systems of the day have a hierarchical structure (see Figure 1.2). A cluster of computing systems are connected by a network. These systems are also called nodes. The network topology will be discussed in Section 1.6. These systems usually, each, have their own operating system and name-space.[5] They may also share a common global name-space. The computing system itself contains a number of processors connected with each other in a more tightly knit unit (see Figure 1.3). This may include central processing units (CPUs), graphics

[5] *Defined*: Name-space is a unique naming system where different objects do not have the same name or label. Labels across name-space are not necessarily unique.

processing units (GPUs), *direct memory access* (DMA)[6] controllers, caches, and an underlying memory system. A computing system is usually under the overall control

[6] *Defined*: A DMA controller contains hardware to copy blocks of data from one memory location to another.

of a single operating system, even though there may exist separate controllers for different components, each capable of executing independently from others.[7] Thus we have many processors within a single computing system as well. Further, multiple streams of data can be read from and written into the memory concurrently, and even in parallel.

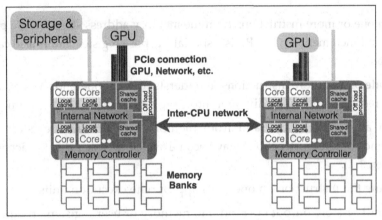

**Figure 1.3** Computing system

Thus, both cluster as well as single node are common examples of the MIMD architecture.

## 1.3 CPU Architecture

We next focus on the computation core. It comprises registers[8] in addition to control and execution logic. Some registers are general purpose, and their addresses (or names) may

[8] *Defined*: A register is a small but fast local memory. A CPU has access to a small number of registers.

be used in user programs. Others are for special purposes. Different parts of the core, all, perform their steps simultaneously in parallel and are synchronized to a CPU-wide clock. In principle, we may use this clock to measure time. In other words, "at the same time" would mean at the same clock tick or in the same clock cycle.

---

[7] We do not delve into virtualization in this book, where cores and memory may be virtually partitioned into multiple nodes, each under the apparent control of a different operating system.

The core's main controller fetches streams of instructions and affects their execution, sometimes seeking assistance from other controllers. Instructions indicate the operations and data on which to operate, which we call operands. Examples of operations are *add*, *read, write, branch*, and so on. Operands are data or addresses, and provide input to the operation or store its output. These operands may be provided as literal values, or taken from a specified register or a specified memory address. For example, "ADDM R1, R2, 3" may mean "considering the value in general register R2 as an address, fetch the value from that memory address, add 3 to it, and store the result in R1." The perpetual iteration of a core is as follows:

1. **Fetch** one or more instructions from the memory address stored in the program counter (PC) and increment the PC. PC is a special-purpose register, and is also called instruction pointer.

2. **Decode** one or more instructions to understand what operands and execution units are required, and optionally divide it into simpler sub-instructions (or micro-operations).

3. **Fetch** any required operand from memory into operand registers. Note that the operands of later instructions may become available earlier due to caches (see Caches in Section 1.4).

4. **Execute** the instruction on one of its appropriate execution units.

5. **Commit** or store output operand into memory or user registers if required.

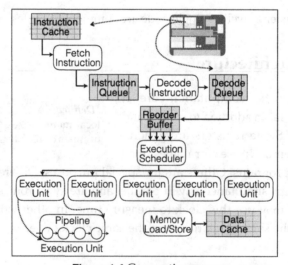

**Figure 1.4** Computing core

The core's functional pipeline[9] is illustrated in Figure 1.4. Each stage of the pipeline passes its results on to the next stage on completion and immediately seeks its next task from the previous stage.

[9] *Defined*: A pipeline is like an assembly line: a sequence of sub-operations that together complete a given operation.

The front end of a core's controller fetches instructions from memory, decodes them, and schedules them on one of the several execution units. These units are designed to perform logical and arithmetic operations on one or more pieces of data at a time. This front end may fetch and interleave instructions from multiple code-streams.[10] A given code-stream's instructions are fetched usually in that stream's order. They are also fetched speculatively by predicting the outcomes of conditional branch instructions. A conditional branch continues execution sequentially as usual, or from a new address listed as an operand. The choice is determined by the value of a second operand associated with the instruction. For example, "BRANCH R1 R3" may reset the PC to the address stored in register R1 if the value stored in R3 is 0.

The front end stores the decoded instructions in order in a decode buffer, which acts as a conduit to the execution engine. The execution engine allocates appropriate execution units to each instruction. It may reorder the instructions to achieve faster completion times. However, it *retires*, meaning completes, them in the order of the decode buffer, committing the results of the execution. Multiple commits may occur in the same clock cycle. It is important to note that execution units themselves consist of pipelined sub-units holding multiple instructions in different stages simultaneously. However, an instruction cannot begin to be executed until its operands are available. Note that some input operand of an instruction may be the output of a previous one. Such operand is available only after the earlier instruction is completed. The later instruction is said to *depend* on the earlier one as shown:

```
1   R1 = read address A;
2   R2 = read address B; // Independent of instruction 1: can begin before 1 is complete.
3   R3 = R1+R2; // Depends on instruction 1 and 2
```

The description above is only at a rather high level of abstraction. Architectural details are intricate, but the following repercussions are important to note. The "execution" of an instruction takes finite and variable time. Not only does a computing system have many cores, potentially executing different parts of the same program at any given instant, but each core also has multiple instructions in flight at any given time. These in-flight instructions do not necessarily follow each other sequentially through the various stages of the core's pipeline, but they retire sequentially. This parallel execution, or start, of multiple instructions in the same clock cycle is called *instruction-level parallelism*.

---

[10] A code-stream may be thought of as a program.

From the discussion in this section, it should be clear that even a single core follows the MIMD principle at some level. It can indeed execute multiple instructions (on its multiple execution units) in the same step. Some of these execution units process only a single data-stream and are examples of SISD. At the same time, some modern cores also contain execution units that are SIMD. Intel's AVX and AVX2, and nVIDIA's SMX are examples of such execution units.

## 1.4   Memory and Cache

CPUs are invariably attached to large memory systems, which we sometimes refer to as the main memory. Main memory latency[11]

**Question:** Where all is data stored? How is it fetched by various execution engines?

is significantly larger than that of computation unit pipelines. Memory instructions are also processed as shown in Figure 1.4. The execution of a memory *read* or *write* instruction that started on a core is not completed for a relatively long period, possibly delaying the start of subsequent instructions.

Hence, it is common for the hardware to maintain copies of a subset of the data in fast local memory, called a *cache*. Indeed, an entire cache hierarchy – a series of caches – is maintained with an eye on the cost. A cache too small may not be of much help, and a cache large enough to be helpful may be too expensive. Therefore the cache is often divided into multiple levels. Level 1 (L1 for short) cache is small but could have a latency comparable to registers, with a high per-unit cost. A level 2 cache may be larger with a slightly higher latency and a slightly lower per-unit cost, and so on. Often, higher-level caches are also shared by more cores.

If a given piece of data is in the level $i$ cache, it must also exist in level $i + 1$. Thus, the same data has many proxies. The goal is to try and retain the frequently used data in the lower levels, and to operate on that copy. Data reuse and locality of use within a program is a common reason why this is possible.

With a cache hierarchy, if a data item is not found in the level $i$ cache, meaning it is a *cache-miss*, it is allocated space in that cache. That space is populated by bringing the item from level $i + 1$ (and recursively from higher levels if necessary). This means that any data previously resident in that allocated space in level $i$ must be *evicted* first, possibly by updating its proxies at higher levels. The performance of a program's memory operations depends on the allocations and eviction policy. Some systems allow the program to control both policies. More often, though, a fixed policy is available.

---

[11] Latency is the time taken for an activity (like memory write) to complete from the time it is started (i.e. the write request is made).

For example, in *direct-mapped caches*, the cache location of an item is uniquely determined by its memory address. Another item already occupying that location must be evicted to bring in the new item before the core can access it. In the more pervasive *associative caches*, an item is allowed to be placed in one of several cache locations. If all those candidate locations are occupied, one must be vacated to make space for the new item. The *cache replacement policy* governs which item is evicted. *FIFO eviction policy* (FIFO stands for first in, first out) dictates that the item that came into the cache before other candidates is evicted. In the *LRU eviction policy* (LRU stands for least recently used), the evicted cache entry is the one that was last accessed before every other candidate.

Even if a fixed policy is in effect, programs can be written to adapt to it. For example, a program may ensure that multiple SIMD cores that share a cache do not incessantly evict each other's data. Suppose a direct-mapped cache addressing is used. In a cache with $k$ locations, the memory address $m$ occupies the cache location $m\%k$. This means that up to $k$ contiguous memory items can coexist in the cache and can be read simultaneously by $k$ SIMD cores. On the other hand, accesses to memory addresses $A$ and $A + k$ conflict, and would evict each other.

When updating data resident in a cache, it can be written to its next higher-level cache (*write-through* cache) before the write is considered complete. Alternate write policies also exist. For example, in *write-back* caches, data is written only into that cache level and the instruction is completed. Writing to the higher cache levels is deferred until later. Write-back caches are simpler and complete updates faster, but can lead to harder cache coherence problems when memory is shared by multiple processors and multiple cache hierarchies.

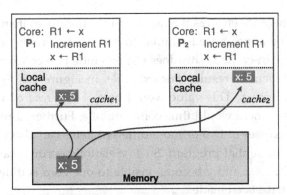

**Figure 1.5** Cache coherence: two cores are shown with separate caches. R1 is a local register in each core. $x$ and $y$ are memory items

Each cache level is divided into *cache-lines*: equal-sized blocks of contiguous bytes. The policies are implemented in terms of entire lines. So organizing a cache into lines helps reduce the hardware cost of the query about whether a data item accessed by a core is in that cache, that is, whether there is a cache-hit or a cache-miss. However, dealing in cache-lines means that an entire cache-line must be fetched in order to access a smaller memory item. This acts to prefetch certain data, in case the other items in that cache-line are accessed in the near future.

Caches impose significant complexity in parallel computing environments. Note in Figure 1.3 that each computing core has its own cache. These multiple cores may retain their own copies of some data, or write to it. This duplication can lead to different parts of the same program executing on those cores to see different – and hence inconsistent – data in the same memory location at the "same time." Such inconsistency is hardly surprising if each part assumes that there is only one data item in one memory location at a time. This consistency is called *cache coherence*. Coherence is maintained by ensuring that two cores do not modify their copies concurrently. If a core modifies its copy, other copies are invalidated or updated with the new value.

These updates cannot be instantaneous, meaning there are periods when the copies do not have the same values. However, it suffices to make them consistent before the next access of that memory item. If a memory item is updated through its proxies in multiple caches, those updates only need to be observed by the cores (i.e. by readers executing on each core) to have been made in the same order. In other words, if a reader observes the update $A$ to have occurred before update $B$ to a location, no other reader may observe update $B$ before update $A$.

Figure 1.5 demonstrates cache coherence. Cores $P_1$ and $P_2$ read $x$, whose initial value 5 is cached both in $cache_1$ and $cache_2$. $P_1$ now stores 6 in $cache_1$, which is propagated to $cache_2$. If the second access to $x$ by $P_2$ happens before this update, it receives 5. Otherwise, it receives 6.

Recall that coherence ensures that any modification to an item is propagated to all its cached copies. The appearance is similar to the case where the item is directly accessed from the memory un-cached. This does not preclude two concurrent changes to an item leading to unpredictable results. For example, in Figure 1.5, $P_2$ could write the value of its register R1 into $x$. This value would be 6 if $P_2$'s *read* of $x$ completes before $P_1$'s *write* to $x$. $P_1$'s increment would thus come undone. Furthermore, the interplay between cache-coherent accesses of two or more different items can also violate expectations that are routine in a sequential program. Such violations occur because the order in which updates to two items $x$ and $y$ become visible to one core is different from the order in which they may have been made.

We will later study this larger issue of memory-wide consistency in more detail in Section 4.2. One must understand the type of memory consistency guaranteed by a parallel programming environment to design programs that execute correctly in that environment. In fact, some programming environments even allow incoherent caches in an attempt to bolster performance. After all, coherence comes at a performance cost. Such environments leave it to the program to manage consistency as needed. We will see such examples in Chapter 6.

Recall that caches operate in units of cache-lines, meaning coherence protocols deal in lines. If item $x$ in $P_2$'s cache needs to be invalidated, its entire line – including items not written by $P_1$ – is invalidated. This is called *false-sharing* and is discussed in Chapter 6.

## 1.5  GPU Architecture

Graphics processing units, popularly called GPUs, are named so due to their historical roots in graphics processing. They nevertheless comprise general-purpose parallel processors, which are used to accelerate parts of a program, and sometimes just to off-load a subset of the work from the CPU. A computing system may have one or more GPUs, just as it may have one or more CPUs. CPUs on a system communicate through an inter-CPU network. GPUs may also communicate through an inter-GPU network. Finally, there is a third network connecting the CPUs to the GPUs. The design of a uniform and integrated structure for these networks are on the horizon, but multiple networks with divergent characteristics are commonplace, and should be considered in parallel program design. The CPU–GPU network is usually much slower than the other two. A program that reduces CPU–GPU communication, then, would be more suited to this situation.

GPUs reside within a computing system and are usually connected to CPU cores through an internal network called PCI express (see Figure 1.3). The general architecture of GPUs is shown in Figure 1.6. GPU cores are organized in a hierarchy of groups. GPU execution engines comprise SIMD cores. For example, one engine may consist of, say, 32 floating-point execution units, and all may be used to execute the next floating-point instruction in some instruction stream with its 32 data-streams. Just like CPU execution units, each core of the SIMD group consists of a pipeline of subunits.

Similarly, another execution unit may cause *read* or *write* of, say, 32 memory addresses. GPUs have a memory separate from the CPU memory. This memory is accessible by all GPU cores. Due to a higher number of concurrent operations, GPU memory pipelines tend to be even longer (i.e. they are *deep pipelines*) than CPU memory pipelines, even as the cache hierarchy may have fewer levels. On the other hand, the GPU's execution unit pipelines are often shorter than the CPU's, and the imbalance in GPU memory and compute latencies is significant. (See Section 6.5 for its impact on GPU programming.)

Stream processors (SPs) are grouped into clusters variously called streaming multi-processors (SM), or compute-unit (CU). SPs within an SM usually share an L0 or L1 level cache local to that SM. In addition, SMs may also contain a user-managed cache shared by its cores. This cache is referred to as scratchpad, local data-share (LDS), or sometimes merely shared memory. Sometimes, groups of SMs may be further organized into "super-clusters," for example, for sharing graphics-related hardware. Several of these super-clusters may share higher levels of cache. At other times, the processors of an SM (or CU) may be partitioned into multiple subsets, each subset operating in SIMD fashion. Thus, there is a hierarchy of cores and a hierarchy of caches. Again, due to the possible replication of data into multiple local caches, their coherence is an important consideration.

In terms of instruction execution, this GPU architecture is not substantially different from the CPU architecture shown in Figure 1.4. Only, there is a preponderance of SIMD execution engines in GPU, but of SISD engines in the case of CPU. The difference is larger in the organization of cores and the resulting design parameters. Much of this difference can be attributed to the fact that the GPUs tend to carry many more execution units. They also are likely to have somewhat smaller memory and cache, particularly on a per-core basis. Many more simultaneous memory reads and writes need to be sustained by GPUs, and hence they need to lay a greater emphasis on efficient memory operations. The hierarchical organization of cores and caches into clusters aids this effort.

For example, each SM has a separate shared-memory unit (see block marked local cache in Figure 1.6), and each shared-memory unit may be further divided into several banks. Each bank of each unit can be accessed simultaneously. The SIMD nature of instructions allows a program to control the banks accessed by a single instruction and thus improve its memory performance. For example, a 32-core SIMD instruction could read up to 32 contiguous elements of an array in parallel if those elements reside in different banks. Similarly, all items accessed by an instruction could occupy the same cache-line, thus requiring a single cache transaction.

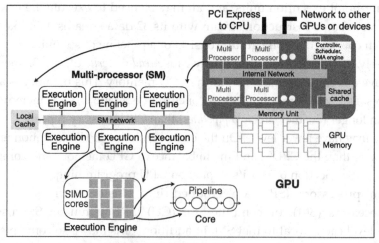

**Figure 1.6** GPU architecture

## 1.6   Interconnect Architecture

A network interconnects processors, which we can call network nodes. Note that these network nodes need not be units that directly

*Question*: How is data communicated among execution engines?

execute program instructions, but they all have the ability to consume, produce, or collate data. The memory controller is an example. Multiple cores connect to the memory controller using a network. They send requests to the controller, which returns the response after performing memory operations on the cores' behalf.

Sometimes, a unit contains multiple connections, each of which we may call endpoints or *ports*. Transmission *links* connect the ports allowing messages to travel from one port to another. In general, the network structure can be represented as a graph, as discussed in Section 1.1. Vertices of this graph may be the nodes themselves, or simply intermediate routers that forward data incoming on one link to another. Edges are the links. Networks containing such routers, or switches, are called switched or indirect networks. Such switches necessarily have multiple ports. On the other hand, nodes in a direct network themselves contain multiple ports (see Figure 1.9). It is common for general-purpose networks to employ modular design and populate ports into switches and employ switched networks. Internal, on-chip networks on devices like CPUs and GPUs can often be direct networks instead.

### Routing

Messages are routed either using circuit switching or packet switching. For circuit switching, the entire path between the sender and the recipient is reserved and may not be shared by any other pair until that

[12] *Defined*: A packet is a small amount of data. Larger "messages" may be subdivided into multiple "packets." We will use these terms interchangeably.

communication is complete. For packet switching, each switch routes incoming packets[12] "toward" the recipient at each step. Sometimes switches are equipped with buffers to store and then forward packets in a later step. This is useful to resolve *contention* when two messages from two different sources arrive at the same time-step and are required to be forwarded onto the same link on the way to their respective destinations. One alternative is to drop one of the messages and require it to be retransmitted. That is a high-level overview. We will not discuss detailed routing issues in this book.

### Links

Most network topologies support bidirectional links that can carry data in both directions simultaneously. These are called *full-duplex links*. It is in many ways similar to having two *simplex links* instead – simplex links are unidirectional. In contrast, *half-duplex* links are bidirectional but carry data in only one direction at a time. In this section, we will not separately discuss the duplex variants of the described topologies, but it may be easier to understand the discussion assuming half-duplex links.

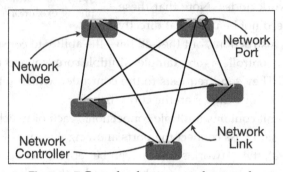

**Figure 1.7** Completely connected network

## Types and Quality of Networks

The simplest network is a completely connected one: each node is directly connected to every other with a dedicated link (see Figure 1.7). However, if the number of nodes is $n$, up to $\frac{n(n-1)}{2}$ links would be required in addition to $n-1$ ports per node. This is expensive. Another convenient interconnect is a bus (Figure 1.8): a pervasive channel to which each endpoint attaches. This method is cost-effective but hard to extend over large distances. Bus communication is also slowed by a large number of endpoints, as only one endpoint may send its data on a fully shared bus at one time, and some bus access arbitration is required for conflict-free communication.

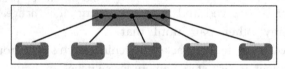

**Figure 1.8** A bus network

One measure of such conflict is whether a network is blocking. A *nonblocking network* exhibits no contention or conflict for any combination of sender–recipient pairs as long as no two senders seek to communicate with the same recipient. In other words, disjoint pairs can communicate simultaneously. A completely connected network is nonblocking, and a bus is blocking. Note that having separate paths between each pair is not required in packet-switched networks, but the independent paths do provide lower communication latency on average. Network latency is the time taken by a single packet to reach its destination.

There are many possible network designs. In general, as more links are added, less link-sharing is required, but the topology of the links can have a significant bearing on the types of traffic that a network can handle well. An understanding of the available network's properties helps a programmer ensure that programs are designed to exploit its strengths and avoid its weaknesses. First, we need a way to describe the properties of networks. The following metrics are useful:

1. **Number of links:** It is fair to assume that each link incurs a cost. Fewer links also imply simplicity of the network layout. On the other hand, the lack of links often leads to inefficient communication, and programs may benefit from reducing or batching communication.

2. **Degree:** The degree of a node refers to the number of links connected to it. It translates to the number of ports on the node. A large degree, particularly for computation nodes, increases network cost and complexity. It can also support higher concurrency among messages to different recipients. Formally, the degree of a network is the highest degree among its nodes. In common high-degree networks, many nodes have high degrees. However, extremes are possible, where only one or a few nodes have a high degree. For example, in a star network, a "hub" is connected to every other node. Any program on the hub in such cases have to account for its high degree. A hub can also be a source of high contention, not unlike a bus.

3. **Total bandwidth:** The maximum rate at which data can be handled by the entire network is its bandwidth. For an $l$ link network with link bandwidth $b$, the maximum *network bandwidth* is $bl$. However, in many practical networks, all links cannot be active at the same time, and the network bandwidth is usually smaller than $bl$. The bandwidth can be brought near $bl$ with good routing protocols and contention resolution. Programs able to limit communication to the total bandwidth do not suffer from this bottleneck.

4. **Minimum throughput:** The maximum rate at which data can be sent between a given pair of nodes is called the pair's throughput. The minimum such throughput of any pair of nodes is called the minimum *network throughput*.

5. **Diameter:** The minimum number of links traversed by a message from node $a$ to node $b$ is the minimum path length $p_{ab}$ for that pair. The diameter of a network is the longest minimum path: $\max(p_{ij})$, among all node-pairs $i, j$ in the network. The diameter indicates the maximum latency of messages. Programs that block while the communication completes can be severely limited by long latency.

6. **Average path length:** The lengths of paths between pairs of nodes can vary significantly from pair to pair. In such cases, the average path length is a useful metric. The minimum

path length between node pairs, averaged across all pairs, is called the average *network path length*.

7. **Bisection width:** The minimum number of links that must be severed for one-half of the nodes to be completely separated from the other half. While a high *bisection width* suggests robustness in the face of failing links, this metric also identifies communication bottleneck.

   Consider any equi-partition of $n$ communicating nodes – each receiving as well as sending across half-duplex links in a given step. On average $\frac{n}{2}$ pairs would straddle partitions. Thus a bisection width less than $\frac{n}{2}$ is certain to block some pairs from communicating. Again, a bisection width of $\frac{n}{2}$ is not guaranteed to allow all pairs to proceed, as the network may be blocking, and there may be other conflicts along the paths between different pairs.

8. **Bisection bandwidth:** The minimum bandwidth available between two halves. As a global metric focusing on the bottleneck, the *bisection bandwidth* is generally more meaningful than the minimum bandwidth.

   In addition to the above metrics, for switched networks, the number and complexity of switches (e.g. the number of ports in each switch) are also important. Let us now evaluate a few common network topologies, particularly ones with a higher performance than the bus and a lower cost than the complete network.

## Torus Network

A simple network that reduces the bus bottleneck is a ring (see Figure 1.9). Each node in a ring is connected to the next node in a wrap-around configuration. The two diagrams in Figure 1.9 show the direct and switched variants of the ring network. A ring uses $n$ links to connect $n$ nodes. With unidirectional communication, the latency can be as high as $n-1$ with simplex, and $\frac{n}{2}$ with duplex links. The bisection bandwidth is also quite low: $2b$ for link bandwidth of $b$. We will improve these parameters by adding more links next.

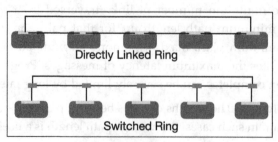

**Figure 1.9** Ring network

A ring is a special case of the more general mesh or torus topology. A 2D mesh is simply the nodes arranged in a 2D grid, with links connecting each node to neighbors in its row as well as the neighbors in its column. Figure 1.10 shows a 3D mesh. If the corresponding nodes in extremal rows are linked to each other, and the extremal columns are similarly linked (as shown with dashed links in Figure 1.11), the network is called a 2D torus. A ring is simply a 1D torus.

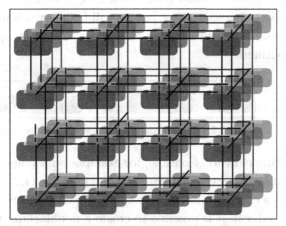

**Figure 1.10** 4 × 4 × 4 3D Mesh network

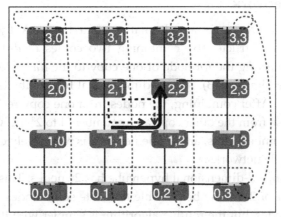

**Figure 1.11** A 4 × 4 2D torus, showing conflicting routes from node $(1,1)$ to $(2,2)$ and from node $(2,1)$ to $(1,2)$

A $d$-dimensional torus network of $n$ nodes has $k = \lceil \sqrt[d]{n} \rceil$ nodes along each dimension and $dn$ links, each node having $2d$ ports. We call such tori $k$-way tori. The diameter of such a network is $\frac{kd}{2}$: the furthest node from a node is at a distance of $\frac{k}{2}$ along each dimension.

The bisection width is $2k^{d-1}$: a $(d-1)$-dimensional slice through the middle would divide the nodes into two.

One benefit of the torus is its short link lengths except for the wrap-around links – all $dk^{d-1}$ of them. However, in the context of networks inside a chip, not only is the long delay in long links undesirable, variable delay in variable link lengths causes a significant impediment to speed and throughput. On the other hand, it is possible to lay tori out to alleviate the link length variability problem at a slight cost to the overall lengths. Figure 1.12 demonstrates one simple strategy, but we will not discuss it in detail here. Regardless, laying out high link counts, particularly on a plane, or on a few planar layers, or even in 3D, is quite complicated.

**Figure 1.12** A 1D torus layout with no long links

Torus is a blocking network. Consider, for example, a message from node $(1,1)$ to node $(2,2)$ at the same time as a message from node $(2,1)$ to node $(1,2)$ as marked in Figure 1.11. Both must employ a common link (unless a longer path is taken but there may be similar conflicts on other edges). It is possible to create a nonblocking torus network, but that requires many more links and additional switches.

## Hypercube Network

The hypercube network[13] is an alternative to a torus. A hypercube of dimension $d+1, d \geq 0$, is constructed by combining two copies of $d$-dimensional hypercubes by mutually connecting the $ith$ node of one copy to the $ith$ node of the other copy, by a link, for all $i$ (see Figure 1.13). A zero-dimensional hypercube is a single node with no links and index 0. After combining, the nodes from one copy retain their previous index numbers and those from the other copy are renumbered to $2^d + i$, where $i$ is a given node's previous index number. Thus, an $n$-node network is recursively constructed by adding $\frac{n}{2}$ links to two $\frac{n}{2}$-node networks.

By construction, a $d$-dimensional hypercube has $2^d$ nodes. This restricts the number of nodes to a power of 2. It may be possible to delete some nodes and their links to allow any number of nodes, but the routing algorithm is simpler with the power of 2 restriction. The degree of each node is $\log n$ for an $n$-node network. This is somewhat high. The total number of links for a hypercube of $n$ nodes is $\frac{1}{2}(n \log n)$, and the bisection width is $\frac{n}{2}$. Hypercubes have a good performance at moderate cost and are a good choice for small to

---

[13] Squire and Palais, "Programming and design considerations."

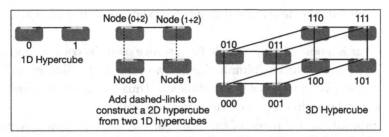

**Figure 1.13** Hypercube network: Construction from 1D to 2D to 3D hypercubes is shown

medium networks. For larger node counts, however, the node degree becomes unwieldy, and the constraint that the total number of nodes be a power of 2 precludes most node counts.

## Cross-Bar Network

The cross-bar seeks to reduce the cost of the completely connected network. A cross-bar switch has $2n$ ports connecting $n$ nodes as shown in Figure 1.14.

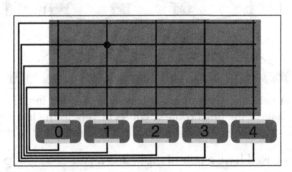

**Figure 1.14** Cross-bar: Dots designate that crossing wires are closed (meaning connected). Other crossings are open (only one dot may appear in any row or column).

The cross-bar switch can connect at most one pair of cross-wires in any row or column. For example, the connections depicted by dark circles in Figure 1.14[14] allow node 0 to communicate with node 2, at the same time node 1 communicates with node 3. Thus, up to $\frac{n}{2}$ separate pairs can be connected simultaneously, but one node can communicate with only one other node at a time. A cross-bar requires $2n$ links to connect $n$ nodes in addition to the $2n$ port cross-bar switch. The bisection width is $n$. If the link bandwidth is $b$, the bisection bandwidth is $nb$. Cross-bar switches are also expensive due to the need for $n^2$

---

[14] In these diagrams, wire crossings do not depict junctions, except when a circle indicates a connection.

cross-wire connector switches. The data must also be able to travel larger distances on links with increasing $n$.

A cross-bar is a nonblocking switch. Each source owns its column, and no other source may set any junction in its column. Similarly, every destination owns its row and no junction in row $d$ is set unless $d$ is a destination. Thus the junction in row $s$ and column $d$ is reserved for the exclusive use of $s$ to $d$ communications.

The complexity and expense of the cross-bar can be ameliorated by using a modular multistage connector at the expense of latency. Shuffle-exchange networks are one such class of multistage switches.

## Shuffle-Exchange Network

Shuffle-exchange networks are of many types. Let us consider an example. The Omega network is a multistage network, as shown in Figure 1.15.

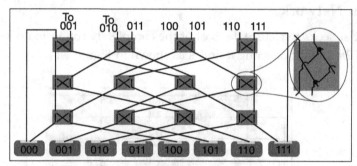

**Figure 1.15** Omega network: Output of switches are shuffled into the inputs at the next stage. The first half of the links connect consecutively to the left input ports of the next level switches. The second half connect to the right ports.

All the switches used have a pair of input and a pair of output ports. Each switch can be separately controlled to either let both its inputs pass straight through to its corresponding outputs or to swap them. This is really a $2 \times 2$ cross-bar, also called a *Banyan switch* element, as shown in the inset in Figure 1.15 (although other implementations are possible). In the figure, cross-connects (or exchanges) are set up for swap (i.e. cross). Connecting the other diagonal junctions instead would result in a pass-through (i.e. bar).

An $n$-node Omega network requires $\log n$ stages,[15] with $\frac{n}{2}$ switches per stage. The output of a stage is shuffled into the input of the next stage – the left half of the links connect consecutively to the left input of each switch and the right half of the links connect to the right input of consecutive switches. In other words, if we number[16] the output from

---

[15] Logarithm base 2 is implied in this book.

[16] Numberings start at 0.

left to right, output $i$, for $i < \frac{n}{2}$, connects to the left input of switch $i$. Output $i$, for $i \geq \frac{n}{2}$, similarly connects to the right input of switch $\frac{i}{2}$.

Omega networks are examples of a family of multistage shuffle-exchange networks,[17] like Butterfly[18] or Benes.[19] Different members of the family mainly have different shuffle patterns. Figure 1.16 shows a butterfly topology, for example. It contains $(\log n - 1)$ shuffle stages consisting of $n$ exchange switches each. This leads to a slightly lower diameter than Omega ($\log n$ vs. $\log n + 1$) and a higher bisection width ($2n$ vs. $n$) at the cost of almost doubling the number of links ($2n \log n$ vs. $n \log n + n$). One practical advantage of Omega network is that the shuffle pattern does not change from stage to stage allowing a more modular design. Also note that although the diagrams apparently show unidirectional data flow, it does not have to be. This is demonstrated later in this section.

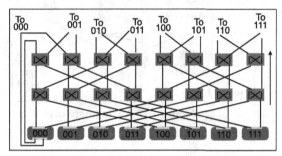

**Figure 1.16** Butterfly network

## Clos Network

Clos networks take a different approach to reduce the cost of the cross-bar. The main idea is to reduce the size and complexity by dividing the ports into smaller groups, say of size $k$, and use a cross-bar within the smaller groups as shown in Figure 1.17. In a way, Clos is also a generalization of the shuffle-exchange network. Recall that exchange is but a $2 \times 2$ cross-bar. Clos allows larger cross-bars. In this three-stage network, the shuffle is a perfect $r$-way shuffle, for a chosen $r$. The $ith$ output of switch $j$ is connected to the $jth$ input of switch $i$ of the next stage.

The bottom stage uses $k \times l$ cross-bars. The middle stage uses $r \times r$ cross-bars, $r = \lceil \frac{n}{k} \rceil$. The top stage uses $l \times k$ cross-bars. Clos has shown[20] that if $l \geq 2k - 1$, this network is nonblocking, retaining the contention-free routing of the cross-bar. For a large number

---

[17] Stone, "Parallel processing."

[18] LeBlanc et al., "Large-scale parallel programming."

[19] Benes, *Mathematical Theory*.

[20] Clos, "A study of non-blocking switching networks."

of ports $n$, a Clos network requires multiple but significantly smaller cross-bars than a full $n \times n$ cross-bar at the cost of a few more links. For example, a 1,024-node cross-bar requires 1,048,576 cross-connects. In contrast, we can use 64 $16 \times 31$ cross-bars in the first stage, 31 $64 \times 64$ cross-bars in the second stage, and 64 $31 \times 16$ cross-bars in the third stage, for a total of only 190,464 cross-connects and 1,984 additional links, albeit of smaller lengths than those inside a $1,024 \times 1,024$ cross-bar.

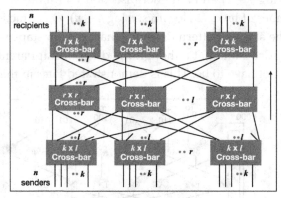

**Figure 1.17** A Clos network

## Tree Network

One of the simplest networks to design and route is a binary tree as shown in Figure 1.18. Possibly, the root can be removed (depicted with dashed lines), and its two children directly connected. Network complexity is small. The link count is only $2n - 3$ for $n$ nodes. Switches are simple three-port connectors able to route between any two ports in one step. The tree network has major bottlenecks owing to this simplicity. For example, the bisection width is just 1 – the link at the root can be severed to partition the nodes into equal halves. The diameter is $(2 \log n - 1)$.

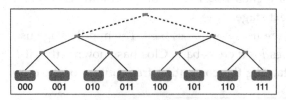

**Figure 1.18** Tree network

Some of these bottlenecks can be improved by recognizing that the bottlenecks are worse near the top of the tree. The root switch must be used by all the traffic going from the left subtree to the right subtree, and vice versa. This problem can be addressed by adding more links at the higher levels of the tree. For example, double the number of links going up at the level above the leaf, quadruple above that, and so on. See Figure 1.19. So modified, it is called the Fat tree network. Of course, the tree need not necessarily be a binary tree but may have any degree $d > 1$.

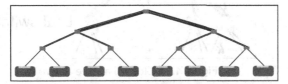

**Figure 1.19** Fat tree network

Surprisingly, the Fat tree is a close relative of the Clos network. Let us quickly revisit the Clos network just described, where a Clos network is presented as a unidirectional network communicating data upwards. Three stages are shown. Now, suppose we allow the links to be full-duplex and fold the figure down the middle, as shown in Figure 1.20. The middle stage $r \times r$ cross-bars of Figure 1.17 now looks like the top row of Figure 1.20. On folding, this row now has $r$ "output" links on the same side as $r$ "input" links, making $2r$ full-duplex links. All $l$ switches at this stage are folded. After folding, the cross-bar in the top and the bottom stages of Figure 1.17 occupy the bottom row of Figure 1.20. Thus the two rows of Figure 1.20 together make for a root node with $2n$ links. Given the duplex links, the network becomes symmetric. Any port can send or receive in a given step – possibly both if the links are full-duplex.

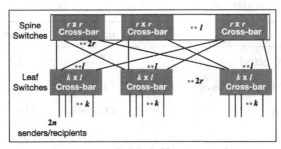

**Figure 1.20** Folded Clos network

We can reinterpret Figure 1.20 as demonstrated in Figure 1.21, integrating the $l$ $r \times r$ cross-bars of the top row into a single node with $l$ links to each of the $2r$ nodes in the bottom row. The topology reduces to that of a three-level Fat tree topology. The root's degree is $2r$ and that of each switch in the bottom row is $k$. In this configuration, the root is often referred to as the spine and its children as leaf switches. If $l = k$, $k$ links between each leaf switch and the spine are sufficient to support the combined throughput of the leaf's $k$ children.

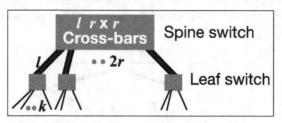

**Figure 1.21** Clos = Fat tree network

## Network Comparison

We have discussed a few popular network topologies in this section. Each has its pluses and minuses. Broadly speaking, the performance increases with increasing complexity and cost. Ideally, these details are hidden from a parallel application programmer, whose main concern should be to send data from a producer to a consumer. Nonetheless, certain topologies are more suited to specific communication patterns than others. A smart program exploits the knowledge of the underlying topology to situate consumers and producers in nodes that are more likely at a short communication distance. In general, shorter communications also incur – and cause – fewer conflicts. Table 1.1 lists some of the network metrics for selected topologies.

**Table 1.1** Network Comparison

| Network | Link count | Diameter | Bisection width |
|---|---|---|---|
| Completely connected | $\frac{n(n-1)}{2}$ | 1 | $\frac{n}{2} \times \frac{n}{2}$ |
| $d$-dimensional $k$-way Torus, $k^d = n$ | $nd$ | $\frac{dk}{2}$ | $2k^{d-1}$ |
| Fat Tree (Binary) | $n \log n$ | $2 \log n$ | $\frac{n}{2}$ |
| Hypercube | $\frac{n \log n}{2}$ | $\log(n)$ | $n/2$ |

## 1.7  Summary

Parallel processors are ubiquitous. These include CPUs with nearly 10 or 20 cores, GPUs with a few thousand cores, and clusters with up to a million cores and more. Each core usually accepts a sequence of instructions and executes them ostensibly in that order.

Each instruction may execute on a single set of operands (scalar operation) or an array of them at a time (vector operation). Some of these instructions read from or write to memory locations. Cores communicate with other cores through these memory operations. In some systems, communication ports connect cores to help them communicate. Often, cores communicate with these ports through special memory operations.

A parallel program that runs on multiple cores decides:

1. which core executes what instructions on what operands (and in what order)

2. which cores communicate what data with which other cores

This decision should account for heterogeneity: varying network characteristics between pairs of cores, or the difference in capabilities of the cores. At the same time, the interference of the cores' operations with each other has a major impact on the overall efficiency of a parallel program. For example, two cores sharing a common cache would impact each other's cache-hit rates. A core attempting to communicate with another must wait if that other core is busy completing a different operation. This chapter introduces the architectural framework for these decisions. The key lessons include:

- Sequential execution of instruction on a core is usually pipelined. Systems commonly allow out-of-order execution of certain instructions as long as the result is consistent with ordered execution.

- Overlapping the execution of multiple instructions allows better utilization of hardware components because they can be simultaneously busy operating on different parts of a program.

- Parallel MIMD cores execute independent instructions. SIMD cores all execute the same instruction simultaneously on different data.

- Somewhat refined terminology is also in vogue. The SIMT – single instruction multiple threads – architecture allows a variable number of virtual cores to apparently execute an instruction "simultaneously." If the available number of physical cores is smaller than the requested SIMT width, each SIMT instruction is serialized into multiple SIMD instructions.

- Similarly, SPMD (single program multiple data) and MPMD (multiple programs multiple data) are variants of MIMD, except the definition works at the level of the entire user program, rather than that of individual instructions. For example, in an SPMD architecture, the same program is executed on multiple cores, and at each core it operates on its own data. The executions together solve a problem. It is up to the program to determine at the time of execution which part of the solution each core undertakes.

- Processors may share memory, or maintain private memory whose data is communicated using a network.

- Memory caches are used to improve access times to a subset of data. These caches may be directly managed by the user program or transparently managed by the underlying system.

- Different parts of a program may share caches and may interfere with the residency of each other's data in the shared cache.

- In a parallel computing system, cores may be hierarchically organized into groups (and subgroups). Groups may have different architectures and capabilities from each other. For example, a computing system in a networked cluster of systems may comprise a group of CPU cores, all sharing a common memory; a group of GPU cores sharing another memory; and a network between the two groups.

- Large networks have a structured topology, such as tree, torus, or cube.

- Network latency and throughput are not necessarily uniform in a network connecting many processors. For example, in a network, processor $P_1$ may have a shorter communication distance to processor $P_2$ than any other processor. If more communication happens between topologically nearby pairs than between faraway pairs, the total communication time can be lower.

Textbooks on parallel architecture[21] are good sources for a deeper study of these topics. GPU architecture evolves at such a fast pace that any textbook[22] quickly becomes out of date. However, architecture vendors usually release white papers and programming guides, which are up-to-date sources of detailed information. A detailed analysis of design and performance issues of interconnects have been discussed in several books.[23]

Large-scale computing systems have many components. They add up to large power consumption. That is a major concern in high-performance computing. A large number of components also translates into a large chance of failure: even one component failing could abort a long-running program if the failure is not handled. Significant effort is devoted to designing a low-power and fault-tolerant architecture. Programs designed to

---

[21] Hennessy and Patterson, *Computer Architecture*.
Sarangi, *Computer Organisation and Architecture*.
Hwang, *Computer Architecture and Parallel Processing*.
[22] Kirk and Hwu, *Programming Massively Parallel Processors*.
Wilt, *The CUDA Handbook*.
[23] Leighton, *Introduction to Parallel Algorithms*.
Duato, Yalamanchili, and Ni, *Interconnection Networks*.
Yalamanchili, "Interconnection networks."

take advantage of these features can reduce power consumption and can respond to certain failures. These topics are out of the scope of this book, but several overviews of recent techniques have been published.[24] Please refer to these to learn about such topics.

# Exercise

1.1. What is NUMA memory configuration?

1.2. What is false-sharing?

1.3. What are the reasons that multiple levels of cache may be employed?

1.4. Does memory in a UMA configuration with four attached cores require four ports for the four cores to attach to? If a single port exists, how can the four cores connect to the same port?

1.5. What is the instruction fetch-commit pipeline?

1.6. Once an instruction is decoded, operands require fetching from memory. This fetch takes variable time (due to cache misses, coherence protocols, memory contention, etc.). Thus, operands of instruction $i + 1$ may arrive before those of instruction $i$ do. What is the condition under which instruction $i + 1$ may be started before instruction $i$?

1.7. Consider the conditions when instruction $i$ and instruction $i + 1$ of a sequential program may be swapped by a compiler without affecting the result. Can they be swapped also if another program may access the same memory? Explain with an example.

1.8. Suppose the execution of an instruction is divided into seven pipelines stages: $stage_1$ to $stage_7$. Each stage is able to complete its operation in a single clock cycle. What is the instruction latency? Suppose a new instruction may start only two clock cycles after the previous one does. What is the maximum execution throughput?

1.9. What is the difference between a switch and a port?

1.10. What is the role of instruction execution engines in a switched network?

1.11. All SIMD cores perform the same operation in any clock cycle. However, branches can complicate this. For example, consider a group of 32 SIMD cores executing the following program. (ID is the core number in the range 0..31).

---

[24] Mittal, "A survey of architectural techniques."
Cho and Melhem, "On the interplay of parallelization."
Obrien et al., "A survey of power."
Ma et al., "Greengpu."
Egwutuoha et al., "A survey of fault tolerance mechanisms."
Radetzki et al., "Methods for fault tolerance."

```
1    int aincr = b[id] - a[id];
2    int s = sign(aincr); // s is 0 if aincr is +ve and 1 if it is -ve
3    if(s) {
4        b[id] = b[id] + bfactor;
5        a[id] = a[id] + afactor * aincr;
6    } else {
7        a[id] = a[id] - afactor * aincr;
8    }
```

All cores can execute the test on line 3 and then branch to their corresponding lines (4 or 7), depending on the result of the test. However, if some cores take the branch to line 4 and others to line 7, they have different instructions to execute next. The groups execute them taking turns. In each turn, the nonexecuting subset remains idle. In the example above, the first group executes line 4 and the second execute lines 7 and 8, leading to a total of six separate instructions.

Rewrite the code so that cores do not separate (or diverge) into groups, and all execute only five lines in total. Assume that the multiplication and addition on a line can be performed together in one instruction.

1.12. Which of the following two pieces of code is more cache-friendly (meaning they use caches well), assuming that the matrix mat is laid out in the row-major order in memory?

```
for(int r=0; r<m; r++)                    for(int c=0; c<n; c++)
    for(int c=0; c<n; c++)                    for(int r=0; r<m; r++)
        mat[r][c] *= factor;                      mat[r][c] *= factor;
}                                         }
```

1.13. Assume a single-level cache with a cache line of 16 integers. What is the total number of memory operations performed in the following code? What percentage of those operations are cache-hits? Assume the cache holds $1,024$ lines, and there is only one processor. Assume direct mapping of addresses, such that the integer at index $i$ always maps to the cache location $i\%160$, given that the cache can hold up to 160 integers. (This would be in the cache-line number $(i\%60)/16$.)

```
void func(int *a, int *b) {
    for(int i=0,j=16; i<40; i++,j+=8)
        a[i] += b[j];
}
```

1.14. What is the hit-rate in Exercise 1.13, if the cache can only hold 10 lines? Assume FIFO eviction policy.

1.15. Let two cores, respectively with ID = 0 and ID = 1, share memory but maintain their own caches as described in Exercise 1.14, with 10 cache-lines each and using direct mapping with FIFO eviction policy. What is the maximum and the minimum cache-hit rate for the following code in each core?

```
void func(int *a, int *b) {
    for(int i=0,j=16; i<40; i++,j+=16)
        a[id] += b[j*id];
}
```

1.16. Explain the statement: "CPU instruction to send data to GPU is executed with the help of DMA controllers."

1.17. A GPU has a single address on the CPU PCI-express network, to which CPUs may send instructions and data. Recall that a GPU has many SIMD units, meaning different SIMD units may execute different instructions. In the SPMD model, a single program is sent to the GPU by one CPU, and all SIMD units execute this program at their own pace.

What are the reasons the progress of these SIMD units can get arbitrarily out of pace with each other?

1.18. One way to increase the memory bandwidth is to have many memory units so that each can be read in parallel. For example, the SM on a GPU may contain 32 banks to support a 32-wide SIMD instruction. All banks are accessible to each SIMD-core so that they can share memory. However, only one data item can be requested from one bank in a single clock cycle. If two different items are requested by two cores in the same cycle, these requests are in conflict, and they are issued serially. Assume that $data[i]$ resides in bank $i\%32$, Also assume that $i$, $j$, and $tmp$ are local to each core and reside, respectively, in three of the registers of that core.

```
int data[][33]
    for(int i=0; i<32; i++)
    for(int j=i+1; j<32; j++)
        int tmp = data[i][id];
        data[i][id] = data[id][i];
        data[id][i] = tmp;
}
```

Prove that the code above causes no bank conflict.

1.19. Assign binary addresses to nodes on a cube network in a way that the addresses of any pair of nodes directly connected by a link differ in exactly one bit. Suppose the neighbor that is different in bit $i$ is called neighbor $i$.

Now devise a routing algorithm to send a packet from the node with address $A$ to that with address $B$. Routing must be through the shortest path. What is the maximum number of links traversed by any packet?

1.20. Consider the addressing scheme shown in Figure 1.18 but for a tree network with degree 32. Devise the routing algorithm. Find the maximum number of links traversed by any packet.

1.21. For the tree network in Exercise 1.20, find the maximum network latency observed if each device sends one packet to one other device. Assume that a packet takes one time-step to traverse each link. Two packets may not traverse the same link at any time-step. In addition, a node may only perform a single operation on a single link at one time-step. Thus, it may accept one packet at any time-step on one of its links, or send one out on one link.

1.22. For a $16 \times 16 \times 16$ 3D torus network, where each node is addressed with its 3D coordinate $(i, j, k)$, devise the routing algorithm to send a packet from node $(i_s, j_s, k_s)$ to node $(i_d, j_d, k_d)$ using the shortest route.

1.23. Show that the Butterfly network shown in Figure 1.16 is equivalent to an Omega network.

1.24. Reimagine the folded Clos network in Figure 1.20 with $2r \times 2r$ cross-bars at the spine level and $(l + k) \times (l + k)$ cross-bars at the leaf level so that incoming data on any full-duplex link can be routed to any other link. Design a nonblocking network supporting 648 computing systems. You may choose an appropriate $r$, $l$, and $k$.

# CHAPTER 2

# Parallel Programming Models

You have the hardware and understand its architecture. You have a large problem to solve. You suspect that a parallel program

*Question*: How are execution engines and data organized into a parallel program?

may be helpful. Where do you begin? Before we can answer that question, an understanding of the software infrastructure is required. In this chapter, we will discuss general organization of parallel programs, that is, typical software architecture. Chapter 5 elaborates this further and discusses how to design solutions to different types of problems.

As we have noted, truly sequential processors hardly exist, but they execute sequential programs fully well. Some parts of the

*Question*: What are some common types of parallel programs?

sequential program may even be executed in parallel, either directly by the hardware's design, or with the help of a parallelizing compiler. On the other hand, we are likely to achieve severely sub-par performance by relying solely on the hardware and the compiler. With only a little more thought, it is often possible to simply organize a sequential program into multiple components and turn it into a truly parallel program.

This chapter introduces parallel programming models. Parallel programming models characterize the anatomy or structure of parallel programs. This structure is somewhat more complex than that of a sequential program, and one must understand this structure to develop parallel programs. These programming models will also provide the context for the performance analysis methodology discussed in Chapter 3 as well as the parallel design techniques described in Chapter 5.

We will see in Chapter 7 that many efficient sequential algorithms are not so efficient if trivially parallelized. Many problems instead require specially designed parallel algorithms suitable for the underlying system architecture. These parallel algorithms are often designed directly in terms of these programming models.

A program broadly consists of executable parts and memory where data is held, in addition to input and output. A large parallel program usually performs input and output through a parallel file system. We will discuss parallel file systems in Section 5.4, but in the context of the current discussion they behave much like memory – data of some size can be fetched from an address or written to an address by executable parts. At a high level then, programs can be characterized by the relationship between memory parts and executable parts. Two broad categories exist: distributed-memory model and shared-memory model.

## 2.1  Distributed-Memory Programming Model

The distributed-memory programming model is demonstrated in Figure 2.1. Each execution part – let us call it a fragment[1] – is able to

> [1] *Defined*: A fragment is sequence of executed instructions

address one or more memory areas. However, addresses accessed by different fragments, even if those addresses happen to have the same value, refer to different locations. In other words, they have separate address spaces. Notice the similarity of Figure 2.1 to Figure 1.1b, which describes a similar hardware architecture.

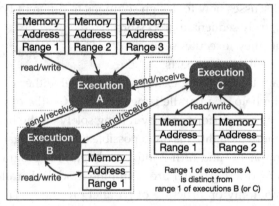

**Figure 2.1** Distributed-memory programming model

The two are independent, however. Programs based on the distributed-memory model may be executed on shared-memory hardware. Similarly, shared-memory programs may be executed on distributed-memory hardware using software abstractions like what we will study in Chapter 6. Computing hardware can contain both distributed and shared memory components. Similarly, programs may also be a mix – different groups of fragments may have separate address spaces, with all fragments in a group sharing its address space. However, many programmers exclusively select one style over the other in the interest of simplicity, even when the hybrid model may yield the better performance.

In distributed-memory programming, fragments intercommunicate through explicit instructions executed by each fragment, for example, *send* and *receive*. This is called *message-passing* and necessarily requires that each fragment has a name or identifier using which other fragments address it. Send and receive are point-to-point communicators and symmetric. A send function in one fragment must match a receive function in another. Thus a degree of "synchronization" between the sender and recipient is required.

A rudimentary program skeleton in the distributed-memory style is shown below. We defer until later the details of how to start and execute multiple programs.

| Fragment 0 |
| --- |
| x = 5; |
| receive(1, y); |
| send(1, x + y); |

| Fragment 1 |
| --- |
| send(0, 10); |
| receive(0, x); |

The first argument to both the receive and send functions is the name of the fragment to which the second argument is communicated. Both fragments have variables called $x$ and $y$, but they contain different data and are not shared. Note that Fragment 0, on its second line, is ready to receive in its variable $y$, some data from Fragment 1. At the same time, Fragment 1 on line 1 sends the value 10 to Fragment 0. Both must execute complementary instructions. Managing such handshakes is an important part of distributed-memory programming. Later in their codes, Fragment 0 sends back the sum of its variables $x$ and $y$ (i.e. 15) to Fragment 1, which it receives in its variable $x$.

We will study enhancements to this model where the synchronization in handshakes is loose, or where explicit send and receive functions are not required. We will also see examples of higher-order communication primitives that allow more intricate data transfer patterns involving more than two participants, for example, scatter-gather and reduce.

## 2.2   Shared-Memory Programming Model

As the name suggests, fragments of a program based on the shared-memory model can access the same memory. Programs in this category look structurally similar to the traditional sequential style, as the fragments simply read and write in a similar fashion. In the following shared-memory program example, values written by Fragment 0 are simply read by Fragment 1.

| Fragment 0 |
| --- |
| x = 1; |

| Fragment 1 |
| --- |
| while(x == 0); |
| x = 2; |

Both fragments refer to the same $x$. Assuming that $x$ is initially set to 0, Fragment 0 first sets it to 1, and after Fragment 2 observes this change, it sets it to 2. They can communicate thus, and no send–receive handshake is required and each fragment may appear similar to a sequential program.

This can be deceptive. Although these fragments would behave similarly to sequential programs if executed in isolation when no other fragments exist, the presence of others can impact each in both obvious and subtle ways. Since memory locations are shared by fragments, the oft-implicit assumption breaks that a memory location remains what it was when it was last read (or written) by a given fragment. Not accounting for this possibility can – and does – have disastrous consequences. Consider the following listing for the system shown in Figure 2.2.

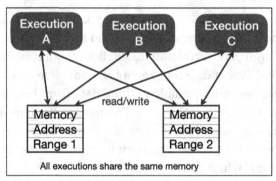

**Figure 2.2** Shared-memory programming model

**Listing 2.1** Incorrect Shared Operation

```
1 void withdraw(int amount)
2 {
3    if(balance - amount > 0)
4       balance -= amount;
5 }
```

On line 4, the program assumes that *balance* remains what it was observed on line 3. This may not be so if another thread modifies it. That is why, the send–receive handshake must be replaced here by a different type of synchronization. This synchronization is not directly between two specific fragments, but rather between a fragment that accesses a given memory location and any other fragment that accesses the same memory location. Indeed, we may say that the synchronization is specific to that memory location, or any such shared resource in general. Chapter 4 describes several common synchronization primitives, but the notion of *atomicity* is the most basic ingredient in any synchronization.

An atomic activity is a list of instructions executed by a fragment that appears to have occurred instantaneously with respect to other atomic activities. In other words, two atomic activities with respect to some shared resource are strictly sequential and never overlapping or concurrent. Hence, during an atomic activity by a fragment, the otherwise shared resource becomes exclusive to it. For example, if the following sequence of instructions is atomically performed by some fragment,

**Atomic:**

> 1. Location $x = 1$;
>
> 2. Location $y = 5$;

no other fragment referring to $x$ and $y$ may read the value 1 in $x$ but not the value 5 in $y$ – assuming that $x$ had a value other than 1, and $y$ had a value other than 5 before this fragment updated those variables. This holds as long as the other threads also use atomic operations to access $x$ and $y$.

In general, synchrony has to do with time or time-step. Recall that this time-step is related to clock ticks. However, there may not be a universal clock in a parallel system. Indeed, unsynchronized clocks ticking at different rates is the norm. Nevertheless, a fragment can observe the impact of other fragments' activities. For example, a recipient observes the sender's activity. Similarly, a reader observes a writer's activity. Of course, each fragment directly observes its own activities. Synchronization then can be defined by ordering of such observations by any fragment with respect to its own steps. The two accesses in the example above being atomic, other fragments that access $x$ and $y$ atomically must always observe both updates or neither at any of its own steps. We will study synchronization in more detail in Chapter 4.

Shared-memory programs map quite well to shared-memory hardware. However, the performance of shared-memory hardware does not generally scale well with increasing processor counts. Hence, large systems are likely to contain many hardware memory modules, usually distributed among the processors. Executing shared-memory programs on distributed-memory hardware is more complex and usually relies on significant software infrastructure. We will see examples in Chapter 6.

## 2.3  Task Graph Model

Other than the relationship between executing fragments and memory, the relationship among the fragments themselves is one way to think about program organization. We have already seen one such explicit inter-fragment relationship in Section 2.1. The other important relationship is their synchronization. Two executing fragments may proceed in parallel but in complete synchrony, completely independently (i.e. *asynchronously*) or in occasional synchrony.

These relationships can be captured in a task graph. We define a *task* as a sequential execution, or more accurately: instructions retired sequentially. It is worth noting that different connotations of the term "task" are applied in different contexts. Ours is not a universal definition, but it is useful. A parallel program consists of many such tasks. In the extreme case, a task may consist of a single instruction's execution, but given that hardware comprises sequential execution engines, it is common for parallel programs to consist of longer tasks. The number of steps in a task relative to those in the complete parallel program is called its *granularity*. Coarse-grained tasks are relatively longer; fine-grained tasks are shorter. We will discuss their trade-offs in more detail in Chapter 5.

We have informally used the term "executing fragment" in the previous sections. In general, these fragments could be parallel constructs in those cases, but an executing task is always sequential by our definition. The relationships among the tasks are encoded in directed edges of the task graph. These edges are of two types:

Communicate: Edge from task A to task B indicates that A sends one or more messages that B receives. We will assume that the messages are received by B in the order they are sent by A. If B also sends messages to A, we may use a bi-directional arrow instead of two separate arrows.[2]

Start: Edge from task A to task B indicates that B starts after A finishes. Communication is also implicit in start edges: message from A to B may, for example, communicate A's program state to B so it may proceed from there, or simply say "start."

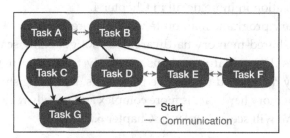

**Figure 2.3** Task graph

Figure 2.3 shows an example. Tasks A and B communicate. Tasks C to F start on completion of task B. Task G may begin only after every one of tasks A and C–F completes.

---

[2] This communication may be through shared memory or as explicit messages. In that sense, task graphs unify shared-memory and distributed-memory programming. Alternatively, a task graph may be considered a high-level structure that hides the memory relationship, and exposes the fragment relationship.

The graph is necessarily acyclic with respect to the start edges. The program ends when all tasks are completed. Communication edges may have implicit synchronization. Start edges also require synchronization.

In the expanded task graph, we also represent memory as special vertices. A task has an edge to a memory vertex if it can write to it and an edge from a memory vertex if it can read from it. Further, memory locations may be locked and thus synchronized by tasks with an edge to or from that memory. Memory edges are usually bi-directional. Some tasks may share memory with each other, while other tasks share data only through communication edges.

Task graph programming is based on, for example, primitives to create, start, terminate, suspend, merge, or continue tasks. We defer detailed discussion about how tasks start, where they execute, and how edges are managed to Chapter 6, where we will discuss practical tools for task graph programming. In particular, we will discuss higher-level primitives that create and manage multiple tasks in one shot, for example, fork-join and task-arrays. We will also discuss in Chapter 5 how to decompose a problem into tasks in the first place.

## 2.4   Variants of Task Parallelism

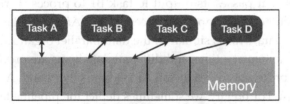

**Figure 2.4** Data parallelism

*Data-parallel* model can be thought of as a variant of the task graph in which multiple similar tasks are created. Each task operates on one of many similar data items as shown in Figure 2.4. Usually, these data are in shared memory that all tasks directly read. The focus on data-parallel programs is mainly to determine which pieces of data each task must process. Usually, this is a simple mapping, like task $i$ processes array element $i$. Many times, one task per data-item is created, and they execute independently of each other, repeating the same computation on their data.

Task decomposition and mapping are parts of solution design, and we will discuss them in detail in Chapter 6. Purely data-parallel tasks have no edges among them. Since such tasks generally perform work equal to each other, assigning tasks to processors in an equitable way is easy.

Another variant is called *model parallelism*. In this, the tasks are not necessarily the same, but they all work on the same piece of data, and each task's work is predetermined. Such parallelism is often employed when, say, multiple different search algorithms are employed to locate a pattern in given data. Machine learning applications often employ this technique.

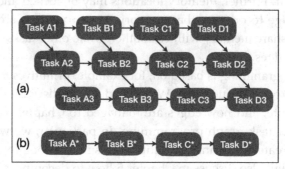

**Figure 2.5** Task pipeline

*Pipeline parallelism* is a different organization of parallel computation, which mirrors the way hardware pipelines are structured (see Section 1.3). Tasks are performed in a sequence, as shown in Figure 2.5a. Each row of tasks is similar to the row below. Once task A1 completes, it passes its output to task B1 to process further. It also starts A2, a copy of A1, which gets new input to process. Tasks A$i$ are similar to each other; they just process different data. This is similar to the data-parallel organization, except only one A$i$ processes one data item at a time, and different data items are processed in sequence. (This allows the same processor to execute all A$i$.) On the other hand, A2 can proceed in parallel with B1 and so on. For brevity, we sometimes depict the pipeline task graph by folding the lower rows into the top row, as shown in Figure 2.5b.

*Stream processing* is a particular type of pipeline parallelism that focuses on organizing the data as a sequence of items streamed to each processing unit. The unit operates on each item in order, producing an output stream. This output may become an input stream to another processing unit. In addition to such linear streaming, splitting or merging of streams is also possible, creating a directed acyclic graph of stream processors. The management of computation at each processing unit is straightforward once the streams are set up.

*Actors* are another abstraction over the task graphs. Unlike stream processing, which focuses on data, actors stand for independent and arbitrary computational chunks. In both, however, the computation is local to an actor or stream processing unit — and it only maintains its local state. Of course, information about their states can be passed to each other as data.

In the Actors abstraction, actors are named and act in response to messages from other actors. An initial actor receives an implicit start message to begin computation. Actions are encapsulated by a behavior, which operates on each message. Actions can be:

- create a finite number of new actors

- send a finite number of messages to other actors known to this actor

- modify this actor's behavior on the next message

These actions in response to a message are concurrent and self-contained in the behaviour.

In the more general task-parallel programs, the separation of task creation and execution contexts may be unclear or too general. Concerns encompass determining when tasks are created, what work they must perform, and states they share and ensuring arbitrary order and synchronization. General task management can have a significant overhead, increasing the total execution time considerably. Hence, simpler task organizations like data-parallel computation or pipelines are often employed in practical systems.

## 2.5  Summary

Computing clusters used to execute parallel programs are often heterogeneous and complex. They include a variety of computation devices, including CPUs, GPUs, special-purpose hardware like FPGA (field-programmable gate array), programmable network devices, and others. A parallel program effectively requires code components for each of these and necessarily has many different parts (even though some parts may be copies of each other). Programming these different parts and, more importantly, their interactions become somewhat manageable by abstracting the software style.

More than determining how to divide the computation into parts, these styles focus on the organization of those parts. They include:

- Sharing memory – Appropriate ordering constraints must be used to determine when it is safe to access memory that can also be accessed by another execution.

- Exchanging data explicitly – The program must determine when to stop computing to communicate with one or more partner programs. Computation and communication may be in phases. The communication unit is separate from the instruction execution units and can proceed in parallel with it. However, synchronization between them is necessary to determine when it is safe to communicate with a partner.

- Cooperating task – Any number of somewhat autonomous programs collaboratively determine which tasks execute when. Programs accept input from others and produce output to others. Such interactions can be encoded in a task graph program, which a task graph processor executes.

- Pipelined operation – Limits may be imposed on the structure of the task graph. For example, tasks may be processed in a strict pipeline, with a fixed role for each task. Alternatively, a set of tasks may produce "data," while another set accepts the data and performs some operation on it. This amounts to a pipeline of groups. Such organization often requires a work-queue, to which task generators add data, and from which task executors remove items.

- Data-parallel operation – Copies of the same program (or minor variants) each operate on one unit of data. This subdivision can be in terms of operating on one part of the input, one part of the output, or one part of some intermediate data.

It is beyond this book's scope, but a formal study of fragment interaction[3] can help improve the insight into many correctness issues. Shared-memory style programming on distributed-memory hardware requires a careful design of the memory consistency guarantees and synchronization primitives. We will discuss these issues in Chapter 5. There are many examples of shared-memory style programming using distributed-memory hardware.[4] Task graphs are a powerful way to model parallelism, but expressing explicit graphs in programs can be expensive. Task graphs have historically been used for performance analysis and scheduling.[5] They are often used as an internal representation of middleware.[6] Programming APIs[7] for applications to specify explicit task graphs are also emerging.

[3] Hoare, "Communicating sequential processes."
Hewitt et al., "A universal modular ACTOR formalism for artificial intelligence."
[4] Charles et al., "X10: An object-oriented approach."
El-Ghazawi and Smith, "Upc: Unified parallel."
Nieplocha et al., "Global arrays."
Chamberlain et al., "Parallel programmability."
Beri et al., "The unicorn runtime.".
[5] El-Rewini et al., *Task Scheduling*.
Adve and Sakellariou, "Application representations."
Johnson et al., "A concurrent dynamic task graph."
[6] OpenMP Architecture Review Board, *OpenMP Application Program Interface*.
Beri et al., "The unicorn runtime."
Lam and Rinard, "Coarse-grain parallel programming in jade."
Chamberlain et al., "Parallel programmability."
[7] OpenMP Architecture Review Board, *OpenMP Application Program Interface*.
CUDA Development Team, *CUDA Toolkit Documentation*.
Rocklin, "Dask: Parallel computation."

# Exercise

2.1. What is shared-memory programming?

2.2. What is distributed-memory?

2.3. What is message-passing?

2.4. Assuming that the following fragments share memory (and variable name-space), what are the possible output? Assuming that there is a common output device, what is the order in which this output is produced? Ignore any effects of caching.

**Fragment 0**
```
x = 0;
y = 5;
if(x == 1)
y += 20;
output x + y;
```

**Fragment 1**
```
x = 1;
if(x == 0)
y = 10;
output x + y;
```

2.5. What is output by the fragments in Exercise 2.4 if they use distributed memory (and in what order)?

2.6. Shared-memory programs can suffer from subtle memory consistency issues. Exercise 2.4 is an example. One could, however, convert a shared-memory program to distributed memory by ensuring that the memory is partitioned, allocating one partition to each executing fragment. Describe what other changes may be required in the program. What are the shortcomings of this approach?

2.7. Consider the following executing fragments that share variables $x$ and $y$. Their goal is to ensure that both fragments' updates to $y$ are retained at the end. Explain what can go wrong if independent instructions in a fragment may be re-ordered by the compiler.

**Fragment 0**
```
while(x == 0);
y += 5;
x = 1;
```

**Fragment 1**
```
while(x == 1);
y += 50;
x = 0;
```

Assume for simplicity that there is no data caching. The value of $x$ may be 0 or 1 initially.

2.8.  In the following code fragments (each executing sequentially), each message-passing operation requires complete handshake. Argue that neither fragment progresses to its output statement.

| Fragment 0 |
| --- |
| send(1, $x$); |
| receive(1, $y$); |
| output $x + y$; |

| Fragment 1 |
| --- |
| send(0, $x$); |
| receive(0, $y$); |
| output $x + y$; |

2.9.  Communication usually has a higher latency than computation, whether it is through messages or memory. (Note that caches can reduce the average latency, but they only increase the worst-case latency.) On the other hand, fragments retire instructions sequentially. However, instead of waiting for the communication instruction to complete, suppose the instructions immediately after a memory/send/receive instruction do not depend on its result. These later instructions can then start executing before the communication is complete. (This usually requires additional registers to store operands for later use.) Propose a technique to perform the send–receive handshake to enable such out-of-order instruction execution.

2.10.  The tasks on the longest chain of dependencies in a task graph are said to form its critical path. Tasks on this chain must proceed one after the other. The maximum concurrency of a task graph is the maximum number of tasks that can execute in parallel with each other. For the tasks in Figure 2.6, compute their critical paths, and the maximum concurrency. You may assume that the inter-task communication occurs only at the task start and end times.

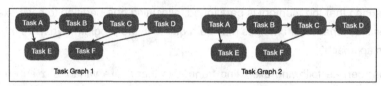

**Figure 2.6** Example task graphs

2.11.  Task design for a program organized in a data-parallel fashion is usually straightforward. Data are equally partitioned into some $P$ parts, and each assigned to one of $P$ task copies. Each task is independent of others. Design such a task graph for computing the product of two $n \times n$ matrices.

2.12.  Provide the task graph for the reduction algorithm in Section 3.2, assuming each node is a task.

2.13. In a work-queue organization, tasks are often generated dynamically on the fly and are usually independent of each other. Write pseudo-code showing how these generated tasks may be added to a common list of waiting tasks and later removed for execution. You may assume an "atomic" construct as follows:

```
atomic{
   - lines of code -
}
```

This construct ensures that the "lines of code" is executed atomically.

# CHAPTER 3

# Parallel Performance Analysis

Programs need to be correct. Programs also need to be fast. In order to write efficient programs, one surely must know how to

**Question**: How do you reason about how long an algorithm or program takes?

evaluate efficiency. One might take recourse to our prior understanding of efficiency in the sequential context and compare observed parallel performance to observed sequential performance. Or, we can define parallel efficiency independent of sequential performance. We may yet draw inspiration from the way efficiency is evaluated in a sequential context. Into that scheme, we would need to incorporate the impact of an increasing number of processors deployed to solve the given problem.

Efficiency has two metrics. The first is in an abstract setting, for example, the asymptotic analysis[1] of the underlying algorithm. The second is concrete – how well does the algorithm's implementation behave in practice on the available hardware and on data sizes of interest. Both are important.

There is no substitute for measuring the performance of the real implementation on real data. On the other hand, developing and testing iteratively on large parallel systems is prohibitively expensive. Most development occurs on a small scale: using only a few processors, $p$, on small input of size $n$. The extrapolation of these tests to a much larger scale is deceptively hard, and we often must resort to simplified models and analysis tools.

Asymptotic analysis on simple models is sometimes criticized because it oversimplifies several complex dynamics (like cache behavior, out-of-order execution on multiple execution engines, instruction dependencies, etc.) and conceals constant multipliers. Nonetheless, with large input sizes that are common in parallel applications, asymptotic measures do have value. They can be computed somewhat easily, in a standardized setting and without requiring iterations on large supercomputers. And, concealing constants is a choice to some degree. Useful constants can and should be retained. Nonetheless, the abstract part of our analysis will employ the big-$O$ notation to describe the number of steps an algorithm takes. It is a function of the input size $n$ and the number of processors $p$.

---

[1] The notion of asymptotic complexity is not described here. Readers not aware of this tool should refer to a book, for example, Cormen et al., *Introduction to Algorithms*.

Asymptotic notation or not, the time $t(n, p)$ to solve a problem in parallel is a function of $n$ and $p$. For this purpose, we will generally count in $p$ the number of sequential processors – they complete their program instructions in sequence. Naturally, we want both $n$ and $p$ to be variable to allow a wider choice of computing platforms. $t(n, p)$ is the number of steps taken by the slowest of the $p$ processors deployed. Like we expect a program to run on varying input sizes, we also must design programs that run well with varying $p$. In reality, $t$ is also a function of the core structure, network topology, cache sizes, and so on, but taking a cue from the sequential analysis style, we will use a simplified model of a parallel system.

## 3.1  Simple Parallel Model

We need a simple model of computation steps to be able to evaluate performance. Random Access Machine (RAM)[2] model is such a sequential model, where simple arithmetic operations and memory operations take a unit time-step. Given that, one may evaluate the total number of time-steps taken by an algorithm in the worst case, or on average.

We seek a similar simple model to capture parallelism.

1. A parallel system consists of $p$ sequential processors, $p$ is variable and may be chosen to be a function of $n$. It may be fixed for the entire duration of the algorithm or could be allowed to vary from step to step.[3]

2. Each processor has access to an unbounded number of constant-sized local memory locations, which are not accessible to other processors.

3. Each processor can read from or write to any local memory location in unit time.

4. Communicating a constant-sized message from processor $i$ to processor $j$ takes unit time.

5. Each processor takes unit time to perform simple arithmetic and logical operations on constant-sized operands.

This model is simple and more useful than it may first seem. Its major shortcoming is that the time taken by the network in message transmission is not modeled. The cost of synchronization is also ignored. Instead, it assumes that if a message addressed to processor $i$ is sent by some other processor, it arrives instantaneously and processor $i$ spends one time-unit reading it. In effect, processor $i$ may receive a message at any time,

---

[2] Cook and Reckhow, "Time-bounded random access machines."
[3] Varying $p$ may seem odd at first, considering that most computing systems have a fixed size. Nonetheless, we do not generally design algorithms and programs for one specific machine. They must be flexible and support the variable $p$. See Section 3.5 for a more detailed explanation.

and only the unit time spent in reading it is counted. This model works reasonably well in practice for programs based on the distributed-memory model. A more precise model accounts for the message transmission delay as well as the synchronization overhead.

## 3.2   Bulk-Synchronous Parallel Model

The bulk-synchronous parallel model (i.e. *BSP* model[4]) addresses those two shortcomings. At the same time, it avoids modeling synchronizations in too great a detail. The BSP model limits synchronization to defined points after every few local steps. Thus recognizing that synchronization is an occasional requirement, it groups instructions into *super-steps*. A super-step consists of a finite number of local arithmetic or memory steps, followed by one synchronization step. Each local step is as in the simple model in Section 3.1 and an arbitrary number of processors is available per super-step. We continue to denote their count by $p$. Each processor has access to an arbitrary number of constant-sized local memory locations.

1. Super-steps proceed in synchrony: all processors complete super-step $s$ before any starts super-step $s + 1$.

2. A super-step consists of local steps, followed by a synchronization step. Synchronization is a global event – all processors take this step, and its end at any processor indicates that all processors have reached the synchronization step. After the synchronization completes, the next super-step may begin. The time taken to synchronize is a function of $p$, the number of processors.

3. The time taken by a super-step includes the local computation time, which is the maximum time taken by any processor, $L_s$ for super-step $s$. This can vary from super-step to super-step. $L_s$ may depend on the input size $n$ and processor count $p$.

4. In super-step $s$, processor $i$ sends $h_{s_i}$ point-to-point messages to other processors. The total number of messages sent in super-step $s$ is $\sum h_{s_i} = h_s$. $h_s$ may be a function of $n$ and $p$.[5]

5. The messages are all received at the synchronization step. Thus the received data is available only in the next super-step. This clearly defines the send–receive synchronization point.

Figure 3.1 depicts the super-steps in a BSP model. All processors perform local computation interspersed with sends. The messages go into the network, which delivers them to their destinations. At the completion of these local steps, each processor proceeds

---

[4] Valiant, "A bridging model."

[5] This cost formulation is slightly different from the original work of Valiant.

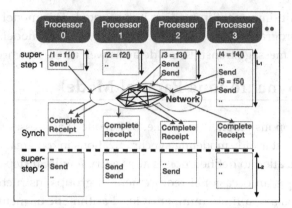

**Figure 3.1** BSP computation model

to the synchronization *barrier*. Formally, no processor may cross this barrier until all processors have reached it and they have all received their messages.

## BSP Computation Time

The time taken by a BSP algorithm is the sum of the times taken by each super-step. The time taken by a super-step varies from step to step. This time includes computation time as well as data transmission and synchronization time. The computation time for super-step $s$ is $L_s$, the maximum time taken by any processor. We assume in this analysis that the processors all execute at the same rate, meaning that a unit time is the same for all processors. The number of steps taken by different processors can then be compared to each other. It's a safe assumption for asymptotic analysis because the clock rates, in reality, do not differ by more than a constant factor. In fact, rates may not differ by much at all in practice, and even with the assumption of a common rate, the performance analysis is meaningful.

The data transmission time is proportional to $h_s$. For example, we might say that the network has the capacity to deliver $\frac{1}{t}$ constant size messages between any pair of processors per unit time. The time taken to deliver $h_s$ message, then, is $t h_s$. One might consider $t$ to be a function of $p$, or let it be a constant for simpler analysis. Finally the synchronization time $S_s$ is a function only of $p$.

Thus the super-step time is $L_s + t h_s + S_s$. The total execution time is given by:

$$\sum_{\forall parallel \text{ super-step } s} (L_s + t h_s + S_s).$$

Each component is potentially a function if $p$. $L_s$ and $h_s$ may also depend on $n$. And, of course, $p$ can itself be a function of $n$. The three terms above separate the measurement of local computation times, communication times, and synchronization times, respectively.

This model does consider the synchronization overhead and idle times of processors. However, the synchronization model may be too restrictive, and it ignores the complexities of network communication. For example, in real systems, multiple messages between a pair of nodes may or may not be batched. Thus, the communication time need not be solely a function of the total number of messages. We have also seen in Chapter 1 that different pairs of nodes could have different latency or throughput. The BSP model also hides communication latency. That may not be possible if $L$ and $t$ are small in comparison to the latency. As a practicum, assuming $p$ to be several times the actual number of physical processors allows an underlying system to schedule communication more efficiently. A cleverly written program attempts to hide communication latency by performing other computation concurrently with the communication.

Assuming complete concurrency between computation and communication, we can account for the overlap by replacing $L_s + th_s$ with $\max(L_s, th_s)$. This would not impact asymptotic analysis as the big-$O$ complexity remains the same. It is desirable for a computational model to abstract away many complexities – particularly ones that vary from system to system. The role of the model is to help with a gross analysis of the parallel algorithm. This algorithm may then be suitably adapted to the actual hardware architecture, at which point some of the abstracted details can be reconsidered. Furthermore, a universally accepted model allows programs to be written to the model and architecture to be designed to support its primitive operations.

## BSP Example

Let us consider an illustrative example of performance analysis using the BSP model. Take the problem of computing the dot product of two vectors.

Assume that the $n$ elements of vectors $A$ and $B$ are initially equally divided among $p$ processors. The vector segments are in arrays referred to locally as $lA$ and $lB$ in all processors. The number of elements in each local array $= \frac{n}{p}$. Assume $n$ is divisible by $p$ and consider the following code:

Input:  Array $A$ and $B$ with $n$ integers each.

Output:

$$A \cdot B = \sum_{i=0}^{n-1} A[i] \times B[i]$$

Solution:

```
forall⁶ processor i < p {// in parallel
  { // Super-step local computation:
```

---

[6] forall means that all indicated processors perform the loop in parallel. The range of forall index variable (i here), along with an optional condition indicates how many processors are used. The lower end of the range defaults to 0. The use of the index variable i in the enclosed body indicates what each processor does. We sometimes omit the keyword processor to emphasize the data-parallelism.

```
int lc = 0; // Local at each processor
int lC[p]; // Only needed at processor 0. Used for Receipt.
for(int idx=0; idx<n/p; idx++)
    lc += lA[idx] * lB[idx];
send lc to processor 0
} { // Super-step synchronization:
barrier; // The barrier is always there for BSP, listed or not.
Receive any item from processor i into lC[i] // Only processor 0 has any
}
}
//-- All receipts have now been completed into lC --
forall processor i == 0 { // A single virtual processor is active.
{ // Super-step local computation
    for(int idx=1; idx<p; idx++)
        lc += lC[idx];
    output lc;
} {// The barrier is implicit.
}
}
```

We can now analyze the time complexity of this algorithm. The first super-step requires $k_1 \frac{n}{p}$ local time, $k_2 p$ communication time, and $k_3 p$ synchronization time, assuming the network throughput to be a constant independent of $p$ and the barrier to be a linear function of $p$. $k_1, k_2, k_3$ are constants. The second super-step takes time $k_4 p$. Thus the total time is $\Theta(\frac{n}{p} + p)$.

It is possible to make a different choice for the second super-step, whose goal is to add the $p$ numbers at $p$ processors. Consider the following alternative. Assume for simplicity that $p$ is a power of 2.

```
forall processor i < p {// Assume p is a power of 2
    { // Super-step local computation
        int lc2; // Designate for receipt of 1 item
        int lc = 0;
        for(int idx=0; idx<n/p; idx++)
            lc += lA[idx] * lB[idx];
        if(i >= p/2)
            send lc to processor i - p/2 // 2nd half sends to 1st half
        p = p/2; // Halve the processor count for the next super-step
    }{ // Super-step synchronization
        barrier;
        receive any item into lc2
    }
}
```

```
while(p > 0) { // Super-step loop
  // Data sent in the previous step have now been received into lc2
  forall processor i < p { // Only those that remain active
    { // Super-step local computation
      lc += lc2; // Accumulate the received value
      if(i >= p/2)
        send lc to processor i - p/2 // 2nd half sends to 1st half
      p = p/2; // Halve the processors active at the next super-step
    }{ // Super-step synchronization
      barrier;
      receive any item into lc2 // to accumulate further in the next iteration
    }
  }
}
// -- Last super-step --
forall processor i == 0 {
  output lc; // Implicit barrier is after this local step
}
```

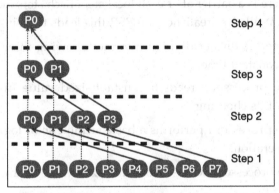

**Figure 3.2** Binary tree–like computation tree

Now, there are more super-steps. The super-step loop has log $p$ iterations. The structure of the computation is that of a binary tree, as shown in Figure 3.2. This process, where values in a vector are combined to produce a single scalar value, is called reduction.[7] In this variant of reduction, the number of processors employed in each super-step halves from that at the previous step, until it goes down to 1 in the final step. In this

> [7] **Defined**: Values in a vector are combined to produce a single scalar value. This is called reduction.

example, each active processor sends a single message in each iteration. Thus the total time is again $\Theta(\frac{n}{p} + p + \log p) = \Theta(\frac{n}{p} + p)$:

1. The first super-step takes $k_1 \frac{n}{p}$ local time, $k_2 \frac{p}{2}$ communication time, and $k_3 p$ synchronizatio time.

2. The iterative super-step $s$ takes $\Theta(1)$ local time and $\Theta(2^{(\log p - s)})$ communication and synchronization time. This sums to $\Theta(\log p + p)$ over the $\log p$ super-steps.

3. The final super-step takes $\Theta(1)$ total time.

## 3.3  PRAM Model

The parallel RAM (i.e. *PRAM*)[8] model mirrors the shared-memory programming model. Like the BSP model, the PRAM model also assumes an arbitrary number of processors, $p$, each with an arbitrary number of constant-sized local memory locations. Further:

1. An arbitrary number of shared memory locations are accessible to all processors.

2. All processors proceed in complete synchrony: all complete step $s$ before any starts step $s + 1$. Thus, there is a barrier after each local step. Each step, including the barrier, takes constant time. While less realistic than BSP, this leads to a simpler analysis.

3. Each PRAM step is further divided into the following three synchronous sub-steps, each taking a constant time:

   i Each active processor $i$ reads a constant-sized value from any shared-memory location $r_i$ of its choosing.

   ii Each active processor $i$ performs a basic arithmetic or logical operation, or a local memory operation.

   iii Each active processor $i$ writes a constant-sized value to any shared location $w_i$ of its choosing.

The processors that are active at any step depends on the algorithm. Not all active processors are required to perform each sub-step. Some processors may remain idle in some sub-step.

The imposition of lock-step progress eliminates the need for explicit synchronization by the program, but it may yet result in conflicting writes by two processors to the same memory location in the same step. One solution is simply to disallow such shared reads and writes. This variant of the model is called *EREW* PRAM model: $r_i \neq r_j$ and $w_i \neq w_j$ in any sub-step if $i \neq j$. Algorithms in this model must respect this restriction. Thus, each

---

[8] Fortune and Wyllie, "Parallelism in random access machines."

reader has exclusive access to its read location and each writer has exclusive access to its write location. Conflict is hence ruled out by the definition of the model. This restriction on the model (and hence the algorithms that assume this model) actually does not limit its generality. Algorithms designed for models that do not have these restrictions can be automatically translated into algorithms that do respect these restrictions. Only, the number of steps required by the resulting algorithm may be higher.

A more general variant is *CREW* PRAM, which allows two processors to read values from the same location in the same step. Writes remain exclusive. *CRCW* PRAM models, which allow conflicting writes as well, are also meaningful if the result of such conflicts are well defined. Several CRCW models have been proposed.[9] These allow $w_i$ to equal $w_j$ for any number of different $i, j$ pairs, but with certain restrictions. Some examples are:

1. Common-CRCW: If $w_i = w_j$, both processors $i$ and $j$ must write the same value. So, there is no data conflict.

2. Arbitrary-CRCW: If $w_i = w_j$, either of the conflicting values may be written. The other is discarded. If more than two processors conflict, any one write may succeed. The algorithm's correctness must not depend on which value is actually written.

3. Priority-CRCW: If $w_i = w_j$, the smaller of $i$ and $j$ succeeds. If more than two processors conflict, the smallest-indexed processor among all conflicting processors has priority and its value is written.

Figure 3.3 demonstrates the PRAM model. Step 1 shows that processors 2 and 3 read from the same location $w$. This would not be possible in an EREW PRAM. All the writes in step 1 are to different locations – they do not conflict. Hence this step would be allowed by a CREW PRAM. Note that processor 2 writing to location $w$ and other processors reading from $w$ in the read sub-step of the same step is not considered common or conflicting. The read fetches the older value.

Step 2 shows a succinct way to write instructions. Each processor reads from a shared-memory location, optionally adds two values, and then writes to a shared-memory location. Notice that processors 0–2 all write to location $y$. This is not possible in CREW or EREW PRAM. It is possible only in CRCW PRAM. Again note that the reading of $x$ by processor 0 happens strictly before its update by processor 3 in the write sub-step of this step.

The third step shows that processors 1 and 2 have a common write to location $z$. Since the two values are the same, all three CRCW variants support this. Processors 0 and

---

[9] Kučera, "Parallel computation."
Shiloach and Vishkin, "An o(logn) parallel connectivity algorithm."

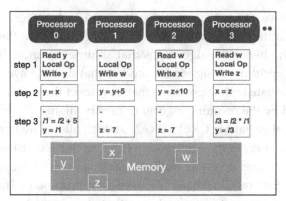

**Figure 3.3** PRAM computation model

3 must also have the same values in their respective local variables $l1$ and $l3$ for this program to be supported by Common CRCW. In case they do not have the same values, only Priority-CRCW and Arbitrary-CRCW would allow that. In Priority-CRCW PRAM, the value in variable $l1$ of processor 0 is expected to be written by this program. In Arbitrary-CRCW PRAM, this program must produce the correct result irrespective of the value ($l1$ or $l3$) written into $y$ at the end of this step.

All the listed PRAM variants are generally equal, and an algorithm designed in any model can be translated into any other.[10] The difference is in their execution times and the simplicity of designing algorithms. Priority-CRCW is the most useful since any algorithm of other models can be executed in this model *as is* without any translation. We could choose this model for our design. However, in practice, this model is the furthest from practical hardware, and hides more cost than the others. Detecting and prioritizing conflicts of an arbitrary number of processors in constant time is not feasible. Comparatively, Common-CRCW and Arbitrary-CRCW are safer models to design algorithms with, being more representative of the hardware. However, the cost of supporting conflicting reads and writes can be nontrivial in a distributed-memory setting, where the EREW model may be more effective.

Regardless, all models assume perfect synchrony, which is hard to achieve in hardware in constant time for a large number of processors. This means that that communication and synchronization costs are not accounted for in PRAM analysis.

---

[10] Chlebus et al., "New simulations between CRCW PRAMS."
Jájá, *Introduction to Parallel Algorithms*.

## PRAM Computation Time

Each step of PRAM takes a constant time-unit. The total time taken is then proportional to the number of PRAM steps.

There is a local step in PRAM, quite like BSP does. The communication step maps to reads and writes. Processors "send" in the PRAM model by writing to a shared location, and "recipients" read from there. In a sense, the (read, local step, write) triplet is analogous to the BSP super-step, except that each of the three sub-steps is synchronous in PRAM, whereas only the full super-step is synchronous in BSP. Also, the cost of synchronization is hidden in PRAM, while BSP accounts for synchronization and also allows arbitrary local computation between synchronizations.

Thus, accounting is simpler in PRAM: assume each step takes unit time. One can equivalently say that each of the three sub-steps takes unit time, and the step takes "3" units. Asymptotically, they lead to the same analysis. Note that each processor is allowed local memory in PRAM, just like BSP. It may be tempting to allow the middle sub-step to include an arbitrary number of sub-steps, as BSP does. On the other hand, that is equivalent to having those local sub-steps to be simply associated with "NULL" read and write steps (i.e. all processors remain inactive in those sub-steps). The difference effectively is that BSP accounts for the increased cost of shared reads and writes, and PRAM does not.

Let us analyze the same dot product example, now in the PRAM model. This time $A$ and $B$ are in shared memory accessible to all processors.

## PRAM Example

Input: Array $A$ and $B$ with $n$ integers each in shared memory.

Output:

$$A \cdot B = \sum_{i=0}^{n-1} A[i] \times B[i]$$

Solution:

```
int C[p]; // C is a shared int array of size p
forall processor i < p {
    C[i] = 0;
    for(int idx=0; idx<n/p; idx++)
        C[i] += A[i*n/p+idx] * B[i*n/p+idx];
}
forall processor i == 0 {
    for(int idx=1; idx<p; idx++)
        C[0] += C[idx];
    output C[0];
}
```

At each iteration of the first loop, processor $i$ reads from $A, B,$ and $C$ in three consecutive steps. The local computation of the product and sum as well as the write-back of $C[i]$ also takes place in the third step. Thus the processors all take $\Theta(\frac{n}{p})$ steps in the first loop. The second loop employs only a single processor, which takes $\Theta(p)$ time. Thus the total time complexity of this PRAM algorithm is $\Theta(\frac{n}{p} + p)$. This matches the complexity of the equivalent algorithm in the BSP model. Note that only exclusive reads and writes are required.

We can also do a tree-like reduction in the EREW PRAM model, as we did in the BSP model, as follows:

```
int C[p]; // C is a shared int array of size p
forall processor i < p {
    C[i] = 0;
    for(int idx=0; idx<n/p; idx++) // Assume n is divisible by p
        C[i] += A[i*n/p+idx] * B[i*n/p+idx];
}

p = p/2; // Halve the number of processors used
while(p > 0) {
    forall processor i < p {
        C[i] += C[i+p/2];
        p = p/2;
    }
}

forall processor i == 0
    output C[0];
```

The first loop is unchanged from the previous version and takes time $\Theta(\frac{n}{p})$. The second loop takes $\Theta(1)$ time per iteration and $\log p$ iterations, taking total time $\Theta(\log p)$. The last step takes $\Theta(1)$ time by processor 0. Notice that the total time based on this analysis, that is, $\Theta(\frac{n}{p} + \log p)$, is different from the time taken by the analogous algorithm in the BSP model. This is because the extra messages passed in the reduction variant are exposed and counted in the BSP model. This count remains hidden in the PRAM model because more processors are able to perform more shared-memory accesses in parallel in the same time-step. In this aspect, PRAM is like the simple parallel model. In the case of shared-memory hardware, this unit time-step for shared-memory read is a reasonable assumption. Note that we sometimes allow $p$ to be a suitable function of $n$ for unified analysis. This allows us to count the number of inherently parallel operations in an algorithm. For example, if $p = \Theta(n)$ in the example above, the time complexity is $\Theta(\log n)$ even if $p$ is unlimited.

For distributed-memory setting, PRAM is simpler, but BSP may be better suited. Particularly so for algorithms that are communication-heavy. Other more elaborate computational models exist, but they also increase the complexity of algorithm analysis without necessarily providing significantly more realistic prediction of hardware performance. We discuss practical performance metrics next, which encompass measured running times of programs.

## 3.4   Parallel Performance Evaluation

If we describe a parallel program using the simple parallel model or one of the other models, we can compute the time it takes in the context of that model. We may next

> *Question:* What are the different aspects of measuring a parallel program's performance?

translate such a description to actual program implementation and measure the time it takes on real hardware. Either way, we can compare the speeds of two programs, given an input size $n$ and a processor count $p$. We can also chart the speed of one program with increasing processor counts. How are these varying speeds to be evaluated? This behavior or performance with increasing processor count is a critical ingredient of parallel programming and is called *scalability*. Scalability is important because it predicts performance on large input and on large systems (that may not be immediately available).

The following definitions are useful to study various aspects of parallel performance evaluation. These may be measured by executing implemented programs. They can be equally well defined in terms of algorithms and computational models we have just studied. In the context of programs, we may use measured wall clock times, and for algorithms, we talk of the number of model steps as described above.

### Latency and Throughput

The time taken to complete one program, call it job execution, from the time it began is also called the elapsed time or job *latency*. Often, many jobs are executed on a parallel system. They may be processed one at a time from a queue, or several could execute concurrently on a large parallel system. These could be unrelated programs, related programs, or different executions of the same program. In all cases, the number of jobs retired per unit time is known as the job *throughput*. Job throughput is related to average job latency. If jobs take less time on average, more jobs are processed per unit time. However, the latency of different jobs may vary wildly from job to job, without impacting the throughput. The worst-case latency, that is, the longest latency of any job, is an important metric.

## Speed-up

The *speed-up* $S$ of a program $\mathcal{P}$ taking time $t(n, p)$ with respect to another program $\mathcal{P}_1$ taking time $t_1(n_1, p_1)$ is the ratio of their speeds, which is the inverse of their execution times:

$$S = \frac{t_1(n_1, p_1)}{t(n, p)} \tag{3.1}$$

Like before, $n$ is the size of the input and $p$ is the number of processors deployed by an algorithm. So are $n_1$ and $p_1$, respectively. Although not explicit in the notation, $S$ is clearly a function of $\mathcal{P}$, $\mathcal{P}_1$, $n$, $n_1$, $p$, and $p_1$. We will keep this notation for brevity; it should be clear from the context. We often consider *parallel speed-up*, the special case of the speed-up with respect to the sequential execution of a parallel program, that is, $p_1 = 1$ and $n_1 = n$:

$$S_{par} = \frac{t(n, 1)}{t(n, p)} \tag{3.2}$$

Similarly, *maximum speed-up* may be defined as the maximum speed with respect to the "best-known" sequential program (let us say that is $\mathcal{P}_1$).

$$S_{max} = \frac{t_1(n, 1)}{t(n, p)} \tag{3.3}$$

$S_{max} \geq 1$ in principle, because a parallel program may simply choose to inactivate $p - 1$ processors and degenerate to a sequential version. Thus, a parallel program should always be able to beat the sequential version. In fact, the speed-up of parallel program $\mathcal{P}$ using $p$ processors with respect to it using $p_1$ processors, $p_1 < p$ for the same input size should be greater than 1.

## Cost

Speed-up can increase with increasing $p$. On the other hand, deploying more processors is costly. We define the cost $\mathcal{C}$ of a parallel program as the product of its time and the processor count:

$$\mathcal{C} = t(n, p) \times p \tag{3.4}$$

A parallel program is *cost-optimal* if $\mathcal{C} = t_1(n, 1)$, the cost of the best sequential program. Cost-optimality means the speed-up gained by deploying a large $p$ is commensurate with their increased cost. For example, doubling the number of available processors doubles the speed, that is, halves the execution time.

Often, we do not know $t_1(n, 1)$ precisely, but only in an asymptotic sense. In such a situation a definition of asymptotic optimality is useful. A parallel program (or algorithm) is *asymptotically cost-optimal* if $\mathcal{C} = O(t_1(n, 1))$.

## Efficiency

Another way to express the "quality" of speed-up is efficiency. Expected speed-up over a sequential program is higher for a higher value of $p$. The quality of this speed-up, or the speed-up efficiency $\mathcal{E}$, is the maximum speed-up per deployed processor:

$$\mathcal{E} = \frac{\mathcal{S}_{max}}{p} \tag{3.5}$$

$\mathcal{E} \leq 1$, because any speed-up larger than $p$ implies the discovery of a better sequential algorithm than the best-known sequential algorithm (making the newly discovered algorithm the new best). After all, any flexible parallel algorithm can be executed sequentially by setting $p = 1$. $\mathcal{E} = 1$ implies the program is cost-optimal, and the speed-up is proportional to the number of processors used.

In practice, it is quite possible to observe values of efficiency greater than 1. This occurs because the underlying system on which the executions of the sequential program and the parallel program are measured are necessarily different. For example, with larger $p$ may come larger caches, improving data access times. Recall that data access latency is significantly higher than arithmetic operation latency. Hence, the performance of a program with many memory operations can depend heavily on this latency. Consequently, even small improvements in memory access latency can improve the program's performance. There can also be other scenarios, for example, a parallel "multi-pronged" search may serendipitously converge to a solution quicker. The tools we develop next are designed in a more idealized setting and these real effects are ignored. Regardless, they are meaningful and may generally be used even in the presence of these effects.

## Scalability

Scalability is related to efficiency and measures the ability to increase the speed-up linearly with $p$. In particular, if the efficiency of program $\mathcal{P}$ remains 1 with increasing processor count $p$, we say it scales perfectly with the size of the computing system. Most problems cannot be solved this efficiently, and those that can are often said to be embarrassingly parallel. Indeed, the program may begin to slow down for larger values of $p$, as shown in Figure 3.4, for $p = 17$ and $n = 10^4$. This can happen due to several reasons. For example, communication may increase, or more processors remain idle. Of course, the efficiency may also depend on the size of the input, $n$. For example, a $\Theta(n)$ sequential program, on parallelization, might not get faster for $p > n$. It is often the case that performance scales better for larger values of $n$. For example, Figure 3.4 shows higher speed-up for $n = 10^6$. In some cases, however, the speed-up may even reduce for larger $n$, for example, because caches become less effective.

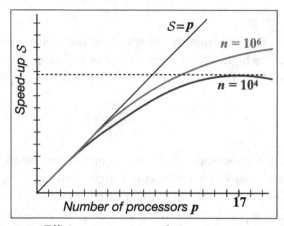

**Figure 3.4** Efficiency curve: speed-up vs. processor count

When efficiency remains high with increasing $p$, regardless of $n$, we say the program exhibits *strong scaling*. On the other hand, if efficiency for higher values of $p$ remains high only if $n$ is also increased, we call it *weak scaling*. If efficiency is low regardless, we say the program does not scale. But how high is high? For the efficiency to remain 1 is unrealistic, and such definition would hardly be useful. One might instead say, if the speed-up for a higher value of $p$ is lower than that for a lower value of $p$, the efficiency is low, and scaling is poor. This seems too low a bar. A slightly tighter definition says that the efficiency $\mathcal{E}$ does not reduce with increasing $p$ – it remains constant. This means the efficiency curve remains linear, even if its slope may be somewhat less than 1. We refine this quantitative measure of scalability next.

## Iso-efficiency

The *iso-efficiency* of a scalable program indicates how (and if) the problem size must grow to maintain efficiency on increasingly larger computing systems. Iso-efficiency is, in reality, a restating of the sequential execution time as a function of $p$, the processor count. Recall from Eqs. (3.3) and (3.5):

$$t_1(n, 1) = \mathcal{E}(n, p)\, t(n, p)\, p \tag{3.6}$$

$t_1(n, 1)$, the best sequential execution time, is a measure of the problem's size and complexity. Given $p$ and the time-function for a parallel program $t(n, p)$, we want to derive $t_1$, which would ensure a constant efficiency $\mathcal{E}$. $t_1$ changes because $n$ changes. Thus, deriving $t_1$ really amounts to finding the appropriate input size $n$ that takes time $t_1$. To emphasize that we seek to find the problem size for a given $p$, we use the notation $\mathcal{I}(p)$ for problem size in place of $t_1$. $\mathcal{I}(p)$ is called the iso-efficiency function. The parameterization with $p$ signifies that we adapt the problem size to $p$. A rapid growth in $\mathcal{I}$ with increasing $p$ means that only much larger problems can be efficiently solved on larger machines. This is poor scalability.

We can relate $\mathcal{I}$ to the overhead of parallelization $\bar{o}(n, p)$: the computation that is not required in the sequential solution. In other words, $\bar{o}(n, p)$ is the "extra" time collectively spent by the parallel processors compared to the best sequential program. This may include idle processors, communication time, and so on.

Hence,

$$\bar{o}(n, p) = t(n, p) \, p - t_1(n, 1) \tag{3.7}$$

and

$$\mathcal{I}(p) = t_1(n, 1) = t(n, p) \, p - \bar{o}(n, p) \tag{3.8}$$

Substituting $\mathcal{E}$ from Eqs. (3.3) and (3.5)

$$\Rightarrow \mathcal{I}(p) = \left[ \frac{\mathcal{E}(n, p)}{1 - \mathcal{E}(n, p)} \right] \bar{o}(n, p) \tag{3.9}$$

This means that if $\mathcal{I}$ increases proportionally to the overhead $\bar{o}$, the term within [] above – call it $K$ – remains constant, that is, the efficiency remains constant. In other words, if the overhead grows rapidly with increasing $p$, the problem size also must grow as rapidly to maintain the same efficiency. That indicates poor iso-efficiency.

For illustration, consider the BSP example of parallel reduction in Section 3.2: $t(n, p) = \Theta(\frac{n}{p} + p)$. We know the optimal sequential algorithm is linear in $n$: $t_1(n, 1) = \Theta(n)$. This means:

$$\bar{o}(n, p) = \Omega(p^2)$$

$$\Rightarrow \mathcal{I}(p) = K\Omega(p^2)$$

This means that the problem size must grow at least quadratically with increasing $p$ to maintain constant efficiency. Check this in the PRAM model; $\mathcal{I}$ is bounded sub-quadratically (see Exercise 3.11) in $p$.

Note that by Eqs. (3.6) and (3.7), for embarrassingly parallel problems, $\bar{o}$ remains 0, and $\mathcal{E}$ remains 1 because $t_1(n, 1) = t(n, p) \, p$. The problem size apparently does not need to grow to keep $\mathcal{E}$ constant. However, there is a limit. If $p > t_1(n, 1)$, there is not enough work to go around. Hence, the problem size must eventually grow at least as fast as $p$, that is, asymptotically $\mathcal{I}(p) = \Omega(p)$. Practically speaking also, the overhead usually grows at least in proportion to $p$, and often faster. In other words, we expect that the input size $n$ needs to grow at least as fast as the processor count $p$ to maintain efficiency. Similarly, if $\bar{o}(n, p) = O(t_1(n, 1))$, Eq. (3.7) indicates that $t(n, p) \, p = O(t_1(n, 1))$ meaning that the solution is asymptotically cost-optimal.

Note that $p$ is bounded in practice. Surely, there is not an unlimited supply of processors. Nonetheless, scalability with increasing $p$ is a useful measure. Of course, it indicates the possibility of speed-up with increasing system size. It is also often the case that better scaling programs – and better scaling algorithms – tend to perform better on a wider variety of systems and system architecture. Indeed, if high-level programs support several times the actual number of physical processors, their execution and communication can often be optimized better.

## 3.5   Parallel Work

The final metric we will study is called *parallel work*. This is the total sum of work done by processors actually employed at different steps of an algorithm. Recall, the cost is the time taken by an algorithm multiplied by the maximum number of processors available for use at any step. Work is a more thorough accounting of the processors actually used. In other words, parallel work required for input of size $n$,

$$W(n) = \sum_{s=1}^{t(n,p)} p_s(n), \tag{3.10}$$

where $p_s(n)$ processors are active at step $s$. Recall that we allow the number of active processors to be a function of input size $n$. Each processor takes unit time per step, and the algorithm takes $t(n, p)$ steps. Note also that in $t(n, p)$, $p$ varies at each step. We leave this intricacy out of the notation for $p$ and let it imply the maximum number of processors used at any step. The actual value of $p$ at each step is specified for algorithms, however.

As an example, the initial number of processors assumed in the binary tree reduction algorithm is $\frac{n}{2}$. The algorithm requires $\log n$ steps, but the number of active processors halves at each step. For instance, in the first step of the PRAM algorithm $\frac{n}{2}$ processors each performs unit work (a single addition in this example). $\frac{n}{4}$ processors are used in the second step and so on. Thus the total work, W(n) is:

$$\sum_{s=0}^{\log n - 1} 2^s = n$$

The total parallel work performed in the reduction algorithm is $\Theta(n)$, but the cost is $\Theta(n \log n)$. One may question the logic of using work as a performance metric. If $n$ processors were available and not used in step two, that seems like a wasted opportunity. Maybe, it is not so because the unused processors are available to a different job. However, there is a more fundamental reason this work complexity is important. It measures the actual number of operations.

Counting work guides us to design highly scalable algorithms that allow an arbitrarily large value for $p_s$, sometimes even equal to or greater than $n$. An implementation would, of course, have a limited number $P_r$ of real processors available. We then map each step of the algorithm to $P_r$ processors simply by each real processor performing the work of $\frac{p_s}{P_r}$ assumed processors in a loop. What can we say about the expected time taken by such an execution then? This is given by Brent's work-time scheduling principle.

## Brent's Work-Time Scheduling Principle

Let us assume the PRAM model to take a specific example, but other models are equally compliant. Step $s$ of the original algorithm takes $\Theta(1)$ using $p_s$ processors. In its execution, step $s$ is scheduled on $P_r$ processors taking $\left\lceil \frac{p_s}{P_r} \right\rceil$ steps. Note that $p_s$ can be less than $P_r$ for some step; all steps still require at least one time unit. The total number of steps are:

$$\sum_{s=1}^{t(n,p)} \left\lceil \frac{p_s}{P_r} \right\rceil \leq \sum_{s=1}^{t(n,p)} (\frac{p_s}{P_r} + 1) = \sum_{s=1}^{t(n,p)} \frac{p_s}{P_r} + \sum_{s=1}^{t(n,p)} 1 = \frac{W(n)}{P_r} + t(n,p) \qquad (3.11)$$

The work and time both impact the actual performance. For many algorithms $t(n,p) = O(W(n))$, and hence work is the main determinant of the execution time. Another useful way to think about this is that with $P_r$ processors, the algorithm takes time $O(\frac{W(n)}{P_r})$, for $P_r \leq W(n)/t(n)$. This ratio can be thought of as average parallelism. Contrast this with cost, where a single highly parallel step can skew its value. Hence, cost is meaningful mainly in the context of $P_r$, the number of real processors.

We can also now define the notion of work optimality. A parallel algorithm is called *work-optimal*, if $W(n) = O(t_1(n,1))$. Further, a work-optimal algorithm for which $t(n,p)$ is a lower bound on the running time and cannot be further reduced is called *work-time optimal*.

## 3.6 Amdahl's Law

There are certain limits to the speed-up and scalability of algorithms. Sometimes the problem itself is limited by its definition. Such

> **Question:** Is this the best performance achievable?

limits may exist, for example, because there may be dependencies that reduce or preclude concurrency. Recall that concurrency is a prerequisite for parallelism. Reconsider, for example, the problem of moving vans described in the introduction to this book. Boxes can be transported in vans, but before they can be moved, they must be loaded, say, at the warehouse. There is no way to perform the task of loading a van at the warehouse and driving it to its destination in parallel with each other. Driving must happen after loading and is dependent on it.

Sometimes, the dependency is imposed by the algorithm. For example, in hopes of better packing, the loaders may load large boxes first and the small ones later. Possibly, the large boxes may be loaded in parallel by multiple loaders. However, the small boxes' loading may only begin after a certain minimum number of large boxes are loaded.

Here is a more "computational" example, called the prefix-sum problem.

Input: Array $A$ with $n$ integers

Output: Array $B$ with $n$ integers such that

$$B[i] = \sum_{j=0}^{i} A[i]$$

Solution:

```
B[0] = A[0];
for(int i=1; i<n; i++)
    B[i] = A[i] + B[i-1];
```

This solution has each iteration $i$ dependant on the value of $B[i-1]$ computed in the previous iteration. Thus, different entries of B cannot be filled in parallel; rather, the entire loop is sequential. We will later see that this is a shortcoming of the chosen algorithm and not a limitation of the problem itself. There do exist parallel solutions to this problem.

Amdahl's law[11] is an idealization of such sequential constraints. Suppose fraction $f$ of a program is sequential. That may be because of inherent limits to parallelization or because that fraction was simply not parallelized. The fraction is in terms of the problem size (i.e. the fraction of time taken by the sequential program). This implies that fraction $f$ would take time $t_1(n,1)f$. Assuming that the rest is perfectly parallelizable, it can be speeded up by factor up to $p$. This means that time $t(n,p)$ taken by a parallel program can be no lower than $t_1(n,1)f + \frac{t_1(n,1)}{p}(1-f)$. This implies a maximum speed-up of:

$$S_{max} = \frac{t_1(n,1)}{t_1(n,1)f + \frac{t_1(n,1)}{p}(1-f)} = \frac{1}{f + \frac{1-f}{p}} \tag{3.12}$$

No matter how many processors we apply (say, $p \to \infty$), a speed-up greater than $\frac{1}{f}$ could never be achieved. Even that is possible only if the parallel part scales strongly with an efficiency of 1 for an unlimited number of processors. This equation may seem hardly surprising, but looking at the actual value of such limits can be eye-opening.

The graph in Figure 3.5 plots the maximum speed-up that is theoretically possible for a varying number of processors. The different plots are for different values of $f$. Notice

---

[11] Amdahl, "Validity of the single processor approach."

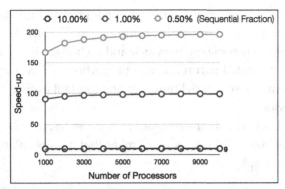

**Figure 3.5** Maximum speed-up possible with different processor counts (in an idealized setting)

how much limit even small values of $f$ can place. If the sequential fraction is only 10%, the parallel speed-up could never be more than 10. It would seem that there is little benefit of using, say, more than 100 processors, which would yield a speed-up greater than 9. This is rarely true in practice. First, the formula assumes an efficiency of 1. If the efficiency is less, even the speed-up of 9 likely requires many more than 100 processors. Second, for weakly scaling solutions, larger problems could be solved efficiently on larger machines, even if the small problem does not scale beyond a hundred processors. Gustafson's law accounts for precisely that.

## 3.7 Gustafson's Law

Gustafson[12] redirects Amdahl's equation to bring the size of the problem into the mix. Suppose that the time spent in sequential components by a parallel program is $t(n, p) f$, and the time spent in the parallel part is $t(n, p)(1 - f)$. The fraction is now in terms of the execution time of the parallel program (and can vary with $p$ and $n$). The sequential fraction also includes all overheads, meaning the $(1 - f)$ fraction of the time is spent in fully parallel computation keeping all processors busy.

Given that breakup, any sequential implementation must take $t(n, p) f + pt(n, p)(1 - f)$ time. After all, a single processor must perform the work of each of the $p$ processors, one at a time. This means that the speed-up of the parallel implementation over the sequential one is:

$$\frac{t(n, p) f + t(n, p)(1 - f) p}{t(n, p)} = f + p(1 - f) \tag{3.13}$$

Note that the fractions $f$ used by Amdahl and Gustafson are different. In Amdahl's treatment, $f$ represents the fraction of a sequential program that is not parallelized, and $f$

---

[12] Gustafson, "Reevaluating Amdahl's law."

does not vary with $p$, whether the problem size $n$ grows or not. In Gustafson's treatment, $f$ accounts for the overheads of parallel computation. This fraction, relative to the parallel execution time, remains constant even as $n$ and $p$ change. This effectively means that the time spent in the sequential part reduces in proportion to that spent in the parallel part. In Amdahl's treatment, the sequential time remains constant even as the parallel time reduces with more processors.

If Gustafson's fraction remains constant as $p$ increases, the obtained speed-up $S$ grows linearly with $p$, as Figure 3.6 shows. Remember that $n$ grows along with $p$, but that is not highlighted in the graph.

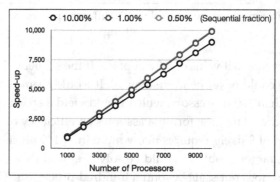

**Figure 3.6** Maximum speed-up possible by scaling problem size with processor count (in an idealized setting)

In practice, it is possible that Gustafson's $f$ does not remain constant but grows more slowly than envisaged by Amdahl. This would lead to a sub-linear growth of speed-up with increasing $p$, but possibly not as slow as Amdahl envisages. In any case, neither law accounts for the higher overhead with more processors. This overhead has a major impact on real program execution times, and causes the efficiency to decrease with increasing $p$.

## 3.8  Karp–Flatt Metric

Karp–Flatt Metric[13] turns the discussion around and seeks to estimate the unparallelized part $f$ in a program, given the measured speed-up over the sequential execution $S$:

$$f = \frac{\frac{1}{S} - \frac{1}{p}}{1 - \frac{1}{p}} \tag{3.14}$$

It is not hard to verify that this metric is consistent with Amdahl's law. Just reorganize Eq. 3.12 to bring $f$ to the left-hand side. According to this equation, if the speed-up obtained

---

[13] Karp and Flatt, "Measuring parallel processor performance."

by a program using 100 processors is 10, the sequential part takes approximately 9.1% of the execution time. How this fraction varies with $p$ can now be computed by running the experiment with different processor counts.

Again, it is possible that the actual sequential part is lower than the value of $f$ so computed. This means that the observed speed-up is less than the maximum possible. That can happen due to the overheads of parallelization. In that sense, $f$ may thus generically represent the overhead $\bar{o}$.

## 3.9   Summary

An understanding of performance issues is fundamental to the exercise of designing parallel algorithms and writing programs. Measuring actual execution time is useful, but one must design programs that perform well on all $n$ and $p$, or at least many $n$ and $p$. It is not practical to measure the performance on all instances. Rather, one must argue about the performance on $n$ and $p$ that are anticipated.

Hence, modeling and analyzing performance are prerequisites for writing efficient parallel programs. This chapter discusses a few abstract models of computation, which can be used to express and analyze parallel algorithms. It also introduces practical metrics to evaluate parallel programs' design and performance in comparison to, say, sequential programs, as it relates to the number of processors used. These lessons include:

- The PRAM model relies on an arbitrary number of synchronous processors. Each has local memory, and they together share global memory. Simple computation and memory operations take a single time-unit each. Since the processors proceed in lock-step and share memory, there is no synchronization or explicit communication. As a result, such overheads are ignored in the analysis.

- Variants of the PRAM model control the possibility of different processors read from or writing to the same memory location or address in a single time-step. Either common address is supported (e.g. EREW, CREW), or the addresses must be exclusive (e.g. CREW, CRCW). Such support is set separately for reading and writing operations.

- For CRCW PRAM, different semantics are possible. In Common-CRCW PRAM, if multiple processors write to a common address at the same time-step, they must all present the same value to write. Alternatively, in Arbitrary-CRCW PRAM, if multiple processors write to a common address, any of their values may be written. The algorithm's correctness must not depend on which value is written. In the Priority-CRCW PRAM, each processor is accorded a distinct priority. If multiple processors write to a common address, the value presented by the one with the highest priority is always written.

- All variants of the PRAM model are functionally equivalent, for each can simulate the behavior of others. However, such simulation may not take constant time per time-step. Priority-CRCW model, for example, can simulate the steps of every other model in constant time each. Other models cannot simulate Priority-CRCW steps in constant time each. In that sense, the Priority-CRCW is more powerful than others.

- The BSP model maintains the synchronizing characteristic of PRAM, but it does not require complete lock-step progress of processors. Instead, processors may take an arbitrary number of local steps before synchronizing. Further, data is exchanged by the processors explicitly – there is no shared memory. BSP counts the number of messages communicated. The lack of per-step synchrony does not make algorithms much more complicated than in the PRAM model, but the communication overhead is counted. BSP does not consider batching of messages or varying latency.

- Work is an important metric to measure parallel performance. We start by exposing the entire parallelism inherent in an algorithm by normally assuming as many processors as the number of independent steps. Recall that two steps are independent if there is no order required between them, and they can be taken simultaneously. At different time-steps, different numbers of independent steps may be possible. This means that the number of processors used at each time-step varies. The total of all processor-steps in this manner is called the work. Work complexity on its own is not sufficient to indicate the level of parallelism. After all, a sequential algorithm has a low work complexity. Our goal is to keep work complexity similar to that of the sequential solution while minimizing the time complexity.

- Brent's scheduling principle shows how work translates to the real execution time on a specific machine with $p$ processors. If the number of sequential time-steps is $t$ and the number of processor-steps (i.e. work) is $w$, a $p$-processor machine takes time $\frac{w}{p} + t$.

- Speed-up measures the ratio of the speed of one algorithm or implementation with another. When comparing algorithms in a PRAM or BSP setting, asymptotic speed-up is usually of concern. With measured execution times of implementations, the actual speed-up value on specific computing systems becomes possible.

- Although absolute speed-up on specific computing systems is the primary statistic for the user of an application, the efficiency with which it is obtained is a more meaningful metric for the program designer and developer: the speed-up per processor used to obtain it. The same speed-up obtained on a smaller machine indicates a higher efficiency than when more processors are required.

- The cost of an execution is related to its efficiency. Cost is the product of the time taken by a program and the number of processors used. The cost does not require a comparison to the speed of another program. Low-cost implementations take low time or use very few processors. In other words, efficient programs are likely to be cost-effective because the speed per processor is high.

- The speed of a program or algorithm relative to the number of processors used is important. However, some programs are efficient only if a small number of processors are used. Parallelism could be limited. Or, as the number of processors grows, so do the overheads of synchronizing them, exchanging data, or simply waiting for a certain action by other processors. This overhead can be detrimental to both efficiency and cost. More the number of processors, more the overheads. In fact, the overheads from using too many processors can outweigh the entire benefit of the extra execution engines. Scalable programs limit such overheads. As a result, they continue to get faster with more processors. Some even continue to maintain the speed-up per processor, meaning they continue to remain efficient, for large values of $p$.

- A strongly scaling program gets faster if more processors are available. A weakly scaling program roughly maintains speed with more processors if the problem size grows as well. The same program may scale strongly for smaller $p$, scale weakly for medium $p$, and stop scaling altogether for larger $p$.

- The notion of iso-efficiency formalizes scalability. The iso-efficiency of an algorithm or program measures the growth required in the problem size as a function of the number of processors to maintain constant efficiency. Iso-efficiency combines the impact of $n$ and $p$ on scalability, and a slow-growing iso-efficiency function indicates better performance for a large number of processors than a fast growing one.

- There are limits to scaling in most situations. Amdahl's law states one fundamental limit: the limit to the parallel speed-up of problems (or their solution), if they contain strictly sequential components. Such sequential components must be processed on a single processor, while all other processors wait for it to finish. Amdahl's law assumes that the problem of a certain size is solved using increasingly more processors. In this case, the sequential components remain a fixed fraction of the entire problem and do not get faster with more processors. On the other hand, the parallel components do get faster. Consequently, the sequential components start to dominate the total execution time, limiting total speed-up.

- Gustafson's law instead considers the case when the sequential components are a fixed fraction of the parallel execution time. Thus, as more processors are employed to solve larger problems, the sequential components' execution time keeps pace with the parallel components. Linear scaling of speed-up is possible in this scenario.

- Instead of debating the components' sizes, the Karp–Flatt metric estimates them. Rather, it estimates the entire parallelization overhead by observing the speed-up with an increasing number of processors. Growth of this overhead with an increasing number of processors while keeping the problem size constant indicates that the overhead is significant. This suggest that attempts to reduce overhead may be useful.

The abstract computation models that this chapter focuses on are the BSP model and the PRAM model. Historically, the PRAM model was proposed first by Fortune and Wylie.[14] Valiant later proposed the BSP model as a "bridge" between the abstract model and practical architecture. These two are popular, but others that account for more overheads and parameters have also been proposed. For example, block-transfer and communication latency have been considered.[15] Mehlhorn and Vishkin proposed an extension: the *module parallel computer*[16] (MPC). In MPC, shared memory is divided into modules (i.e. banks) and only one word may be accessed from each module in one time-step. Limitations of perfect synchrony have also been addressed.[17]

The BSP model also addresses both synchrony and communication shortcomings of the PRAM model. The BSPRAM model[18] attempts to combine the PRAM and BSP models. Others like the LogP model[19] account the message cost more realistically by considering detailed parameters like the communication bandwidth and overhead and message delay. Barrier is still supported but not required. Others have also focussed on removing the synchronous barrier by supporting higher-level communication primitives, for example, the *coarse-grained multi-computer* model.[20]

Other than shared-memory style and message-passing style models, purely task graph–based models have also been used[21] using parameters like task time, message complexity, and communication delay. All these models can simulate each other and are equivalent in that sense. That may be the reason why the simplest models like PRAM and BSP have gained prevalence. However, the models do differ in their performance analysis. A case can be made that a more realistic model discourages algorithms from taking steps that are costly on real machines by making such cost explicit in the model. More importantly, though, it is the awareness of the differences between the model and the target hardware that drives good algorithm design.

---

[14] Fortune and Wyllie, "Parallelism in random access machines."
[15] Aggarwal et al., "Hierarchical memory."
   Aggarwal et al., "Communication complexity of prams."
[16] Mehlhorn and Vishkin, "Randomized and deterministic simulations."
[17] Gibbons, "A more practical pram model."
   Cole and Zajicek, "The expected advantage."
[18] Tiskin, "The bulk-synchronous parallel."
[19] Culler et al., "Logp."
[20] Dehne et al., "Scalable parallel geometric algorithms for coarse grained multicomputers."
[21] Ullman and Papadimitriou, "A communication-time tradeoff."
   Papadimitriou and Yannakakis, "Towards an architecture-independent analysis of parallel algorithms."

Besides designing efficient algorithms suitable for specific hardware and software architecture, one must also select the number of the processors before execution begins. Large supercomputers may be available, but they are generally partitioned among many applications. It is important for applications not to oversubscribe to processors. As many processors should be used as needed to provide the best speed-up and efficiency trade-off. Sometimes speed-up can reduce with large $p$. At other times speed-up increases, but the efficiency reduces rapidly beyond a certain value of $p$. In many applications, the size of the problem, $n$, can also be configured. Further, the memory reserved for an application, $m$, may also be configured. Optimally choosing $\mathcal{S}$, $\mathcal{E}$, $p$, $n$, and $m$ is hard. A study of time- and memory- constrained scaling[22] is useful in this regard. In particular, Sun-Ni law[23] extends Amdahl's and Gustafson's laws to study limits on scaling due to memory limits.

Multiple studies[24] have shown the utility of optimizing the product of efficiency and speed-up: $\mathcal{E}\mathcal{S}$. Several of these conclude that there exists a maximum value of $p$ beyond which the speed-up inevitably plateaus or decreases for a given problem. In general, seeking to obtain an efficiency of 0.5 provides a good trade-off between speed-up and efficiency.[25]

# Exercise

3.1. Consider the following steps in a three-processor PRAM. Explain the effect of each instruction for each of the following models. Note that some instruction may be illegal under certain models; indicate so. All variables are in shared memory.

(a) EREW PRAM

(b) CREW PRAM

(c) Common-CRCW PRAM

(d) Aribitray-CRCW PRAM

(e) Priority-CRCW PRAM (assume priority diminishes from left to right).

---

[22] Gustafson et al., "Development of parallel methods."
  Worley, "The effect of time constraints."
[23] Sun and Ni, "Scalable problems and memory-bounded speedup."
[24] Kuck, "Parallel processing."
  Eager et al., "Speedup versus efficiency."
  Flatt and Kennedy, "Performance of parallel processors."
[25] Eager et al., "Speedup versus efficiency."
  Flatt and Kennedy, "Performance of parallel processors."

| PO | P1 | P2 |
|---|---|---|
| $x = 5;$ | $x = 5;$ | $x = z;$ |
| $y = z;$ | $y = z;$ | $y = z;$ |

3.2. Show that each step of $p$-processor Common-CRCW PRAM is also valid for $p$-processor Arbitrary-CRCW PRAM.

3.3. Show that each step of $p$-processor Arbitrary-CRCW PRAM is also valid for $p$-processor Priority-CRCW PRAM.

3.4. Show that each step of a $p$-processor Priority-CRCW PRAM can be completed in up to $O(\log p)$ steps of $p$-processor EREW PRAM. (The number of memory locations is allowed to change.)

3.5. Show that every BSP algorithm can be converted to a PRAM algorithm.

3.6. Write a pseudo-code to multiply two $n \times n$ matrices A and B, assuming the PRAM model. Analyze its time and work complexity. Assume that the input matrices A and B are stored in the shared memory in row-major order. Assume as many processors as you need.

3.7. Write a pseudo-code to multiply two $n \times n$ matrices A and B, assuming the BSP model. Analyze its time complexity. The entire input matrices A and B initially reside in the processor 0. Assume as many processors as you need.

3.8. Consider the following BSP algorithm to distribute $n$ items equally among $p$ processors (assume $n$ is divisible by $p$).

Input: Array $B_0$ with $n$ integers in the memory of processor 0

Output: Array $B_i$ in the memory of each processor $i$ such that $B_i = A[i * b..(i + 1) * b - 1]$, where $b = \frac{n}{p}$

Algorithm:

```
for(step i=0; step<logn; step++)
    forall processor i {
        {
            len = 2^step
            if i < len
                send B_i[n/(2*len)] .. B_i[n/len-1] to processor i + len
        } {
            Barrier
            if len <= i < 2*len
                receive n/(2*len) items into B_i[0..n/(2*len)-1]
        }
    }
```

This is called a scatter operation. Analyze its time complexity. You may assume that $p$ is a power of 2.

3.9. Devise an EREW PRAM algorithm for the problem in Exercise 3.8 Analyze its time complexity.

3.10. Consider a parallel sorting algorithm *psort* with PRAM work complexity $O(\log^2 n)$ and time complexity $O(\log n)$. Assume a PRAM limited to $p$ processors. Compute $t(n, p)$ in the asymptotic sense. What is the efficiency compared to the best sequential sorting algorithm of $O(\log n)$?

3.11. Show that the iso-efficiency function $\mathcal{I}(p)$ for the PRAM reduction algorithm in Section 3.3 is $\Omega(p \log p)$.

3.12. The following table lists execution times of two different solutions (Program 1 and Program 2) to a problem. The executions times were recorded with varying number of processors $p$ and varying input size $n$. This table applies to many following questions.

| Input size $n$ (million) | Processor count $p$ | Time $t(n, p)$ (minutes) | |
|---|---|---|---|
| | | Program 1 | Program 2 |
| 1 | 1 | 12 | 12 |
| | 10 | 3.5 | 5.28 |
| | 50 | 3.2 | 17.0 |
| | 100 | 3.0 | 26.5 |
| | 500 | 3.1 | 126.6 |
| 10 | 1 | 22 | 22 |
| | 10 | 8.6 | 10.5 |
| | 50 | 7.1 | 11.9 |
| | 100 | 7.0 | 31.5 |
| | 500 | 7.2 | 126.2 |
| 50 | 1 | 263 | 263 |
| | 10 | 63.2 | 64.9 |
| | 50 | 43.2 | 57.9 |
| | 100 | 40.6 | 59.9 |
| | 500 | 40.3 | 158.6 |
| 100 | 1 | 1021 | 1021 |
| | 10 | 189 | 191 |
| | 50 | 110.5 | 125 |
| | 100 | 100.7 | 118.5 |
| | 500 | 94.5 | 211.9 |

Find the cost of the implementation for each $n$ and $p$.

3.13. Referring to the table in Exercise 3.12, what is the latency of Program 1 for $n = 10$ million and $p = 10$?

3.14. Referring to the table in Exercise 3.12, what is the minimum latency of Program 1 execution for $n = 10$ million.

3.15. Refer to the table in Exercise 3.12 Consider a computing system with 50 total processors. What is the maximum throughput of Program 1 for $n = 10$ million?

3.16. Referring to the table in Exercise 3.12, find the maximum speed-up $S$ of Program 2 over the sequential implementation for each given value of $n$.

3.17. Referring to the table in Exercise 3.12, find the maximum speed-up $S$ of Program 1 over Program 2 for $n = 10$ million.

3.18. Referring to the table in Exercise 3.12, find the efficiency $\mathcal{E}$ of Program 1 and Program 2 for $n = 10$ million and $p = 100$.

3.19. Referring to the table in Exercise 3.12, estimate the iso-efficiency function $\mathcal{I}$ for Program 1 and Program 2.

3.20. Analyze the scalability of Program 1 and Program 2 in the table in Exercise 3.12 (Discuss strong vs. weak scalability and the iso-efficiency function.)

3.21. Discuss how well Amdahl's law and Gustafson's law hold for Programs 1 and 2 for the table in Exercise 3.12. Do they accurately estimate the bounds on the speed-up?

3.22. Refer to the table in Exercise 3.12 Using the Karp–Flatt metric, estimate the overhead (including any sequential components) in Program 2 for each value of $p$ and $n = 10$ million. Discuss how the overhead grows with $p$.

# CHAPTER 4

# Synchronization and Communication Primitives

Interaction between concurrently executing fragments is an essential characteristic of parallel programs and the major source of difference between sequential programming and parallel programming. Synchronization

> *Question:* Who controls the executing fragments? How do different executing fragments interact and impact each other's execution?

and communication are the two ways in which fragments directly interact, and these are the subjects of this chapter. We begin with a brief review of basic operating system concepts, particularly in the context of parallel and concurrent execution. If you already have a good knowledge of operating systems concepts, browse lightly or skip ahead.

## 4.1 Threads and Processes

Computing systems are managed by a program: an operating system. *Process* is the mechanism that operating systems use to start and control the execution of other programs. A process provides one or more ranges of addresses for the executing program to use. Each address has a value (which remains undefined until it is initialized). Each range is mapped to a block of memory (which may reside on one or more attached devices). These blocks of memory are under management of the operating system. A range of addresses and the data that they map to are collectively called an *address space*. An address space is divided into fixed-size units called *pages*. Address space and pages provide a logical or a *virtual* view of the memory. This view is also called *virtual memory*. The operating system maintains a mapping between pages and their locations on the device. One advantage of virtual memory is that not all pages need to be resident in the physical memory device – some may be relegated to slower storage (not unlike the cache strategy), while others that remain undefined need not be mapped to any storage at all.

Being an executing program, the operating system comprises a set of processes, which start and schedule other processes. For example, an application starts with some running process launching a new process to execute that application's code. These processes may execute concurrently, sharing the available hardware by turn. An executing process may be forced to turn over to a waiting process via a mechanism of hardware interrupts. Some types of interrupts may terminate the process altogether. Others allow it to await a new turn. Processes may also request termination – there own or others'.

A process may create or *fork* child processes, with each executing its own instructions. The parent may share none, some, or all of its address space with the child.[1] Additionally, at the time of the fork, a copy of the parent's address space may be created for the child. The child then owns the copy, which is hidden from the parent. Creating such copies is time consuming. Hence noncopy variants are sometimes called lightweight processes.

There is thus a spectrum of relationships between processes, but we will use this broad distinction: each process has its own address space, *threads* within a process all share that address space. A process comprises one or more threads. We say that a process that only executes sequentially is a single thread, and its code shares the address space with no other thread. In this sense, a single-threaded process may be conveniently called a thread. Hence, we will commonly use the term thread when referring to a sequential execution. In other words, an executing fragment is a part of some thread's execution. Two threads from different processes do not share an address space, but through page-mapping mechanisms, they may yet be able to share memory.

There are intricacies we will not delve into. For example, the execution of *kernel* threads are scheduled directly and separately by the operating system, whereas *user* threads may be scheduled as a single unit, leaving them to coordinate each other's scheduling among themselves. Be aware though that documents of different operating systems may differ slightly in their use of these terminologies. Generally, a programming platform, which includes the hardware, the operating systems, compilers, and any middleware, determines the schedulable unit of program. It tries to schedule as many units at a time as the number of cores available for execution. Different execution engines within a core can then be used in parallel only when the unit's code explicitly has multiple threads, or one thread is implicitly parallelized by the system architecture. In this book, we will assume that a thread is a schedulable program unit. (When discussing cases where a set of threads are scheduled together, e.g. in graphic processing units [GPUs], we will make the distinction clearer.)

There exist simple interfaces to start processes. For example, the location of an executable file may be provided to the operating system. Already executing processes can, in turn, request to start other processes, sometimes remotely at another operating system. Such remote start requires communication with a running process at that operating system. We will discuss these later in Chapter 6.

---

[1] There are page-mapping mechanisms for unrelated processes to also share address space with each other. We will not discuss their details.

## 4.2   Race Condition and Consistency of State

Using terminology introduced in Section 4.1, threads can share addresses or variables with other threads, and hence may read values written by other threads. Each thread executes its sequence of instructions at its own pace. Recall that in a parallel system, no universal clock may be available. We will assume that there is a universal time that continually increases, but threads may not have any way to know this universal time at any instant. Rather, threads have their own local clocks, possibly ticking at a rate different from other threads' clocks. Even within a thread, there may be an arbitrary lag between its two consecutive instructions (e.g. if the execution is interrupted after the execution of the first). Thus, events occurring in concurrent threads at independent times impact the shared state and progress of a parallel program.

The order in which these events occur is nondeterministic.[2] Consequently, the behavior of the program may be nondeterministic. The program must always produce the expected result even in the presence of such nondeterminism. If this nondeterminism can

> [2] **Defined**: Nondeterminism implies not knowing in advance. For example, nondeterministic order of two events means the order in which they occur changes unpredictably from execution to execution.

lead to incorrect results, we call this *race condition*. A race condition happens when the relative order of events impacts correctness.[3] A simple example of a race condition is shown below in Listing 4.1.

**Listing 4.1** Race Condition

```
counter$ = counter$ + 1;
```

Suppose multiple threads execute this code, each incrementing the shared variable counter$. We will suffix $ to a variable name to highlight that it is shared by multiple threads. (As an aside, even though we emblematically use shared-memory terminology for ease of explanation, the discussion generally applies to any shared resource or state including those accessed through message-passing.) There are three parts to this instruction:

1. Fetch the value of shared resource counter$.

2. Add 1 to the value.

3. Send the result to shared resource counter$.

---

[3] Recall from Chapter 1 that events are not necessarily instantaneous and may overlap. The order may not even be well defined. More generally, we say the relative timing of two events impact correctness.

We assume here that the intent of the variable `counter$` is to maintain the number of increments by all threads. But as different threads' steps occur in a nondeterministic order, counting may suffer errors. For example, if step 1 for thread $i$ occurs between steps 1 and 2 of another thread $j$, both threads would increment the same value and write the same value. One of the two increments is lost. Race conditions can occur due to the nondeterministic order of fetch-and-update (generally called Read-Modify-Write) of shared location, or other events. For example, two threads sending a message to a third thread could also race each other and lead to nondeterministic behavior, and possibly error.

In such cases, enforcing a restriction on interleaving certain parts of the code execution may solve the problem. For example, thread $i$ may be prevented from starting this sequence during the interval any other thread $j$ executes the three-step sequence making them *atomic*. This eliminates the overlap and the race condition. The threads' relative pace or order no longer impacts the correctness. In other words, in the middle of thread $i$ incrementing `count$`, no other thread accesses[4] it. Thus, if thread $j$ follows thread $i$, it necessarily sees the value stored by thread $i$, and vice versa. The nondeterminism in the order in which threads $i$ and $j$ execute their three steps does not impact the final result. In general, a thread may be allowed to cause temporarily inconsistent or transient state within its view, but no other thread should be privy to that view, meaning they should not be able to see or operate on that inconsistent state. Let us understand the broader notion of consistency next. In particular, we seek to understand the behavior of concurrent shared memory operations: they may overlap nondeterministically. This helps us reason about the overall correctness and efficiency.

## Sequential Consistency

Recall that a central processing unit (CPU) core may execute several instructions of a code fragment in parallel, but it ensures that they appear to execute in the sequence in which they are presented – the *program order*. For example, if instructions numbered $i$ and $i+1$ in some code fragment do not depend on each other (as inferred by the compiler/hardware logic), instruction $i+1$ may be completed before $i$ is. On the other hand, if there is a dependency, even if parts of their execution do overlap, the results of the instruction are the same as they would be if instruction $i+1$ started only after instruction $i$ is completed. A way to reconcile parallel execution with strict ordering is that execution of instructions may well overlap with others, but each "takes effect" instantaneously and these instants are in an expected order. For example, in the following instructions:

**Listing 4.2** Taking Effect

```
x = 5;
R1 = x;
```

---

[4] Access refers to a fetch or store of value at an address.

the first instruction may take effect when the value 5 has appeared in all surviving cache instances of address x. The second takes effect when the value 5 appears in Register R1. We will see that this notion of taking effect is too strict in the context of parallel programs, and may require unabated serialization to ensure that effects are instantaneous. Every access to a shared address may need to wait until all other accesses that have begun before it have taken effect. Furthermore, a global mechanism would be required to determine which ones began "before" that access. Some controlled relaxation of the order could eliminate some serialization and yet be "justifiable." Let us discuss some examples.

An easy recourse is to demand equivalence with the sequential models of memory. That would allow us to carry over many reasoning tools and techniques to the parallel context. As mentioned above, however, imposing this sequential constraint incurs significant performance cost. Let us understand this notion of sequential consistency. Consider the following listing, assuming the values in A$ are 0 initially, and two threads with threadID 0 and 1, respectively, execute:

**Listing 4.3** Sequential Expectation

```
A$[threadID] = 1
print A$[1-threadID]
```

With sequential reasoning, it would be natural to expect that at least one of the threads prints 1. After all, whichever thread writes into A$ "later" expects the other thread's location in A$ to already be 1. Hence, its subsequent fetch of that value should yield 1. A parallel platform that fails to meet this expectation is not sequentially consistent. Let us formalize this idea.

We first assign a more practical meaning to "taking effect." A fetch or read operation takes effect when it completes, meaning, for example, that a value at that address at some unknown time in the past arrives in a register ready for use in a subsequent operation. A store or write operation takes effect when a reader fetches the new value – we call that fetch the writer's *read-effect*. In other words, a reader observes other thread's writes through their read-effect. This definition allows different readers to record different read-effects of the same store operation, which could occur at different times.

Concurrent execution of multiple threads is said to be *sequentially consistent*[5] if there exists a global sequence of all operations that access the shared addresses, which is consistent with the order of operation executed by each thread. The global sequence includes operations by every thread. The global sequence is consistent with thread $i$ only if:

1. If thread $i$ executes operation $o_1$ before $o_2$, $o_1$ appears before $o_2$ also in the global sequence.

---

[5] Lamport, "How to make a multiprocessor computer."

2. If operation $o_i$ (read from $x$) of thread $i$ is the read-effect of operation $o_j$ (write to $x$) of thread $j$, $o_i$ must appear after $o_j$ in the global sequence, and no other instance of (write to $x$) may appear between $o_i$ and $o_j$ in it.

This defines that a read from address $x$ in every thread returns the value of the most recent write to $x$ in that global sequence. In this sequence, we do not worry about the time when an operation takes effect but only their order. Operations of different threads are allowed to fully interleave. However, every thread's view of the order in which its operations take effect is consistent with every other thread's view. Figure 4.1 illustrates examples of sequentially consistent and inconsistent executions.

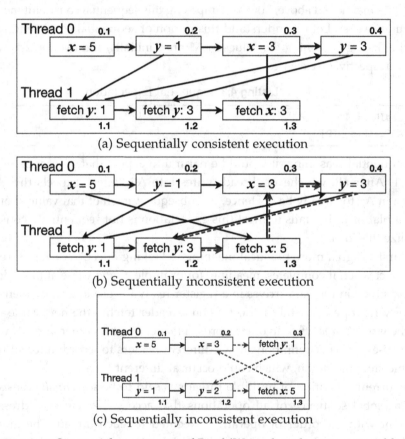

(a) Sequentially consistent execution

(b) Sequentially inconsistent execution

(c) Sequentially inconsistent execution

**Figure 4.1** Sequential consistency of Read/Write shared-memory variables

Figure 4.1(a) shows a sequentially consistent execution; Figures 4.1(b) and (c) show two inconsistent executions. Note that the assignments imply write operations on the shared-memory locations. Values actually obtained by the fetch operations on the listed variables in the given execution are also shown after the colon. We refer to operation number $j$ of thread $i$ by the symbol $i.j$. The arrows show some of the orders that can explain the execution result. For example, 1.2 is the read-effect of 0.4 and must come after it (the value 3 was observed in $y$ by 1.2 and written by 0.4).

There exist several global sequences of operations that the observed behavior is consistent with, for example, $(0.1 \rightarrow 0.2 \rightarrow 0.3 \rightarrow 1.1 \rightarrow 0.4 \rightarrow 1.2 \rightarrow 1.3)$.[6] An execution consistent with any such global sequence is sequentially consistent. If all executions of a program are guaranteed to be sequentially consistent, the program is said to be sequentially consistent. If all programs executable on a programming platform are sequentially consistent, the platform is sequentially consistent.

Figures 4.1(b) and (c) are both inconsistent executions because no consistent global order exists. This can be seen by following the dashed arrows. These arrows form a cycle, meaning there is no way to order them in a sequence. For example, in Figure 4.1(b), 1.3 occurred before 0.3; otherwise, it would have read the value 3 in $x$. Of course, 0.3 always must occur before 0.4, which occurred before 1.2 in this execution, because 1.2 is the read-effect of 0.4. This could occur in an execution if the update to variable $y$ becomes quickly visible to other threads, whereas updates to $x$ travel slower.

This variance in the update speed can also occur due to caches in case of shared memory – even if the caches are coherent. Updates indeed reach all threads, just not in the same order. Keeping all updates in order implies faster updates must wait for slower updates to complete. Moreover, in-order updates do not guarantee sequential consistency, as Figure 4.1(c) shows. Each thread updates different variables – $x$ and $y$, respectively. So, there is no inherent order between 0.2 and 1.2. Still, there exists a cycle as the dashed arrows show, and hence no consistent sequential order can exist. In this case, both updates are just slow. Should we simply block all execution until a *write* becomes visible to all potential readers? Or, is the lack of sequential consistency inconsequential?

There certainly are real-world consequences, as seen in the following example.

**Listing 4.4** Single Producer Consumer

| Thread 0 | Thread 1 |
|---|---|
| `while(! ready$);` | `data$ = generate();` |
| `x = data$;` | `ready$ = true;` |

Thread 1 produces data that thread 0 consumes. This is a simple instance of the *producer–consumer* problem, where one or more threads may produce a sequence of data and one or more threads consume them one at a time. In this example, a single piece of data is produced and consumed. Thread 1 sets ready$ after ensuring that data$ is indeed

---

[6] $a \rightarrow b$ means a is ordered before b.

ready. We assume ready$ is initially false. Accordingly, thread 0 continues checking the value of ready$ until it becomes true. At this point, it reads data$. What if the execution is not sequentially consistent? Thread 0 could read stale data$ even after finding the updated value in ready$.

There are situations, however, when certain pairs of operations may be swapped in the global sequence. For example, if thread $i$ reads $x$ and then reads $y$, it is possible that the results are the same even if those two operations are in the reverse order in the global sequence. We next discuss a few common relaxations to the requirement of complete sequential equivalence. The general idea is to allow the platform to guarantee somewhat relaxed constraints, thus supporting higher performance. The programmer is then responsible for enforcing any other ordering constraints if required, using synchronization techniques discussed in section 4.4.

## Causal Consistency

The idea of causal consistency is to limit the consistent ordering constraint only to what are called *causally* related operations. In particular, there is no requirement of a consistent global sequence of all operations to exist. Rather, each thread views the write operations of other threads in a causally consistent order, meaning two causally related operations are viewed by every thread in the order of their causality, which is defined as follows:

1. Each write of a thread is causally after that thread's earlier reads and writes.
2. A read is causally after the write whose read-effect it is.
3. Causality is transitive, that is, $op_a \rightarrow op_b$ and $op_b \rightarrow op_c$ imply $op_a \rightarrow op_c$.

In particular, two writes (from different threads) that are not causally related may be observed in different orders by different threads: they are truly concurrent. In a given thread's view, its own operations must always appear in its program order. Figure 4.1(c) shows the example of a causally consistent execution. In thread 0's view, only 1.1 needs to happen before 1.2. It sees no evidence to the contrary. For example, the order (0.1 → 0.2 → 1.1 → 0.3 → 1.2) is thread 0's causally consistent view. It does not need to find a consistent place for 1.3 in this ordering. Similarly, the order (1.1 → 1.2 → 0.1 → 1.3 → 0.2) is thread 0's causally consistent view of thread 1. The example in Figure 4.1(b) remains causally inconsistent, however. In thread 1's view, thread 0's operation 0.4 happens before 1.2, but 0.3 happens after 1.3, when 0.3 is causally before 0.4.

## FIFO and Processor Consistency

Guarantee of causal consistency requires a potentially complex evaluation of transitive relationships. On the other hand, further relaxation of certain order constraints provides more opportunity for performance optimization. FIFO[7] (first in, first out) consistency only enforces a consistent order of writes operations of all threads. In other words, writes from a given thread are seen to be in that thread's order by every thread. Read operations and ensuing transitive causalities need not be consistently ordered. The example in Figure 4.1(b) remains FIFO inconsistent, but the example in Figure 4.2(a) exhibits FIFO consistency, even though it violates causal consistency, and hence also sequential consistency. In Figure 4.2(a), the dashed arrows demonstrate transitive causality, which forces a relationship between the otherwise concurrent writes 0.2 and 1.3. Note that 1.3 must occur before 0.1, as 0.1 is its read-effect, and similarly, 1.2 must occur after 0.2. We may assume in these examples that the initial value of variables is, say, 0. Figure 4.2(a) is a FIFO consistent execution because there is only a single write by thread 0, and it only needs to appear before 1.2 in thread 1's view. The two writes to $y$ in thread 1 must appear in that same order in thread 0's view. $(1.1 \rightarrow 1.3 \rightarrow 0.1 \rightarrow 0.2)$ is a FIFO consistent view of thread 0.

The notion of *processor consistency* is a slight tightening of FIFO constraints. In addition to a consistent ordering of all writes by a given thread, all threads must also view all writes to the same variable in the same order no matter which thread makes them. FIFO and processor consistency both allow the execution in Figure 4.2(a). Figure 4.2(b) shows an execution that is FIFO consistent but not processor consistent. It is FIFO consistent because writes to $y$ by thread 1 (i.e. $1.1 \rightarrow 1.3$) are consistent in thread 0's view: $(1.1 \rightarrow 1.3 \rightarrow 0.1 \rightarrow 0.2 \rightarrow 0.3)$. Writes from thread 0 (i.e. $0.2 \rightarrow 0.3$) remain consistent in thread 1's view: $(0.2 \rightarrow 1.1 \rightarrow 0.3 \rightarrow 1.2 \rightarrow 1.3)$.

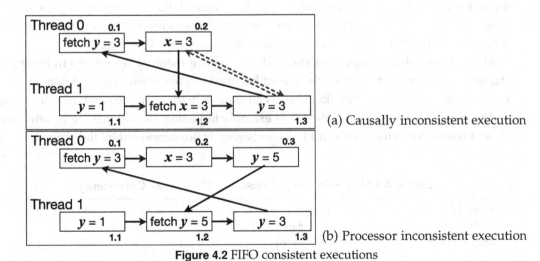

(a) Causally inconsistent execution

(b) Processor inconsistent execution

**Figure 4.2** FIFO consistent executions

---

[7] FIFO consistency model is also known as PRAM consistency.

However, processor consistency additionally requires that all writes to $y$ are seen in by the same order by all threads. This means that the two orders above, which switch 0.3 and 1.3, are not processor consistent. In fact, no consistent order exists for this execution because thread 0 must see 1.3 occur before 0.1 and hence before 0.3. On the other hand, thread 1 must see 0.3 occur before 1.2 and hence before 1.3.

Figure 4.1(b) is neither FIFO consistent nor processor consistent. Thread 1 must see all writes from thread 0 in the order $(0.1 \rightarrow 0.2 \rightarrow 0.3 \rightarrow 0.4)$. However, it sees 0.4 before 1.2, but 0.3 after 1.3.

Check for yourself that a guarantee of FIFO consistency is sufficient to prove the correctness of Listing 4.4 in its every execution.

## Weak Consistency

Finally, there is a practical notion of consistency called weak consistency, under which minimal guarantees are made by the programming platform. The responsibility of maintaining consistency is instead left to the programmer. This follows the principle "programmer knows best" and allows the system to make aggressive optimizations. A programmer in need of enforcing order between two operations then must employ special primitives; an example is *flush*. Another possibility is to enforce sequential or some other form of consistency only on specially designated variables or resources, called *synchronization variables*. Additionally, writes to nonsynchronization-shared variables are allowed to be reordered but only so long as there is no synchronization operation between them. In other words, synchronization operation must all be in a sequentially consistent order, and nonsynchronization operations between two synchronization operations in any thread must appear to happen between those two in all thread's views.

Flush is a synchronization operation. This means all memory operations in flight (i.e. started but not completed) when flush is called must be completed before operations after the flush can begin. This operation is also called *memory fence* – fences that memory reads and writes cannot cross in any view. The example in Listing 4.4 will need to be rewritten thus to ensure correctness, even if FIFO consistency is not supported by the programming platform.

**Listing 4.5** Single Producer Consumer With Weak Consistency

| Thread 0 | Thread 1 |
|---|---|
| `while(! ready$)` | `data$ = generate();` |
| `  memory_fence();` | `memory_fence();` |
| `x = data$;` | `ready$ = true;` |

Fences slow down memory operations and the code above may be an overkill, but it guarantees correctness even if caches are not coherent. By definition, the setting of ready$

must happen after that of data$ in thread 0's view due to their intervening fence in thread 1. A fence ensures that caches are flushed and an updated value of ready$ is indeed fetched by thread 0. Since data$ is read after ready$ is found to be true in thread 0 (guaranteed by its fence), it indeed reads the updated data$ written by thread 1.

## Linearizability

There are several other flavors of the notion of consistency. Linearizability is stronger than sequential consistency. It guarantees not only that all operations have a global order consistent with all the threads' execution, but also that each operation completes within a known time interval. In particular, the operation is supposed to take global effect at some specific instant between its invocation and completion by its thread. It thus requires the notion of a central clock to relate to invocation and completion times and requires arguments about an operation having completed before a certain time $t$. As one consequence, if an execution is linearizable with respect to each variable, the overall execution also becomes linearizable. (We will not prove this statement here.) Sequentially consistent sub-executions are not able to be composed in this manner to produce a longer sequentially consistent execution.

There is a related notion of serializability, mostly used in the context of databases. It's an ordering constraint on *transactions*. A transaction is a set of operations on a set of shared resources. Serializability guarantees that the transactions appear atomic. In other words, there is a sequential order of transactions that produce the same result. Sequential order there means that transactions are performed one at a time without any interleaving.

Now we turn our attention to the general notion of synchronization.

## 4.3  Synchronization

It is not necessary to synchronize individual thread clocks to the universal time. Indeed perfect synchronization is impossible, given that signals may travel only at a finite speed and there may be variable delays. There is a distance even between the clock generator and the execution engines.

However, as discussed in Section 4.2, programs only care about the order of events. A read-effect is so, whether the write started immediately before the read or somewhat earlier. Hence, we focus on enforcing consistency using synchronization to impose order between selected events of two or more threads. We use two types of synchronization: *exclusion* and *inclusion*. Exclusion synchronization precludes mutual execution of two or more threads – rather two or more specific events within those threads. (An event is a sequence of execution steps.) Inclusion synchronization, on the other hand, ensures co-occurrence of events. We will now examine a few important synchronization concepts and tools. Later, we will see some examples.

## Synchronization Condition

With some support from the hardware, operating systems provide several basic synchronization primitives. However, their context is only the system controlled by the operating system. If multiple operating systems are involved, additional primitives must be built, possibly using these basic primitives. In any such primitive, once the execution of a thread encounters a *synchronization event*, it requires certain conditions to be satisfied before it may proceed further. Other fragment executions may impact those conditions. There are two types of conditions: *shared* conditions and *exclusive* conditions. Multiple threads waiting for a shared condition may all see it when the condition becomes satisfied, and therefore all continue their execution. Only one of the waiting threads may continue if the condition is exclusive. There are also hybrids, which allow a fixed number of waiting threads to continue. Usually, the choice of continuing threads is random, but it is also possible to allow continuation based on some priority.

## Protocol Control

A thread completes a synchronized *activity* by following a coordinated protocol involving multiple synchronization events. There are two classes of protocols: *centralized protocol* and *distributed protocol*. In centralized protocols, there is a coordinating entity, for example, another thread, an operating system, or some piece of hardware. This centralized controller flags a thread ahead or stops it, not unlike what a traffic signal does. In parallel computation involving a large number of synchronizing threads, such a centralized controller is often a source of bottleneck. Failure of the coordinator also can be disastrous for the entire program. In distributed protocols, there is no centralized controller. Rather the threads themselves follow a set of steps synchronizing each other. This may involve the use of multiple passive shared resources, for example, memory locations.

As a simple example, concurrent operations on a queue (e.g. insertion or removal) by multiple threads may be activities. Checking whether a queue is full is a synchronization event. Checking whether there are ongoing removals could be another event. A protocol is the set of events designed to ensure that multiple threads may safely add and remove elements without being misled by any transient variables (set by another thread).

In general, the correctness of synchronization depends on all participants following the protocol. However, some fault-tolerant protocols can offer certain guarantees even in the face of failure.

## Progress

A synchronization event is nothing but a sequence of instructions executed by a thread, often via a function call. There are two parts to this call: checking whether the condition is satisfied and then waiting or (eventually) proceeding past the event, depending on the result. Atomicity is required for exclusive conditions because two different threads must not view, and both proceed on the same exclusive condition. This requires some coordination among competing threads, and even the test for the condition in a thread may itself be impacted by the state of a different thread. Still, it is possible to implement synchronization in a way that allows the test to safely complete, independent of action by other threads. Of course, the synchronization protocol still applies, and actions to be taken when the condition is satisfied may still be taken only if the condition is satisfied. Such methods are called *nonblocking*. In particular, a nonblocking function completes in finite time even in the presence of indefinite delays, or failure, in other threads' execution.

This notion of nonblocking functions applies to contexts other than synchronization as well, for example, data communication or file IO. Although similar, this notion is slightly different from that of the nonblocking network topology discussed in Chapter 1. There, messages between one pair of nodes could progress without being blocked by messages between a different pair, that is, one message was not blocked by another as long as the communicators were separate.

A blocking function merely does not return until the synchronization condition is satisfied. The execution proceeds to the next instruction after this return, just as it would after every other function. A nonblocking function, on the other hand, returns even when the condition is not satisfied. The protocol must then account for such unsuccessful return and may, for example, choose to perform some other computation that does not require the condition to hold. We will see examples of such protocols later in this section.

Note that the notion of blocking is a thread-level progress criterion. There are also system-wide progress criteria. A synchronization protocol that guarantees that at least one thread (among all synchronizing threads) always completes its activity irrespective of other threads' behavior is called *lock-free*. In particular, if multiple threads can operate on a shared data structure such that some operation or the other continues to succeed, it is called a lock-free data structure. If every thread following the protocol is guaranteed to complete its activity within a finite number of steps, the data structure is called *wait-free*. A wait-free data structure ensures that each operation eventually completes. We will study examples of lock-free and wait-free synchronization in section 4.3.

Separate from whether a function is nonblocking is the issue of how the condition-checking and progress are managed. In *busy-wait*-based implementation, the fragment repetitively checks until the condition turns favorable. A busy-wait loop can result in blocking if the condition checking depends on action by other threads. The other alternative is *signal-wait*. The calling thread is suspended until the conditions become favorable again, after which an external entity like the operating system wakes the thread and makes it eligible for execution. The signal-wait mechanism is blocking by definition, as the thread can make no progress in the absence of action by the external entity.

When there are many more threads than the number of cores available to execute them, the busy-wait strategy can waste computing cycles in repetitively testing and failing – particularly if the synchronization event involves a large number of threads or long synchronized activities. On the other hand, the latency of such tests is usually much lower than that of signal-wait. In any case, synchronization overhead is not trivial. This overhead includes the time spent in the synchronization primitive as well as the time a thread waits for action by other threads. Hence frequent or fine-grained synchronization is not advisable in parallel programming. A well-designed parallel program tries to reduce synchronization in the first place. We will see that certain busy-wait strategies are suitable for parallel execution.

## Synchronization Hazards

In any synchronization protocol, there are two hazards to guard against: *deadlock* and *starvation*.

Two or more thread are in deadlock if none of them can ever complete the synchronization activity because the condition for each remains permanently unfavorable. Each such unfavorable condition could only be turned favorable by one or more of the other deadlocked threads. But, they cannot, because those other threads are themselves waiting, likely for some other condition. Effectively, they all indefinitely wait for each other. There is a famous abstraction called the dining philosopher's problem demonstrating deadlocks. A modified version goes like this.

Consider five philosophers sitting around a table with five forks alternately laid between them. The philosophers meditate and eat alternately, but they may eat only if they can pick up both forks next to them. After they eat, they clean both forks and put them back in their original setting. Each philosopher eats and meditates for arbitrarily long periods. Their eat–meditate lifecycle goes on indefinitely. No more than two philosophers may eat at the same time (maybe because the food cannot be supplied quickly enough).

Consider the following protocol. The philosophers try to pick the fork on their left and then their right when hungry. If both are picked, they eat. Once full, they put the forks down one at a time and go back to meditating. If only one fork is available, they pick it up. If they do not get the second, they meditate some more before checking again. They do so repeatedly until they get both forks. They then eat before replacing the forks.

This protocol ensures that no philosopher eats with only a single fork. It also ensures that only up to two philosophers can be eating at any given time. Note that a philosopher who is using two forks ensures that neither neighbor may have two forks. A synchronization protocol that guarantees the required behavior at all times, as this eating protocol does, is called *safe*. What happens in this protocol, however, if all philosophers pick up the forks to their left almost simultaneously, and then wait for the fork to their right to become free? Since no one got two, no one eats, and no fork is set down, no matter how many times they check to their right. This is a deadlock. Note that if the philosophers could simultaneously pick two forks, the deadlock could be avoided. Sometimes, such complex atomic instructions may be available for synchronizations. At other times, only simple building blocks, like "pick one fork" are available.

Starvation is the situation when a thread waiting for a condition to become favorable fails to find it so, even if the condition does intermittently become favorable. It either fails to check in time before the condition turns unfavorable again (if it is busy-waiting), or it remains sleeping for a long time, even indefinitely, and some other thread is repeatedly woken up instead. Thus wait-free synchronization must not allow starvation. Protocols that guarantee a lack of starvation are called *fair*. Notice that in the previous example, a dining philosopher could starve in the listed protocol, for there is no guarantee that they check during the period their neighbors left the fork down on the table. The neighbor is allowed to pick the fork back up.

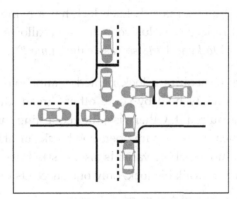

**Figure 4.3** Traffic light deadlock

Considering the traffic light example, the basic purpose of synchronization is that no two vehicles may be in each other's path (following behind is allowed, reversing is not). A protocol like "go only on green" is safe as long as the signals are properly coordinated. There may be a deadlock, however, if a slow vehicle that enters the intersection on green is not able to get through before the light turns green for the cross-traffic. See Figure 4.3 for a deadlocked configuration. One may modify the protocol to prevent these deadlocks. For example, vehicles could go on green only if there is no cross-vehicle in the intersection. Now, there would be no deadlock, but starvation is possible. Too many slow vehicles could ensure that a waiting vehicle continually sees a vehicle in the intersection while its light is green (before it turns red again). Furthermore, the vehicle throughput may reduce. This situation arises in many synchronization protocols, and simple solutions to prevent deadlocks often risk starvation.

## 4.4  Mutual Exclusion

We now introduce a few standard synchronization primitives. *Mutual exclusion* is one such widely used primitive. As the name suggests, it prevents mutual execution of two code fragments. We use the term *critical section* to refer to such a code fragment. Although any part of a thread's execution can be designated as critical, such usage is generally limited to parts of the execution that modify a shared resource or state, for example, a shared-memory location. If a thread is executing any part of its critical section, no other thread may be executing a competing critical section. Rather, critical sections are strictly ordered in their impact on the shared resource. This also means these impacts appear to be atomic to those competing threads.

We next discuss some synchronization methods that support mutual exclusion.

### Lock

A simple synchronization tool is *lock*. Each lock has a name known to all participating threads. The simplest locks are exclusive. A thread is allowed two main operations on a lock: *acquire* (also called *lock*) and *release* (also called *unlock*).

Acquire($x$):  Attempts to acquire a lock named $x$ and hold it. Acquisition succeeds if $x$ is not already held by some other thread, that is, some thread has not already acquired it. Otherwise, the requesting thread waits until the current holder releases $x$. Acquire operation blocks until the acquisition is successful (although nonblocking variants also exist). If two concurrent threads attempt to acquire an available lock, only one succeeds (if the lock is exclusive).

Release($x$):  Allow subsequent acquisitions.

Nonexclusive locks are *counting locks*, which allow up to $n$ holders at a time for some fixed value of $n$. Locks may also be *reentrant*, meaning additional acquisition attempt by the holder is allowed. In such a situation, the definition of holder (e.g. a thread or a process) must be clear. In non-reentrant locks, the holder trying to reacquire an exclusive lock would lead to a deadlock. The following example shows how to safely perform the counter increment operation described in Section 1.4.

**Listing 4.6** Lock-Based Mutual Exclusion

```
Acquire(counter_lock$)
counter$ = counter$ + 1
Release(counter_lock$)
```

If every thread updating counter$ follows this protocol, and updates to counter$ are seen consistently in all threads, counter$ is incremented safely and atomically. Consistent ordering is ensured if Acquire and Release are synchronization operations for the variable counter$. In fact, it is sufficient that these two are processor-consistent write operations.

Notice that deadlock is not possible in fragment 4.6. If thread $i$ waits, that is only because some other thread $j$ holds the lock. Thread $j$ that holds the lock eventually executes the release, since there is no other synchronization it waits for. Of course thread $i$ may yet starve as there is no guarantee that if the lock is released, it won't be repeatedly offered to another requester. In other situations, the holder may fail to release the lock. For example, thread $j$ may crash. Algorithms to recover from such crashes are complex[8] and will not be discussed in this book.

It is sometimes possible to effect synchronization merely with the help of shared-memory locations. We assume that the shared-memory operations are sequentially consistent. A write operation completes at some instant: all threads see the old value before this instant and the new value after that. Two writes may not occur at the same instant.

We describe two algorithms next that ensure mutual exclusion using only shared-memory: Peterson's algorithm and Bakery's algorithm.

## Peterson's Algorithm

Peterson's algorithm guarantees mutual exclusion between two threads. Both execute Listing 4.7, which may be executed any number of times by each thread. This method employs shared variables ready$ (an array of size 2) and defer$ to achieve exclusion. Assume the two threads are identified by IDs 0 and 1, respectively. The value of the ID is always found in an automatic private variable threadID. Private variables, even if they have the same name in each thread, are local to each thread and thus not shared. Initially, ready$[0] = ready$[1] = false.

**Listing 4.7** Peterson's Algorithm for Two-Thread Mutual Exclusion

```
1 other_id = 1 - threadID;
2 ready$[threadID] = true;                        // This thread wants in
3 defer$ = threadID;                              // This thread defers
4 while(ready$[other_id] && defer$ == threadID);  // Busy-wait
5                                                  // Critical Section goes here
6 ready$[threadID] = false;                       // Not critical. Not ready.
```

---

[8] Agrawal and El Abbadi, "An efficient and fault-tolerant solution."
Prvulovic et al., "Revive."
Elnozahy et al., "A survey of rollback – recovery protocols."

A thread indicates its intent to execute the critical section by setting its ready$ flag. It then indicates its willingness to defer to the other thread. The order of these two operations is important. Of course, defer$ is shared, and the other thread could overwrite defer$. However, each thread is willing to busy-wait in the while loop if defer$ remains set to its ID, and the other thread has indicated that it also wants to enter the critical section. A thread remains ready in the critical section and only turns not-ready after it completes its execution of the critical section.

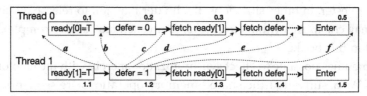

**Figure 4.4** Operation order for Peterson's algorithm

Safety means that if a thread exits its loop and enters the critical section, the other thread is guaranteed to not enter until the first is out of the critical section.

Figure 4.4 demonstrates the possible order of operations on the shared memory. In the top row are operations by thread 0 and the bottom row has those by thread 1. By our assumption that each operation is atomic, no two operations overlap. In particular, $i.j$ occurs before $i.j'$ $\forall j' > j$. Solid arrows from $i.j$ to $i.j'$ help visualize this. (Recall that $i.j$ is the $j$th operation of thread $i$.) Note that we do not, in general, have any predetermined order between $i.j$ and $k.l$ if $i \neq k$. Accordingly in our example, an operation like 1.2 could occur between any $0.j$ and $0.(j+1)$. These possibilities are shown in dashed arrows and marked $a-f$. Regardless, 1.1 must occur before 1.2, which must occur before 1.3, and so on. No two operations on the same shared memory may overlap, as each operation is atomic.

In a given execution, if possibilities $a$ or $b$ materialize, thread 0 must find defer$ == 0 at 0.4. Similarly, if possibilities $c$ or $d$ occur, the value would be 1. Finally, if $e$ or $f$ materialize, thread 0 would still find value 0. Let's analyze each case.

Case $a, b$:  Thread 0 is guaranteed to find ready$[1] to be true at 0.3 as 1.1 is guaranteed to occur before 1.2. Hence, thread 0 does not proceed to the critical section.

Case $c, d$:  In Cases $c$ and $d$, thread 0 finds defer$ == 1. Hence the loop ends, and 0.5 follows. Since 0.1 and 0.2 occur before 1.2, and hence before 1.3, thread 1 cannot get past its loop as it finds thread 0 ready and defer$ == 1.

Case $e$:  The behavior depends on 1.1. If 1.1 occurs before 0.3 (call this Case $e$1), neither thread 0 nor thread 1 may exit their respective loops. Both find the other is ready and both find their own IDs in defer$. However, this cannot last. As both execute the next iteration of their busy-wait loops, thread 0 now finds 1 in defer$ and enters the critical section. Thread 1 does not.

On the other hand, if 1.1 occurs before 0.3 (Case $e2$), thread 0 enters the critical section finding that thread 1 is not ready. This time thread 1 would not enter the critical section as it would find defer$ == 1 at 1.4 and ready$[0] == 1 at 1.3 as long as thread 0 remains in the critical section.

Case $f$: In Case $f$, 1.1 cannot occur before 0.3. If it did, thread 0 would not reach 0.5 as explained for Case $e$. That's a contradiction. Thus 1.1 may only occur before 0.3. This is similar to Case $e2$.

In other words, thread 0 exits its busy-wait loop either because thread 1 was not ready, or thread 0's write to defer$ had been overwritten by 1. If defer$ was indeed found to be 1 by thread 0, thread 1's write to it would have happened *after* thread 0's. This means thread 1 is guaranteed to find 1 in defer$ and wait at its loop as long as thread 0 remains ready.

On the other hand, if thread 0 exits the loop because ready$[1] is false when tested, and if later thread 1 becomes ready and then sets defer$ to 1, it is guaranteed to find defer$ to be 1 in its loop condition. Thus, thread 1 cannot enter the critical section until thread 0 stops being ready, post its execution of the critical section.

The same argument holds for thread 1. Peterson's algorithm is also deadlock-free and starvation-free.

A deadlock could occur only if both threads are indefinitely stuck in their busy-wait loops. This would imply that thread 0 continually finds defer$ == 0 and thread 1 continually finds defer$ == 1. Both cannot be true because neither thread has a chance to change defer$ while busy-waiting.

No thread can starve either. Suppose without loss of generality that thread 0 does. This would imply that thread 1 is able to repeatedly complete its critical section, return for the next round and overtake the busy-waiting loop of thread 1. This means that each time thread 0 checks, defer$ == 0 and ready$[1] is true. But only thread 0 may ever set defer$ to 0, never thread 1. Rather, if thread 1 is able to repeatedly execute the protocol, it is obligated to set defer$ to 1 each time. How then does defer$ become 0 without thread 0 re-setting it? And it couldn't if it is busy-waiting. That's a contradiction.

Peterson's algorithm is not wait-free. If a thread is indefinitely delayed in the critical section, the other thread would not be able to proceed. It is not even lock-free, since a delay in a thread while it is in a critical section, blocks the progress of all competing threads. Indeed, synchronization protocols like mutual exclusion or locks are not lock-free (even as that appears to be a tautology).

In large parallel systems, synchronization is seldom between only two threads. Lamport's Bakery algorithm addresses this problem.

## Bakery Algorithm

Bakery algorithm is based on a ticket system. When a thread becomes ready, it takes a "number," and awaits its turn. The pseudo-code is as follows:

**Listing 4.8** Bakery Algorithm for $n$ Thread Mutual Exclusion

```
1 ready$[threadID] = true;                          // This thread wants in
2 number$[threadID] = maximum(number$) + 1;          // Take a number
3 while(∃ id != threadID s.t. ready$[id] && \        // busy wait
4   number$[id] < number$[threadID] || number$[id] == number$[threadID] && id < threadID);
5                                                     // Critical Section goes here
6 ready$[threadID] = false;                          // Critical no more
```

Its structure is an extension to Peterson's. When ready, a thread takes a number – one more than the maximum number taken by any other thread. It then busy-waits until no ready thread has a smaller number. Note that finding the new number itself is not protected by a critical section or synchronization. This means two (or more) threads may obtain the same number on line 2 of Listing 4.8, say $n$. When this occurs, ID is used to break the tie: the thread with lower ID exits loop first. If that winning thread later wants to enter the critical section again, the next time its number is guaranteed to be greater than $n$ after line 2. Thus number$[i] strictly increases every time thread $i$ completes line 2.

To prove safety, show that two threads may not be in a critical section at the same time. Suppose these are threads $i$ and $j$ with, say, $i < j$. When $j$ exited its busy-wait loop on line 3, either number$[j] < number$[i] or ready$[i] == false.

If ready$[i] was false, thread $i$ set ready$[i] to true later than thread $j$'s condition test. This means thread $i$ also computed its number after $j$'s test and hence number$[i] > number$[j]. Hence, it could not have exited its loop, as ready$[j] remains true until after $j$ completes the critical section.

Instead, if ready$[i] was true, number$[j] < number$[i] at $j$.3 (i.e. at line 3 for thread $j$), meaning $i$.2 occurred after $j$.2. Since $j$ is in the critical section, ready$[j] would be true at $i$.3 and thread $i$ could not exit its busy-wait loop.

Bakery algorithm is also deadlock-free and starvation-free. Deadlocks are avoided because there exists a total order on updates to number$ and some thread with the smallest number is always able to get past the busy-wait loop. At the same time, an increasing number ensures no thread is able to overtake one that got a number earlier. Such a number-based design is common in many wait-free protocols. Interestingly, Bakery algorithm guarantees mutual exclusion even if memory operations are not atomic, and a read overlapping a write may return an old or the new value.

The drawback of Bakery algorithm is the need for large shared arrays (ready$ and number$). It turns out that there exists no algorithm that can guarantee mutual exclusion with a smaller size using only shared-memory reads and writes operations.

## Compare and Swap

Synchronization, as described above, using only shared-memory reads and writes have limited utility. In particular, they have a low consensus number.[9] There exist more powerful primitives that have lower cost and greater generality. The most common one is called Compare and Swap. It atomically performs two shared-memory operations. It compares a given value to a shared-memory location and then operates on the shared-memory location depending on the result of the comparison. Here is an example function for an integer shared variable with address ref$:

> [9] *Defined*: Consensus number indicates the number of threads that can achieve wait-free consensus. See the notion of consensus below.

**Listing 4.9** Compare and Swap

```
boolean compareAndSwap(void *ref$, int expected, int newvalue) {
    Do Atomically —
    int oldvalue;
    fetch *ref$, store the value in oldvalue;
    if(oldvalue == expected) {
        store newvalue into *ref$;
        return true;
    }
    return false;
}
```

The updates to *ref$ are seen in a consistent order by all threads using Compare and Swap. Many hardware-supported implementations of this function exist and are lock-free. Each call or execution returns true after writing the new value to the shared location if the old value was as expected. If the value was not as expected, the function returns false having made no change to the location. Other variants exist. For example, ones that return the old value instead. (The caller may compare the old value to the expected value to decipher what happened inside the function.) This peculiar primitive can help implement a rich set of synchronization functions, including $n$ thread mutual exclusion as shown below (assume turn$ is initially −1):

**Listing 4.10** $n$ Thread Mutual Exclusion Using Compare and Swap

```
while(!compareAndSwap(&turn$, -1, threadID));
    // Critical section
turn$ = -1;
```

If a thread is able to find $-1$ in turn$, it writes its ID in that variable. Since Compare and Swap is atomic, two threads may not both find it to be $-1$. Exactly one succeeds in writing its ID. The others retry. Actually, Compare and Swap primitive's application is much broader than mutual exclusion; it can be used to implement many lock-free and wait-free data structures and algorithms. One important handicap of the Compare and Swap primitive is its fixed granularity, the size of data it operates upon. Sometimes, we need a whole set of variables to remain unchanged, while a thread applies its updates (to one or more locations). Doing this in a lock-free or wait-free manner is harder.

## Transactional Memory

Transactional memory uses a paradigm that seeks to address the challenges of Compare and Swap. The main idea is to define a set of operations on the shared state as a transaction and ensure serialization of these transactions. One way to ensure such serialization is, of course, mutual exclusion. Another is to optimistically perform un-synchronized operations on shared resources. These are performed in a tentative sense, but the risk of races is detected by identifying other instances of transactions. In case no race is detected, the transaction is committed and considered complete. In case a race is detected, the entire transaction is discarded and effectively rolled back. After the discard, an alternate course is followed: simply retry the transaction or apply mutual exclusion this time. Note that multiple conflicting transactions would all be discarded and retried.

Transactions are a higher-order primitive than locks and Compare and Swap. Hence, they may be easier for programmers: it could be as simple as encapsulating a sequence of operations into a transaction that appears to execute atomically. Further, transactions can also be nested – a transaction can consist of sub-transactions, and only the sub-transaction is discarded if it encounters a conflict. Transactions can also be composed. However, they are not do-all. For example, intricate interaction between threads, like in a producer–consumer problem, is not easily expressed as transactions.

It is also worth noting that the catching of all races is an expensive proposition. Data races[10] are a little easier to detect. An implementation of transaction memory may not be able to detect all races. The reality is

> [10] *Defined*: A data race occurs when two or more threads access a shared location in an unsynchronized fashion, and at least one of them is a write operation.

that the more guarantees a transaction memory implementation provides, the slower it can get. Furthermore, interactions between transaction style and traditional synchronization can also become complex to manage. In particular, roll-back of transactions may not be truly possible in all cases, for example, when interaction with a file-system, network, or a user may be involved.

## Barrier and Consensus

Barrier, like transactions, is a higher-order and a collective primitive. It is a contract among a group of threads, which we can call the barrier group. It is collective because each member of the group must reach the barrier event. Every member blocks at the event until they have surety that all the other members have reached their respective barrier events. This is quite clearly not a nonblocking nor a lock-free operation. A stand-alone barrier for an $n$ member barrier group may be implemented as follows. Initially, numt$ is 0.

**Listing 4.11** Barrier

```
void Barrier {
       int num = numt$;
       while(! compareAndSwap(&numt$, num, num+1))
             num = numt$; // Re-read count and retry incrementing
       while(numt$ < n); // Busy-wait
}
```

Each thread reads the then-current value of numt$. If no other thread has modified it in the interim, the thread writes the incremented value into numt$. Otherwise, it re-reads the new value of numt$ and retries incrementing it. It needs to retry no more than $n$ times before it must succeed because a successful thread does not retry. Once the thread succeeds in registering its presence, it moves to check if all threads have registered. It busy-waits until then. This barrier may be used only once. It is possible to modify it so multiple barriers can reuse the same variables. numt$ would need to be reset to 0. But also note that threads may exit their busy-wait loops as soon as numt$ equals $n$, but some could be delayed. Either a thread's next entry into the barrier must be prevented until the last one is out, or the entries would need to be otherwise separated. Implementation is left as an exercise (see Exercise 4.14).

More complex barrier variants perform additional operations once the barrier is reached. For example, the following vote function is a barrier, which each member of the barrier group calls with an argument true or false. The function returns in each thread only after all members have made the call. Further, the returned value is true in each thread if at least half the members call vote(true) and false otherwise.

**Listing 4.12** Voting Barrier

```
// define:
bool vote (bool value);
```

Other fancier versions exist. For example, one returns the sum of integer values supplied by the members. Nonetheless, this simple version is instructive. It is related to *consensus*:

having all threads reach the same value. Consensus is often used to argue about the power of synchronization primitives.[11] In the basic consensus problem, the returned value of vote must be the same for all members of a group, but the semantics of barrier is not required. Threads may provide their values and proceed. Later they may fetch the consensus value. In fact, the only requirements are:

1. the consensus value must be the same for every thread
2. at least one thread must provide the value determined as consensus

Compare and Swap is able to provide wait-free consensus among an arbitrary number of threads, meaning its consensus number is $\infty$. A sample implementation of vote follows. Assume one_value$ is initially $-1$.

**Listing 4.13** Consensus

```
bool consensus (bool value) {
    compareAndSwap(&one_value$, -1, value);
    return one_value$;
}
```

Exactly one thread succeeds in storing its value into one_value$. Others find it to be the value written by the successful thread. It turns out that simple shared-memory reads and writes (of the kind used by Bakery or Peterson's algorithm) cannot be used to achieve consensus of even two threads in a wait-free manner. A solution to the consensus problem can be used to implement solutions of a large variety of concurrent problems. Another important cog in our understanding of concurrency is that consensus is impossible to guarantee if any one of $n > 1$ threads may fail.[12] This is true in the shared-memory model (using only read/write) as well as in the message-passing distributed-memory model. In particular, consensus is not guaranteed if threads (and messages) can be arbitrarily slow. For controlled environments, which a parallel computer system may be, the knowledge of the bound on delays is employed to achieve consensus in a practical manner, even in the presence of failure. In this book, we will not discuss fault-tolerant algorithms, which continue to provide synchronization and safety in the presence of failure.

---

[11] Block-chains are based on the consensus problem.
  Nakamoto, "Bitcoin."
[12] Fischer et al., "Impossibility of distributed consensus."
  Herlihy, "Wait-free synchronization."

## 4.5   Communication

Much of the preceding discussion on synchronization is described in terms of shared memory. That does not restrict it to virtual address space controlled by a single operating system. It also applies to distributed shared-memory systems, which are built on top of message-passing primitives and give the appearance of a unified shared address space across computing systems. Alternatively, a program may explicitly employ message-passing. For example, a message-passing program may unify separate address spaces by annotating an address with the name of the computing system that owns it. A write to a unified shared address now translates to two steps: sending a write message to the corresponding owner, followed by that owner writing the value within its local address space. If such writes are nonblocking on the originator system, the previous discussion on synchronization and consistency directly applies.

Note that scalable and consistent distributed shared-memory implementation is rather complex, and good performance can be hard to achieve. For many applications, direct use of message-passing primitives is easier to design, synchronize, and reason about. There is coordination required for two or more threads to communicate among themselves. Inter-thread interactions are more direct and more explicit compared to the shared-memory model, where a passive memory location has no ability to detect anomalous interactions. Hence, it is important to understand the nature of message-passing-based programming. Broadly speaking, in the message-passing model, shared states and critical sections are eschewed in favor of the synchronization implicit in communication, which has certain features of the barrier. We will see detailed examples in Chapter 6.

As a practical matter, it is useful to realize that synchronization across message-passing threads is likely to be slower as network delays are generally much higher and more variable than local memory latency. We will briefly review the communication system next. With this understanding, we can devise more efficient inter-thread interaction. Common network topologies are discussed in Chapter 1. In this section, we move the discussion to a slightly higher level. We assume the availability of an efficient routing protocol that is able to reliably deliver messages in order from one addressable node to another. We will also abstract address details by simply addressing a thread by its ID. Let us first understand point-to-point communication in some detail.

### Point-to-Point Communication

There are two essential components of communication. A thread must *send* data, and another must *receive* it.

**Listing 4.14** Point-to-Point Communication Primitives

```
Send(IdType destinationID, DataType *buffer);
Receive(IdType sourceID, DataType *buffer);
```

Sender and recipient each must have a local buffer where that data must be stored. The sender sends from its *buffer, and the recipient receives into its *buffer. This means that the recipient must have sufficient space in its buffer to hold the entire data that the sender sends. Possibly, this size is shared in advance. Or, the communication could use fixed-size buffers, but that bounds the size of each message. A sender would have to subdivide larger messages, and that unnecessarily complicates program logic. Moreover, some setup is required to send each message (e.g. route setup or buffer reservation on intermediate switches). Subdividing messages may incur the overhead of repeated setup. The other big concern is synchronization between the sender and the recipient. How does Receive behave if the sender has not reached its corresponding Send and vice versa?

To answer such questions, let us delve deeper into implementation of communication systems. There is at least one network interface card (NIC) in a computing system. A special NIC processor is responsible for the actual sending of data onto an attached network link or receiving data on the link. Links are passive; hence, there must be two active execution units on both ends of a link. These execution units are built into the NIC and usually have their own buffers for temporary storage of data. This means that an application program does not need to concern itself with the transmission details, nor be forced to synchronize simultaneously executing fragments on both ends of the link. For security and generality, the access to NIC operations is through the operating system, and usually through several layers of software, which may have their own limits on message or packet size. This, in turn, implies that the user buffer may be subdivided into multiple packets and copied several times (from user buffer to operating system buffer to NIC buffer). Some of this copying is done by the operating system code on behalf of the application, and some is managed by the direct memory access (DMA) engine (see Section 1.2) associated with the NIC. See Figure 4.5.

Some NICs also support remote DMA, or *RDMA*. The RDMA mechanism is designed to bypass most copies. The DMA engines on the sender NIC and the recipient NIC collaborate to copy data directly from the sender's buffer to the recipient's buffer without an explicit CPU code. Naturally, this method requires that both the send and receive buffers be ready (also called *registered*), before the DMA can begin and remain available for the duration of the transfer. This imposes strict synchronization constraint between the sender and recipient. This constraint can be relaxed by replacing one or both buffers with operating system–owned buffers, but that leads to its own complications.

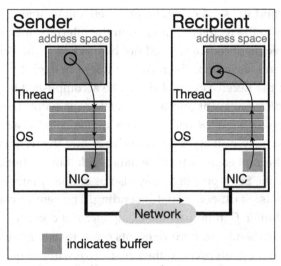

**Figure 4.5** Buffer copying for communication

One problem with DMA-based operations is their interference with the virtual memory paging system. Page management is the operating system's domain and requires CPU instructions, but the DMA engine's job is to off-load the copying from the CPU. Hence the operating system needs to lock or *pin* to real memory the pages that are in use by DMA. Thus memory registration is a heavyweight operation, not to be repeated incessantly. Reusing registered memory for multiple data transfers is important. However, the size of the actual message is known only at the Send event, and preregistered buffers could be too small to accommodate a transfer of the required size. Algorithms[13] exist for dynamic reregistration and pipelined reuse of small parcels of memory, but we will not discuss those in this textbook.

RDMA or not, the separation of concerns between the application program and the network subsystem allows the program to "fire and forget," assuming that the entire message will be delivered "as is" without any loss, corruption, or the need for further intervention or acknowledgments. The network subsystem is also able to guarantee that between one source–destination pair, all messages are delivered in the order they were sent. The use of the network subsystem and NIC buffers also means that a Send primitive may proceed asynchronously with the Receive primitive. A Send without its matching Receive means the message resides in an intermediate buffer, and the sender's execution

---

[13] Woodall et al., "High performance RDMA protocols in HPC."

may proceed beyond the send event. Later, when a matching Receive is finally executed, the data is copied to the recipient buffer from the intermediate buffer.

Similarly, the recipient code also need not be blocked at the Receive event, even if there is no matching Send, as long as the recipient does not expect to access the received data immediately past the Receive event. This can be accomplished by subdividing the Receive event into a *StartReceive* event and a *CompleteReceipt* event. Indeed, analogously to the shared-memory case, *CompleteReceipt* could be implemented as a blocking event, or it might be executed in the busy-wait style. StartReceive allows the recipient to provide the receive buffer. CompleteReceipt ensures that the data is filled in the buffer.

Symmetrically, the Send primitive may also be similarly subdivided into *StartSend* and *CompleteSend* events. StartSend initiates sending. The sender contracts to keep the data unchanged in its buffer. Getting past the CompleteSend event releases the sender from this contract. When both Send and Receive events occur together, the communication is called *synchronous*. When they can occur at their own pace without necessarily overlapping, the communication is called *asynchronous*.

## RPC

*RPC*, or remote procedure call, is a type of point-to-point communication but not described explicitly as a send–receive pair. Rather, a thread makes a function call that looks similar to a local function call, except the call is executed on a remote system. This means that the arguments of the function are packed into a message and sent to the designated recipient. The ID of the recipient may be a part of the call or preregistered with the function's name. On receiving the message, the recipient unpacks the arguments and calls a local function, which in turn may make another RPC. Once the function execution is complete, the function provider packs the value returned by the function into another message and sends it back to the initiator of the RPC. Synchronous RPC requires that the initiator only proceeds beyond the call after receiving the results back. Asynchronous RPC, not unlike asynchronous send and receive, allows the initiator to continue execution beyond the RPC call without receiving the results. The initiator may later invoke a CompleteRPC function to receive the result back. The basic operation is demonstrated in Figure 4.6.

RPC can be thought of as a higher-level communication primitive built on top of the send–receive primitive. RPC is also known as RMI (Remote Method Invocation) in the context of object-oriented programming.

## Collective Communication

Sometimes a more complex pattern of communication can exist among a set of cooperating threads. Describing complex communication among a set in terms of several individual

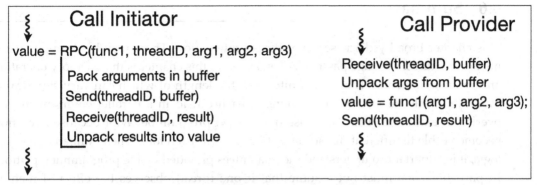

**Figure 4.6** Remote procedure call

point-to-point pairs is wasteful. Such higher-level primitives can again be built on top of the send–receive primitive. That also facilitates their efficient mapping to the underlying network topology, without the user program being concerned with the intricacies. These group level, or *collective communication primitives*, are similar to the barrier: all threads in a group encounter this event. However, unlike the barrier, they need not do so simultaneously. Rather, communication may be asynchronous and strict synchronization mandated by the barrier is not necessary. Some common collective communication primitives are listed below. Chapter 6 describes specific implementations and contains some more detail.

*Broadcast:*
    Message from one sender is received by many recipients

*Scatter:*
    $n$ messages from one sender are distributed to $n$ recipients, one each

*Gather:*
    One message each from $n$ senders is received by a single recipient

*AlltoAll:*
    Each member of a group consisting of $n + 1$ threads scatters $n$ messages (one each to the other members) and consequently gathers $n$ messages (one from each member).

*Reduce:*
    This is a special type of gather, in which one gatherer collects data from $n$ others, but instead of storing these $n$ items in $n$ locations, it reduces the vector of $n$ items to one using a reduce operation (e.g. by taking their sum).

## 4.6  Summary

This chapter broadly discusses inter-thread interaction. These may be through shared-memory or direct message-passing. A key lesson in this chapter is that memory operations are not instantaneous. They take finite time, the length of which can vary significantly. Moreover, multiple memory operations of each thread in a parallel environment may overlap in execution. This can cause unexpected program behavior because operations become visible to different threads at different times. Therefore, when evaluating program logic, it is important to understand the guarantees provided by the programming platform. In particular, one must not assume that if one thread observes the effect of memory operation $o_1$ before $o_2$, all other threads would observe the same order. If the platform does not guarantee so, the program must include explicit synchronization to ensure consistency where needed. Missing synchronization often leads to errors that may be hard to reproduce. Memory consistency errors are among the most obscure. Correct execution in a large number of test cases should not be taken as a proof of correctness. To reiterate the main points:

- Addresses hold values and may be accessed by multiple code fragments. The instructions of two or more code fragments that share addresses may execute in parallel or interleave. Their accesses are hence concurrent, and their order of execution is nondeterministic.

- Two fragments that access a shared address experience a data race if at least one of them updates the value of the address, and the order of their accesses is nondeterministic. Not all data races impact the results. If the relative timing of execution of instructions by fragments impacts the correctness of results, we call it a race condition.

- In parallel execution of threads that share addresses, the sequential nature of memory operations does not hold. The operations by concurrent threads have no defined order between them, and there need not be a common serializing storage, which allows one operation at a time. Hence, the update of shared-memory data by one thread can become visible to other threads at different times. More importantly, two updates may become visible to different threads in different orders. This means, for example, that in the view of one thread, variable $x$ may change from 3 to 5, while in another thread's view, the value 3 may appear later. Thus, their decisions based on the value of $x$ may become inconsistent.

- To avoid such inconsistencies, the order in which the threads view the updates must be consistent. Two views are consistent if they both lead to the same result. However, under what circumstances should the results be the same? We have seen several kinds of circumstances. The brute-force definition leads to sequential consistency: all operations seem to happen in a sequence – one strictly after the previous with no overlap. This means that if in any thread's view, operation $o_1$ seems to occur before $o_2$, no other thread may see the effect of $o_2$ before that of $o_1$, even if the reordering has no impact on the results of the execution. Note that it is not necessary for any specific thread to see $o_2$ before $o_1$. Inconsistency ensues even if, for example, one thread view $o_2$ before $o_3$ and another views $o_3$ before $o_1$. Ordering respects transitivity.

- Other notions of consistency are useful. Examples include causal consistency, processor consistency, FIFO consistency, and so on, which enforce ordering requirement only on certain operations. Many programs can be proven to have the expected behavior even under the relaxed definition. An understanding of memory consistency is important to prove the correctness of shared-memory programs. Indeed, when inspecting shared-memory code, we often unconsciously assume certain consistency. It's important to know when we may be over-assuming. A guarantee of consistency by the platform has performance implications. Hence, in practice, popular programming platforms only guarantee consistency on demand – on certain variables at certain times. This allows the program to increase performance when strict global ordering can be dispensed with. An understanding of memory fences helps this endeavor.

- Memory fences are special operations within threads whose order is globally consistent across threads. This allows threads to ensure global visibility of regular memory accesses at each fence. Thus, accesses are not all individually consistent, but can be grouped into sets such that the order between the sets is globally consistent.

- Like memory fences, computation fences are also useful. Computation fences are more flexible and programmable and are called synchronization in general. Other than serializing execution steps of different threads, synchronization affords the ability to pause and resume the execution of a thread based on a global condition, one that depends on the execution of other threads.

- Some synchronization is possible using consistent shared variables (e.g. Peterson's algorithm). These protocols assume a consistent order of updates visible to all threads, and are often nonblocking (meaning that the execution continues within the program), but not necessarily wait-free (because a thread's progress could be stalled by other threads). Other synchronization protocols require additional scheduling support from the programming platform, where the program is blocked from execution and subsequently resumed only if the synchronization condition holds.

- Tools of synchronization include mutual exclusion (exclusive access by a thread to one or more shared addresses during the execution of a specified code fragment), signal-wait (suspending execution until some variables attain certain values), barrier (suspending until all threads in a group have completed their execution of a related code fragment), and atomic instructions (a small code fragment providing mutual exclusion). Protocols using these tools require care to avoid deadlocks and starvation.

- When designing synchronization protocols, it is useful to be clear about the activity that is being synchronized. In particular, one may formulate global conditions that must remain true after the activity is complete. The design of the synchronization events then depends on the type of activity, performance requirements, and ease of programming.

- Communication between threads through shared memory is somewhat indirect and asynchronous, with the possibility of separate synchronization involving two or more threads. In contrast, some synchronization is built into message-passing – all participating threads must take explicit action for each communication. These actions may be synchronous (akin to a barrier) or asynchronous. Nonetheless, there is a one-to-one matching of actions, meaning that each action of a thread can be associated with a corresponding action of partner threads. Communication through shared memory is often fine-grained, whereas message passing is usually coarse-grained. This is because message-passing requires significant setup and often requires successive copies to a pipeline of buffers.

- Communication can be direct and point to point between a pair of threads. High-order communication involves multiple threads exchanging their data in some pattern. In either kind, the participating threads may choose to enforce synchronization along with communication. Or, they could communicate by leaving messages in a mailbox to be fetched asynchronously. Even then, every receive event must match some send event. Even for collective message-passing, that is, data exchange among a group of threads, the collective event appears in each thread and, they match each other.

The textbook by Herlihy et al.[14] contains an excellent treatise on shared-memory programming and general issues of concurrency. The unifying idea of using consensus numbers to argue about the power of synchronization primitives was introduced by Herlihy.[15] The survey by Adve et al.[16] covers the gamut of memory consistency, whereas Mosberger[17] analyzes the trade-offs of weaker consistency models. Among the most successful high-level message-passing interfaces is MPI,[18] which we will discuss in some detail in Chapter 6. Common communication interfaces[19] offer a deeper look at the breadth of message-passing issues.

---

[14] Herlihy and Shavit, *The Art of Multiprocessor Programming*.

[15] Herlihy, "Wait-free synchronization."

[16] Adve and Gharachorloo, "Shared memory consistency models."

[17] Mosberger, "Memory consistency models."

[18] Gropp et al., "A high-performance."
  By Gropp et al., *Using MPI*.

[19] Atchley et al., "The common communication interface (cci)."

# Exercise

4.1. Explain with an example how a cache-coherent memory system could be sequentially inconsistent.

4.2. Could a cache-coherent memory system be FIFO inconsistent? Explain.

4.3. In most ways, a file shared by multiple threads acts like shared memory. Consider a file system in which, instead of general write operations, a thread may only *append* to the "end" of a shared file. Note that threads may share multiple files. The platform guarantees that the data of two concurrent appends to one file are serialized, meaning their data are not interleaved. Reading threads may read from any address. What additional support from the platform is necessary to ensure that the files are sequentially consistent?

4.4. Provide two examples of situations when a data race may be harmless and does not require synchronization? (Consider memory consistency issues.)

4.5. Rewrite the following dining philosopher's pseudo-code to eliminate the possibility of deadlock, assuming each thread in the group executes this code (place identifies the philosopher).

```
1  philosopher(place, numplaces):
2        left = (place-1)%numplaces
3        right = (place+1)%numplaces
4        Repeat:
5            lock(lock$[left])
6            lock(lock$[right])
7            Eat()
8            unlock(lock$[left])
9            unlock(lock$[right])
10           Ponder()
```

Hint: Change the protocol depending on whether place is odd or even.

4.6. Change the code in Exercise 4.5 to make it nonblocking. Is your code lock-free also?

4.7. Identify the race condition in the following code if multiple threads may execute it concurrently. The lock and unlock act as memory fences.

```
if (Ref$ == null)
    lock(lock1$)
    tmp = allocateMemory()
    initilalize(tmp)
    Ref$ = tmp
    unlock(lock1$)
use(Ref$)
```

4.8. We modify the code in Exercise 4.7 as follows.

```
if (Ref$ == null)
    lock(lock1$)
    if (Ref$ == null)
        tmp = allocateMemory()
        initilalize(tmp)
        Ref$ = tmp
    unlock(lock1$)
use(Ref$)
```

Does it resolve the race condition? On execution by two threads A and B, thread B fails with the error "Uninitialized Ref$." Explain.

4.9. Consider the following code with shared variables A$ and B$.

```
1 X = 2*A$;
2 B$ = A$ + B$
```

Suppose the compiler optimizes away the second read of A$ on line 2, and reuses instead the value read earlier at line 1 (which it had saved in a register). Could that ever violate FIFO consistency if the memory sub-system guarantees FIFO consistency?

4.10. Some languages include syntax to designate a variable as "volatile," which means it is not cached and that the compiler does not reorder or eliminate its read/write. Suppose threads share only volatile variables. Suppose also that a single memory block processes all reads and writes in the order it receives them in. Does that guarantee sequential consistency? If so, prove it. If not, what additional conditions are necessary to meet before sequential consistency can be guaranteed?

4.11. Reconsider the following listing (Listing 4.3):

```
A$[threadID] = 1
print A$[1-threadID]
```

If two threads with threadID 0 and 1, respectively, execute this code concurrently, and both print 0, is the platform FIFO consistent? Is it causally consistent? Explain.

4.12. Rewrite Peterson's algorithm for mutual exclusion using memory fences assuming the platform only guarantees FIFO consistency.

4.13. Compare and Swap depends only on the current value of the associated variable, and not on its history. For example, a thread performs its swap if it sees the value $v$ that it expects. However, the value could have been changed from $v$ to $v'$ by some thread and back to $v$ by some thread. This is often harmless. But if the value is an address, even if the address itself changed back to $v$, the contents at address $v$ could have changed. Propose a modification to the Compare and Swap protocol, which allows a thread a guarantee that there has been no change made to $v$.

4.14. Implement the function barrier described in Section 4.4, which can be called by all members of a thread group any number of times.

4.15. Barriers can exist in shared-memory-based interaction as well as message-passing-based interaction between threads. Message-passing-based barriers may be implemented using point-to-point messages. What is the fewest number of point-to-point messages required to accomplish the barrier functionality in that case? What is the minimum number of shared addresses and accesses required to implement barrier for shared-memory threads?

4.16. Memory fences are also known as memory barriers. How are memory barriers different from (computation) barriers?

4.17. Consider the collective communication primitive: *gather*, in which $n_i$ data items are to be received from thread number $i, i \in 1..N$ by thread 0. Thread 0 must gather these data items contiguously in its local address space in the order of thread numbers from which the data came. Describe the steps required to implement this gather using point-to-point communications. You may use StartSend/CompleteSend and StartReceive/CompleteReceipt primitives.

4.18. Suppose a message transport system is available that subdivides large messages into fixed-size packets and sends them with the guarantee that packets sent by thread $i$ to thread $j$ arrive in the order they are sent. Threads are allowed to use *Send* and *Receive* primitives in the order of their choosing. Under what conditions may *Send* or *Receive* enter a deadlock?

4.19. What is the difference between the terms *lock-free* and *nonblocking*? Could a *barrier* event be lock-free? Could it be nonblocking?

4.20. Provide a protocol to implement *Consensus* among message-passing threads.

4.21. Implement lock-free ATMs. All ATMs share the addresses `Balance$[accountNumber]`. ATMs must provide lock-free methods for:

   i  Withdraw(accountNumber, amount)

   ii  Deposit(accountNumber, amount)

   iii  Transfer(accountNumberFrom, accountNumberTo, amount)

You may use Compare and Swap. Assume that the provided account number is valid, and the same account number may be used at multiple ATMs at one time. Neither the bank nor any account holder should lose money.

# CHAPTER 5

# Parallel Program Design

Parallel programming is challenging. There are many parts interacting in a complex manner: algorithm-imposed dependency,

> *Question*: How to devise the parallel solution to a given problem?

scheduling on multiple execution units, synchronization, data communication capacity, network topology, memory bandwidth limit, cache performance in the presence of multiple independent threads accessing memory, program scalability, heterogeneity of hardware, and so on. It is useful to understand each of these aspects separately. We discuss general parallel design principles in this chapter. These ideas largely apply to both shared-memory style and message-passing style programming, as well as task-centric programs.

At first cut, there are two approaches to start designing parallel applications:

> *Question*: What is the detailed structure of parallel programs?

1. Given a problem, design and implement a sequential algorithm, and then turn it into a parallel program based on the type of available parallel architecture.

2. Start ab initio. Design a parallel algorithm suitable for the underlying architecture and then implement it.

In either case, performance, correctness, reusability, and maintainability are important goals. We will see that for many problems, starting with a sequential algorithm and then dividing it into independent tasks that can execute in parallel leads to a poor parallel algorithm. Instead, another algorithm that is designed to maximize independent parts, may yield better performance. If a good parallel solution cannot be found – and there do exist inherently sequential problems, for which parallel solutions are not sufficiently faster than sequential ones – it may not be a problem worth solving in parallel.

Once a parallel algorithm is designed, it may yet contain parts that are sequential. Further, the parallel parts can also be executed on a sequential machine in an arbitrary sequence. Such "sequentialization" allows the developer to test parts of a parallel program. If a purely sequential version is already available, or can be implemented with only small effort, it can also serve as a starting point for parallel design. The sequential version can be exploited to develop the parallel application incrementally, gradually replacing sequential parts with their parallel versions. The sequential version also provides performance targets for the parallel version and allows debugging by comparing partial results.

Regardless of whether a sequential version is initially employed as a parallel development tool, the core parallel design steps are similar. We will discuss these next.

## 5.1　Design Steps

The major steps in any parallel program design are:

1. Decomposition: subdivide the solution into components
2. Scheduling: allocate cores and communication resources to components

These may be thought of as first designing a general task graph and then scheduling the tasks' execution on computing devices – assigning a device to each task. Not all parallel programming requires these two steps in that way. In exploration-based algorithms, new tasks are discovered during the execution of other tasks. The task graph is dynamically generated on the fly as exploration proceeds. In other problems, tasks remain implicit, with no natural delineation. Instead, small parcels of work may exist, which one might collate into arbitrary tasks. For example, consider inserting a new element at a known position in an array – it may involve copying several elements to their new positions.

Tasks may also be decomposed hierarchically. For example, an algorithm could be completed by a sequential task. Instead, it may be subdivided into two sub-tasks, which could be carried out in parallel with each other. Each sub-task may be further recursively divided into parallel sub-tasks. The simplest problems suggest the task decomposition naturally. Sometimes these tasks can execute independently of each other – these lead to the so-called "embarrassingly parallel" algorithms. The simplest versions of such solutions also naturally decompose into tasks that require a similar amount of computation. These tasks may be allocated to computation devices in a round-robin manner, assigning one or more tasks to each device in each round.

Design is usually a bit more complicated than that. In particular, while performing the two design steps mentioned above, the following interrelated issues have to be considered.

### Granularity

How large are the components, or tasks, relative to the size of the overall problem? Fine-grained decomposition creates more tasks, and hence more concurrency, which usually allows solutions to scale well. Fine-grained decomposition also allows fine-grained scheduling, which often leads to more flexibility, but scheduling many tasks may become costly at too fine a granularity. Also, the finer grained the tasks are, the more inter-task communication or synchronization may be required. There is a balance to achieve. Naturally, the amount of memory available on each device is an important consideration in task sizing. In some situations the entire data of even one task need not fit in the main memory. Instead, they can be processed in batches. In many other situations, the inability to fit the entire address space used by the task can lead to significant thrashing.[1]

Consider the matrix multiplication: $C = A \times B$. Suppose $A$ and $B$ are each $n \times n$. There are $n^2$ tasks if $Task_{ij}$ computes the element $C[i, j]$ with $i$ and $j$ in the range $[0, n)$. $Task_{ij}$ requires row $i$ of matrix $A$ and column $j$ of matrix $B$. $n^2$ tasks fetch $2n$ items each. Alternatively, there are $n$ tasks if $Task_i$

> [1] *Defined*: When data in the address space of a process does not fit in the main memory, parts of it can be evicted and stored in a slower storage by the virtual memory manager. Constant swapping of data between the main memory and the slower storage and back is called thrashing.

computes row $i$ of matrix $C$. In that case, $Task_i$ requires row $i$ of $A$ and the entire matrix $B$. In this decomposition, $n$ tasks fetch $(n + n^2)$ items each, thus requiring fewer fetches. However, it has fewer tasks, and hence a lower degree of parallelism. (We will discuss the characteristics of a task graph in more detail in Section 5.2.) Yet another decomposition could have $n^3$ tasks. $Task_{ijk}$ computes $A[i, k] \times B[k, j]$. $n^3$ tasks fetch two items each. However, they do not compute $C$. Instead, $Task'_{ij}$ adds the result of $Task_{ijk}$ for all $k \in [0, n)$. This method uses the most tasks but also fetches the most amount of data. Moreover, $Task'_{ij}$ must wait for all such $Task_{ijk}$ to complete. This increases the length of the critical path.

## Communication

Communication is costly. Hence, minimizing communication is an important design goal. Tasks that intercommunicate more should preferably execute on the same node or those "close" to each other if they are across a network. Execution of a step that depends on a remote piece of data must wait for the data to be possibly requested and the requested data to subsequently arrive. Request-based communication incurs a round-trip latency. Instead, the program logic may be designed such that the data container knows after which local step to send which data to whom. Some of this communication overhead can be nullified by asynchronous communication, which allows computation to overlap with communication. However, this reduces only the impact of latency. If too many tasks communicate over the network, the throughput capacity can be a bottleneck. Also note that in any communication, whether synchronous or asynchronous, the central processing unit (CPU) has at least some role in the setup of buffers and communication. Hence, recurrent communication has a direct computational cost.

A common characteristic of communication is a per-message overhead. Thus, batching messages has benefits. However, if batching means delaying a message, the latency only increases. Data marshaling is another overhead to consider. Networks inevitably support messages as streams of bytes. On the other hand, the data that a thread $x$ needs to send to thread $y$ may be dispersed in its address space, and not in contiguous locations. A good data structure reduces the need for repeatedly packing such dispersed data into a buffer. Coarse-grained communication design ensures that the computation-to-communication ratio is high, meaning relatively fewer messages are exchanged between large periods of local computation. Also, communication can be point-to-point or collective. Even though a single collective primitive has a larger overhead than a single point-to-point transfer, they accomplish more. Tasks that admit collective communication derive that benefit.

## Synchronization

Synchronization among tasks also has significant overhead. Computation pauses until the synchronization is complete. The overhead is even higher if tasks execute on nodes far from each other. Synchronization requirements can often be reduced by using somewhat larger grained tasks. At other times, breaking dependency by computing partial results in each task and deferring synchronization to a subsequent reduction or prefix-sum primitive is helpful. As a general rule, program design should minimize mutual exclusion. Any related computation that does not impact other threads should remain out of the critical section, which should focus only on accessing the shared resource.

For example, in the fragment below on the left, the function f can be computed outside the critical section assuming Y is not shared and f has no side effect. Only the result of f should be added to A$ within the critical section. In contrast, f must remain inside the critical section in the fragment on the right if the shared A$ is to be read, modified, and written atomically.

```
critical {
    A$ = A$ + f(Y)
}
```

```
critical {
    A$ = A$ + f(A$)
}
```

Fine-grained synchronization is one of the goals. This means that a single critical section should protect as few resources as necessary and contain only direct interactions with those resources. This reduces threads waiting for other threads to complete. However, it may increase the number of synchronization events, and each event has overhead. This overhead is usually smaller using nonblocking primitives like Compare and Swap than for lock-based synchronization. Lock-free synchronization can provide more flexibility and is often more efficient.

## Load Balance

In assigning many tasks to a smaller number of cores, one major concern is to keep all cores busy until no more tasks remain. (This is mainly in the performance-centric context. There exist other considerations. For example, power-conserving algorithms have different design goals.) Cores idle either because task allocation is unbalanced or cores wait too often for memory or network. A proper load-balancing scheme accounts for balancing the compute load as well as the memory and network load. In general, fine-grained tasks are easier to load-balance than coarse-grained ones, just as it is easier to pack sand into a bag than odd-shaped toys. On the other hand, we have seen above that fine-grained tasks may increase the need for communication and synchronization.

Load balancing can be built into the design when all tasks are known in advance, and their approximate computation load can be estimated before starting their execution. For example, if all concurrent tasks perform a similar amount of computation, they may be distributed in a round-robin manner. Alternatively, one may subdivide the task graph into subgraphs in a way that very few edges cross from one subgraph to another. An entire subgraph may then be assigned to a core. Only inter-subgraph edges stand for communication and synchronization. However, there is a trade-off with balancing load. Large subgraphs, particularly ones with varying load, are harder to load balance.

When tasks are created dynamically, more scheduling questions arise. For example, a task generated at node $x$ may have data at that node. Scheduling that task on node $y$ may require communication and synchronization between $x$ and $y$, which would not be needed if the task is scheduled on node $x$. On the other hand, too many such tasks could overload node $x$.

## 5.2  Task Decomposition

As discussed in Section 5.1, the main objective of creating tasks is to assign tasks to processors so that they may proceed concurrently, perhaps independently of other tasks. A large number of tasks is desirable for increased parallelism. Tasks should not require much data that are generated by other tasks. This reduces synchronization with those other tasks. In general, having fewer tasks leads to less such synchronization. After all, a single task – the sequential solution to the problem – requires no communication or synchronization. Thus the two objectives of increased concurrency and reduced synchronization are often in conflict, and a trade-off is required.

Sometimes tasks are implicit in the way a problem or a parallel algorithm is described. This natural decomposition occasionally leads to mostly independent tasks. These tasks may be decomposed further if finer grained tasks are required than those suggested by the algorithm. Consider a problem that amounts to computing function $f(X)$,

$$f(X) = h(g_1(X_1), g_2(X_2), g_3(X_3)..),  \tag{5.1}$$

where $g_i$ and $h$ are other functions. Such constructs are common in functional programming and allow parallel computation of $g_i$. Further, $X$ may be an input vector, and $X_i$ a subset of $X$. We may assume that the output of each function is also a vector. A natural decomposition for this problem is to create tasks $G_i$ computing $g_i$ from each $X_i$, followed by one task H that computes $h$. A preliminary task for generating $X_i$ from $X$ would also be required. Partitioning of data is often referred to as *data decomposition* or *domain decomposition*. On the other hand, subdividing $f$ into H and $G_i$ is referred to as *functional decomposition*. They often go hand in hand, but the design may focus primarily on domain decomposition when such decomposition provides roughly independent tasks. For other problems, functional decomposition may yield good tasks.

Data decomposition, and sometimes functional decomposition, is often manifested in loops. Parallelism implicit in loops is also known as loop-level parallelism.

```
for(int i=0; i<Size; i++)
      for(int j=0; j<Size; j++) {
          Y[i][j] = process(X[i][j], f(i, j));
      }
```

In the above example, each iteration may be a task, or a range $a \leq i < b$ and $c \leq j < d$ may be a task. If all iterations are independent of each other, these tasks are also independent. If subsequent iterations use data produced in earlier iterations, such dependency may not lead to good tasks. Such an example would be if $f(i, j)$ depends on $Y[i-1][j-1]$. If only a small number of iterations depend on an earlier iteration, an iteration-based decomposition may still produce suitable tasks.

## Domain Decomposition

Domain decomposition partitions data and each partition relates to a task. Partitioning may be irregular, in which case $X_i$ is an arbitrary subset of $X$. In this case, domain decomposition requires evaluating a complex function and is a task in its own right. The more common case, however, is a regular pattern. For example, $X$ may be organized as an $n$-dimensional matrix. Let's consider a two-dimensional matrix as an example. There are two basic regular decompositions: *block decomposition* and *cyclic decomposition*. Figure 5.1(a) shows block decomposition. $X_{ij}$ is a contiguous block of indexes. Partition $(i, j)$ is marked in Figure 5.1 for each index of a $12 \times 12$ matrix. Each dimension of the matrix is block

**(a) Block Decomposition**

| | | | | | | | | | | | |
|---|---|---|---|---|---|---|---|---|---|---|---|
| 0,0 | 0,0 | 0,0 | 0,0 | 0,1 | 0,1 | 0,1 | 0,1 | 0,2 | 0,2 | 0,2 | 0,2 |
| 0,0 | 0,0 | 0,0 | 0,0 | 0,1 | 0,1 | 0,1 | 0,1 | 0,2 | 0,2 | 0,2 | 0,2 |
| 0,0 | 0,0 | 0,0 | 0,0 | 0,1 | 0,1 | 0,1 | 0,1 | 0,2 | 0,2 | 0,2 | 0,2 |
| 1,0 | 1,0 | 1,0 | 1,0 | 1,1 | 1,1 | 1,1 | 1,1 | 1,2 | 1,2 | 1,2 | 1,2 |
| 1,0 | 1,0 | 1,0 | 1,0 | 1,1 | 1,1 | 1,1 | 1,1 | 1,2 | 1,2 | 1,2 | 1,2 |
| 1,0 | 1,0 | 1,0 | 1,0 | 1,1 | 1,1 | 1,1 | 1,1 | 1,2 | 1,2 | 1,2 | 1,2 |
| 2,0 | 2,0 | 2,0 | 2,0 | 2,1 | 2,1 | 2,1 | 2,1 | 2,2 | 2,2 | 2,2 | 2,2 |
| 2,0 | 2,0 | 2,0 | 2,0 | 2,1 | 2,1 | 2,1 | 2,1 | 2,2 | 2,2 | 2,2 | 2,2 |
| 2,0 | 2,0 | 2,0 | 2,0 | 2,1 | 2,1 | 2,1 | 2,1 | 2,2 | 2,2 | 2,2 | 2,2 |
| 3,0 | 3,0 | 3,0 | 3,0 | 3,1 | 3,1 | 3,1 | 3,1 | 3,2 | 3,2 | 3,2 | 3,2 |
| 3,0 | 3,0 | 3,0 | 3,0 | 3,1 | 3,1 | 3,1 | 3,1 | 3,2 | 3,2 | 3,2 | 3,2 |
| 3,0 | 3,0 | 3,0 | 3,0 | 3,1 | 3,1 | 3,1 | 3,1 | 3,2 | 3,2 | 3,2 | 3,2 |

**(b) Cyclic Decomposition**

| | | | | | | | | | | | |
|---|---|---|---|---|---|---|---|---|---|---|---|
| 0,0 | 0,1 | 0,2 | 0,0 | 0,1 | 0,2 | 0,0 | 0,1 | 0,2 | 0,0 | 0,1 | 0,2 |
| 1,0 | 1,1 | 1,2 | 1,0 | 1,1 | 1,2 | 1,0 | 1,1 | 1,2 | 1,0 | 1,1 | 1,2 |
| 2,0 | 2,1 | 2,2 | 2,0 | 2,1 | 2,2 | 2,0 | 2,1 | 2,2 | 2,0 | 2,1 | 2,2 |
| 3,0 | 3,1 | 3,2 | 3,0 | 3,1 | 3,2 | 3,0 | 3,1 | 3,2 | 3,0 | 3,1 | 3,2 |
| 0,0 | 0,1 | 0,2 | 0,0 | 0,1 | 0,2 | 0,0 | 0,1 | 0,2 | 0,0 | 0,1 | 0,2 |
| 1,0 | 1,1 | 1,2 | 1,0 | 1,1 | 1,2 | 1,0 | 1,1 | 1,2 | 1,0 | 1,1 | 1,2 |
| 2,0 | 2,1 | 2,2 | 2,0 | 2,1 | 2,2 | 2,0 | 2,1 | 2,2 | 2,0 | 2,1 | 2,2 |
| 3,0 | 3,1 | 3,2 | 3,0 | 3,1 | 3,2 | 3,0 | 3,1 | 3,2 | 3,0 | 3,1 | 3,2 |
| 0,0 | 0,1 | 0,2 | 0,0 | 0,1 | 0,2 | 0,0 | 0,1 | 0,2 | 0,0 | 0,1 | 0,2 |
| 1,0 | 1,1 | 1,2 | 1,0 | 1,1 | 1,2 | 1,0 | 1,1 | 1,2 | 1,0 | 1,1 | 1,2 |
| 2,0 | 2,1 | 2,2 | 2,0 | 2,1 | 2,2 | 2,0 | 2,1 | 2,2 | 2,0 | 2,1 | 2,2 |
| 3,0 | 3,1 | 3,2 | 3,0 | 3,1 | 3,2 | 3,0 | 3,1 | 3,2 | 3,0 | 3,1 | 3,2 |

**Figure 5.1** Block and Cyclic decomposition of domain. Each square lists the block in which the corresponding data location is included.

decomposed – index $i$ in each dimension is in block $\lfloor i/BlockSize \rfloor$. In turn, block $b$ consists of $BlockSize$ indexes starting at $b \times BlockSize$. One advantage of block distribution is that each task gets one or more contiguous chunks, improving data locality and reducing overhead in collecting task's input data at the assigned processor.

Block decomposition can lead to independent tasks, each processing one block. That is not always the case, however. Sometimes, intermediate results are generated by each task, which need to be possibly collated and redistributed. At other times, some intermediate results are interchanged between neighboring blocks. For example, consider intermediate result $Y$, where block $Y_{ij}$ is a function of $X_{ij}$, computed for each $(i, j)$ by the corresponding task. Suppose the left column of block $Y_{ij}$ is sent to the left neighbor for further computation. That left neighbor is the processor responsible for block $Y_{i(j-1)}$. Correspondingly, that left neighbor sends its right column back to the processor with $Y_{ij}$. The top and bottom rows may also be exchanged similarly.

Cyclic decomposition shown in Figure 5.1(b) distributes the data round-robin to tasks. Element $i$ of Block $b$ corresponds to index $i \times BlockSize + b$ in each dimension. Cyclic decomposition often balances load among tasks better than block distribution. It is useful when, say, the matrix is processed iteratively, and only a sub-block of the matrix is processed in the next step. For example, in many factorization algorithms, row $s$ and column $s$ are eliminated from further computation at step $s$. In a block decomposition, $X_{00}$ would be entirely eliminated after the first few steps. This may necessitate a constant reallocation of the remaining tasks to all processors if block decomposition were used. Data access by each processor does not exhibit locality in cyclic decomposition, however.

On the other hand, cyclic decomposition can increase locality when multiple tasks proceed in a lock-step manner, say, on a single instruction, multiple data (SIMD) processor. In that case, at step $i$, SIMD tasks together process contiguous indexes, for example, $i \times BlockSize$ .. $(i + 1) \times BlockSize - 1^2$, thus improving memory access locality. These parallel accesses could even be combined into a single memory transaction.

---

[2] Range "a..b" includes a and b.

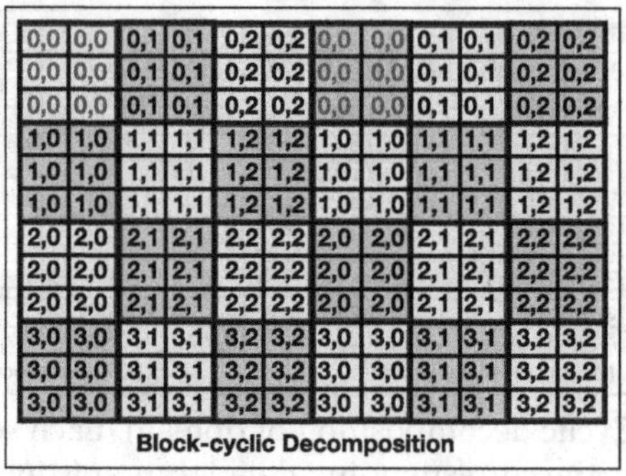

| 0,0 | 0,0 | 0,1 | 0,1 | 0,2 | 0,2 | 0,0 | 0,0 | 0,1 | 0,1 | 0,2 | 0,2 |
|-----|-----|-----|-----|-----|-----|-----|-----|-----|-----|-----|-----|
| 0,0 | 0,0 | 0,1 | 0,1 | 0,2 | 0,2 | 0,0 | 0,0 | 0,1 | 0,1 | 0,2 | 0,2 |
| 0,0 | 0,0 | 0,1 | 0,1 | 0,2 | 0,2 | 0,0 | 0,0 | 0,1 | 0,1 | 0,2 | 0,2 |
| 1,0 | 1,0 | 1,1 | 1,1 | 1,2 | 1,2 | 1,0 | 1,0 | 1,1 | 1,1 | 1,2 | 1,2 |
| 1,0 | 1,0 | 1,1 | 1,1 | 1,2 | 1,2 | 1,0 | 1,0 | 1,1 | 1,1 | 1,2 | 1,2 |
| 1,0 | 1,0 | 1,1 | 1,1 | 1,2 | 1,2 | 1,0 | 1,0 | 1,1 | 1,1 | 1,2 | 1,2 |
| 2,0 | 2,0 | 2,1 | 2,1 | 2,2 | 2,2 | 2,0 | 2,0 | 2,1 | 2,1 | 2,2 | 2,2 |
| 2,0 | 2,0 | 2,1 | 2,1 | 2,2 | 2,2 | 2,0 | 2,0 | 2,1 | 2,1 | 2,2 | 2,2 |
| 2,0 | 2,0 | 2,1 | 2,1 | 2,2 | 2,2 | 2,0 | 2,0 | 2,1 | 2,1 | 2,2 | 2,2 |
| 3,0 | 3,0 | 3,1 | 3,1 | 3,2 | 3,2 | 3,0 | 3,0 | 3,1 | 3,1 | 3,2 | 3,2 |
| 3,0 | 3,0 | 3,1 | 3,1 | 3,2 | 3,2 | 3,0 | 3,0 | 3,1 | 3,1 | 3,2 | 3,2 |
| 3,0 | 3,0 | 3,1 | 3,1 | 3,2 | 3,2 | 3,0 | 3,0 | 3,1 | 3,1 | 3,2 | 3,2 |

**Block-cyclic Decomposition**

**Figure 5.2** Block-cyclic domain decomposition

A combination of block and cyclic decomposition, shown in Figure 5.2, is another commonly used decomposition. This has the benefits of contiguous blocks, but the blocks are smaller than block decomposition. It may be viewed as subdividing the larger blocks into smaller ones, with each task processing the smaller block at a time. Thus, small sections of data may be transferred and processing can begin earlier. The subsequent blocks may be transferred concurrently with the processing of previous blocks. Block-cyclic decomposition, by allowing smaller blocks of data to be processed at a time, also balances the load well.

Not all domains are structured as a regular $n$-dimensional table. Sometimes, the underlying domain has an $n$-dimensional structure, but the data is organized differently if the domain is filled only sparsely – most other entries are a known constant like 0 and need not be explicitly stored. In such cases, a simple block or block-cyclic decomposition of the actually stored values may sometimes be sufficient, but often more customized decompositions are required.

In many problems, the data is organized as a graph. For a dense graph, if an adjacency matrix representation is used, regular decomposition may be employed. However, other more compact representations, like an adjacency list, are more common. Further, the graph may require some per-vertex processing, some per-edge processing, or even-region partitioning. For example, a graph may represent a connected set of triangles representing a surface. One may generate tasks that process a subset of triangles, while other tasks process a subset of vertices. Alternatively, the triangular topology may be thought of as a general graph, and an entire connected subgraph – triangles, vertices, and adjacencies – may be processed by a single task. Such graph partitioning – or *graph cut* – is a common strategy for task decomposition. The underlying assumptions are that:

1. the computation requirement of a task that processes a subgraph is proportional to the size of the subgraph (e.g. the number of its nodes, edges, or both)

2. the additional computation and communication requirements of a task are related to the number of edges connecting nodes in its subgraph with nodes in other tasks' subgraphs

Sometimes, nodes and edges may be assigned weights to reflect added computation for some nodes or edges. The set of edges connecting a subgraph to "neighboring" subgraphs is called a cut. The goal is to partition a graph into roughly equal-sized subgraphs such that the cumulative size of the cuts is minimized. Small cuts lead to less communication and synchronization. Equal-sized partitions are easier to assign to processors in a load-balanced manner, as we will discuss later. An example of a graph and a cut is shown in Figure 5.3(a). The graph is decomposed into two components. The vertices of the two components are shown in different shades. The cut between the two components is shown by the dashed curve. Computation of the minimal cut is an NP-hard problem, but several satisfactory heuristics exist.[3] Cut-based subdivision is particularly useful for static graphs so that it may be performed in a pre-computation step, or if the time to compute the cuts does not dominate the total computation time. The analog for cyclic decomposition is shown in Figure 5.3(b). It uses the concept of graph coloring to subdivide the graph. This example shows four shades denoting four colors and, hence, four components. Each vertex is colored based on its component, and the decomposition ensures that none of its neighbors have the same color.

Domain decomposition need not be always based on the input data, for example, an input matrix or an input graph. Tasks may also be created by partitioning intermediate data, or even the output data. For example, in ray-tracing algorithms for computer graphics, a set of input primitives, for example, triangles, represents a scene. The algorithm projects the scene onto a set of pixels on the screen, producing a color per pixel. Each pixel may be produced (largely) independently of other pixels. Thus, a decomposition based on the output pixels works well. Similarly, two matrices may be multiplied using tasks, each of which produces a block of the product matrix.

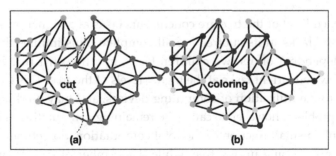

(a)          (b)

**Figure 5.3** Graph decomposition

[3] Karypis and Kumar, "A fast and high quality multilevel scheme."
Bichot and Siarry, *Graph Partitioning: Optimisation and Applications.*

## Functional Decomposition

While domain decomposition focuses on partitioning based on the data that a task processes, functional decomposition focuses on the computation that a task does. Domain decomposition is often conducive to data-parallelism, while functional decomposition is conducive to task parallelism. As seen in Eq. 5.1, dividing $f$ into $h$ and $g_i$, is functional partitioning. Such dependence may even be recursive, leading to *recursive decomposition*. For example:

$$f(X) = g(X), \text{ if } X \text{ is "leaf"}$$
$$= h(f(X_0), f(X_1), f(X_2)..f(X_k)), \text{ otherwise}$$

$g$ terminates the recursion when $X$ need not be subdivided further. Although not necessary, such recursive functional decomposition may also recursively decompose the data: $X$ into $X_0, X_1$, and so on; $X_0$ into $X_{00}, X_{01}$, and so on. The binary tree computation structure shown in Section 3.2 is a common special case of recursive decomposition. Figure 5.4 has a more detailed illustration. The function $h$ in this case is simply a conjunction of its two inputs and $k$ is 2. $g(X)$ is $X$.

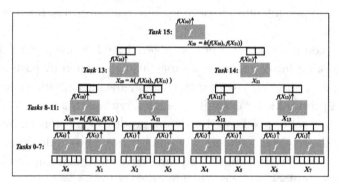

**Figure 5.4** Recursive task decomposition

Tasks at each level of the tree are concurrent. Tasks at a higher level in the tree cannot begin until the tasks in its subtree are all complete. This implies that a parent task in the tree is dependent on its two children tasks. In a tree structure like this, there may remain too few concurrent tasks at the higher levels of the tree. This lack of concurrency is detrimental to the utilization of computing devices, and may hinder scalability. Usually, this is not a problem, however, because the remaining computation at the higher levels of the tree is only a small fraction of the total computation. Sometimes, however, the sizes of the tasks grow going up the tree, while the number of tasks reduces. This requires attention. A secondary decomposition may become necessary in that case, replacing the top few levels of the tree with a different decomposition.

Recursive decomposition applies more generally, even when the solution is not itself expressed recursively. It builds a task hierarchy, perhaps using the divide-and-conquer paradigm. A solution is devised in terms of a small number of mostly independent tasks. These tasks need not be of equal size, but they should preferably communicate and synchronize with each other rarely. Each task is then further divided into component sub-tasks until all remaining sub-tasks are of the desired granularity. The quick-sort algorithm is a classic example of recursive decomposition. At each recursion, an unsorted list is divided into two independent sublists such that all elements in the first sublist are smaller than those in the second sublist. One task is generated for each sublist, which sorts that sublist, possibly by generating more tasks recursively if the sublist size is larger than the target granularity.

In many algorithms, tasks are designed beforehand and then encoded directly into the parallel program. Not always, though. Instead, tasks may be generated dynamically as the algorithm proceeds. This *dynamic task generation* may be by a master generator. More generally, one or more initial tasks generate more tasks, which may, in turn, generate yet more tasks, and so on. For example, these may be tasks that cumulatively traverse a solution space. This is known as *exploratory decomposition*. In the traversal or exploration, some steps lead to the discovery of new potent states, which the algorithm chooses to traverse. Other steps lead to dead ends, and the traversal must backtrack. In sequential breadth-first or depth-first style traversal, these paths would be put on a queue or a stack for later exploration. In the parallel programming context, these are spawned as new tasks to be scheduled and executed according to the resource allocation algorithm.

Discrete event simulation and computing the next best move in a game are examples that suggest exploratory decomposition. For instance, starting from a given chessboard configuration (see Figure 5.5), exploring the next $k$ moves requires exploration of options considering many expected opponent moves. Similarly, in dynamic program analysis, multiple code branches and event orderings are explored to determine if any path leads to a bug or an inconsistent state. Many of these problems can be abstracted as graph traversal – except the graph may be generated as needed on the fly. In such exploratory decompositions, since multiple tasks explore paths concurrently, and they may lead to the same state, proper synchronization is required to ensure that an already explored part is not re-explored by a different task.

Another question for exploratory task decomposition is whether the discovery of each new path indeed requires a new task to explore it. Some exploration may instead be included in the current task itself. Such a decision usually depends on the estimate of the size of state space that the newly discovered paths lead to, or on the estimate of the size of still unexplored space already included in the current task. They may also depend on the location of the data associated with the new paths. Data local to the task may be explored by the task itself. For other data, new tasks may be preferred.

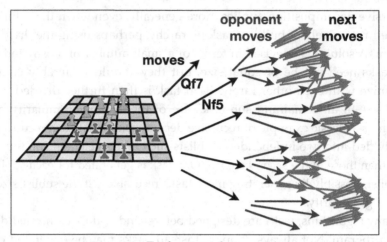

**Figure 5.5** Exploratory decomposition

A special case of explorative decomposition is *speculative decomposition*. In an exploration, many, or even all, possible paths that must be explored from a given task state could be known in advance. For example, the task may be a subgraph, and the edges leading out of the subgraph are known a priori. Not all of these "external" edges eventually require traversal. Sometimes, the task decides whether to explore such an external edge when – and if – the traversal reaches that edge. In speculative exploration, new tasks are spawned aggressively even before the edges are encountered. If it is subsequently determined that the edge does not require traversal, the corresponding speculative task is canceled. Clearly, speculative decomposition has a large downside if too many tasks require cancellation. It is useful mainly for problems where some prior knowledge helps estimate the probability of speculatively chosen edges to eventually require traversal. For example, in the chess move exploration, given a board configuration, certain future opponent moves may be highly likely.

Another method to create tasks is *pipeline decomposition*. This is similar to the hardware pipeline – a task takes one chunk of input from its predecessor task, performs processing, and forwards the results to its successor task. It next processes the next chunk of data fetched from the predecessor. This structure is often used to hide communication latency by overlapping data transfer with computation. Dependency edges in a task graph representing pipeline imply that the dependent task may begin as soon as the first chunk of data is released by its predecessor. They do not need to wait for the predecessor to complete its processing. We refer to such task edges as *communication edges* to differentiate them from regular *dependency edges*. Communication edges usually go in both directions, while dependency is unidirectional.

In practice, task decomposition need not be limited to one of the types described above. Rather, these decompositions can be combined. For example, data decomposition and recursive decomposition may go hand in hand, as shown in Figure 5.4. Or, at some stage of a top-down functional decomposition, one may choose to partition the intermediate results using domain decomposition. Cole's pipelined merge sorting algorithm[4] augments recursive decomposition with pipelining. In this algorithm, tasks are organized in a binary tree manner, as in Figure 5.4, but tasks do not provide their full results to the parent task in one chunk. Instead, previous chunks are incrementally merged with subsequent chunks in $O(1)$ time. And after each merger, the parent task improves its solution in $O(1)$ time, irrespective of the final size of the merged list.

## Task Graph Metrics

Some properties of the task graph generated by a chosen decomposition strategy are related to its performance. A task with long dependency chains has low concurrency. In particular, the tasks in the longest chain of task dependencies in a graph is called its *critical path*. Shorter critical paths are better, as they indicate the minimum time any implementation must take, that is, the sum of times of each task on the critical path and any communication and synchronization overheads between tasks on the path. The cumulative work on the critical path is related to the sequentiality implicit in the solution. That is the number of steps required irrespective of the number of processors. The total work contained in the task graph divided by the work on the critical path indicates the *average concurrency* of the task graph: the average number of tasks that may be processed in parallel.

Another important metric is *task cost variance*. Task graphs with all similar-sized tasks are usually easier to schedule. Complex scheduling algorithms have a cost, and that impacts the overall performance. A related property is the *execution homogeneity* of a task. It is easier to schedule tasks that maintain their load characteristic during their execution. For example, a task that remains compute-intensive during its execution may be assigned to a fast processor. Or a memory-intensive task may be scheduled on a large memory or fast memory device. Also, multiple tasks may be scheduled to execute on a single device if they have a predominance of high latency operations like data transfer. Tasks without execution homogeneity alter their characteristics and are harder to map to the appropriate device.

*Task graph degree* is the maximum out-degree of any task in the graph. When a task with a large out-degree ends, a large number of its successor tasks must be spawned. This imposes a large scheduling overhead, which can be particularly troublesome if the task is on the critical path.

---

[4] Cole, "Parallel merge sort."

Finally, keeping the interface between tasks clean and well defined is important for development and debugging. There are four facets of these interfaces and any design would do well to explicitly answer the following questions:

1. When is a task created?
2. When may the task begin to execute?
3. When does a task acquire data from its predecessors, and when does it send data to its successors?
4. When must a predecessor and successor synchronize and communicate?

## 5.3   Task Execution

A parallel program is typically responsible for both creating tasks and then letting processes, threads, or other primitives execute them. This task-to-processor mapping may be done directly by the application program, or by the programming platform it is built upon (we will discuss a few such platforms in Chapter 6). Either way, this mapping is an important ingredient of parallel programming. We discuss, in this section, some general techniques to perform this mapping. Of primary concern in this mapping is that all resources remain engaged in useful work, reducing idle time. A good mapping strategy also reduces the total work by reducing communication and synchronization overheads. Overall, a good schedule minimizes *makespan* – the end-to-end time since an application is started until its last task completes.

With increasing cluster sizes, power consumption has also become a major optimizing factor. Sometimes, increasing the makespan can reduce the total power consumption noticeably. We do not explore power issues in this textbook, but they are increasingly important, even if they make scheduling more complex.

Some problems allow tasks to be regular, independent, and sized arbitrarily. We have seen such an example above: matrix multiplication. Mapping such tasks to $P$ processors is simple. Size tasks in a way to produce $P$ tasks, and distribute them round-robin to processors. Even these simple cases break down if the devices do not all have the same capability (computation speed, memory bandwidth, network bandwidth, etc.). We discuss general techniques next, where the number of tasks is usually greater than the number of processors. Even when tasks can be sized to requirement, having multiple tasks per processor is helpful in the absence of execution-homogeneity.

We assume that a task is mapped to a single device. For this purpose we may not require that a task always be sequential. A parallel task may occupy multiple computational devices, but it is sufficient for this discussion to treat that set of devices as a single unit. So, we will continue to treat a task as executing on a single device. For computationally intensive tasks, usually only a single task is executed by a device at a time. For non-computationally intensive tasks, like those that perform file input and output, or those facing large memory, synchronization, or network latency, multiple tasks may execute concurrently on a device.

Some programming platforms allow programs to provide an explicit task graph. These graphs are usually static, but may also allow some dynamic updates like adding new tasks and their incoming dependency edges. On other platforms, tasks are managed directly by the program. Even if a platform undertakes the scheduling of tasks, an application program can assist the platform by providing scheduling hints. Thus, an understanding of scheduling issues is vital for platform designers as well as application programmers.

Some time after a task is spawned – statically or dynamically – it is initially *scheduled*, meaning it is mapped to a device. It later begins its execution on that device. It may encounter additional scheduling points when it pauses or resumes execution. A platform may allow the task to migrate to a different device at these subsequent scheduling points. This is not always friendly to data locality, and migration is hardly employed in distributed-memory parallel programming environments. Moreover, a task may specify *affinity* to one or a subset of devices, for example, ones that can access its data efficiently.

Our discussion in this chapter is mainly focused on the initial scheduling, assuming no migration. If migration is allowed, similar ideas apply to subsequent rescheduling. In either case, there are two important goals at each scheduling point:

1. Locality: The task is executed on a device such that its synchronization and communication with other tasks have low overhead.

2. Utilization: No device should be idle when more tasks remain to be executed, meaning device loads are balanced.

These two goals are integrally related to each other, and often in conflict. Both locality and utilization should be high, but the best localization might be achieved by mapping all tasks to the same device, leading to severe load imbalance and low utilization. On the other hand, utilization, or load balancing, is abstracted as the bin-packing problem: group tasks into bins such that the size of each bin is within an $\epsilon$ factor of others, for some small and fixed value of $\epsilon$. Perfect balancing may require assigning frequently interacting tasks to separate devices.

## Preliminary Task Mapping

The mapping of a task to some device may occur at any time after it is spawned. It cannot begin to execute on that device until its task dependencies are satisfied, and the device becomes available. (The device becomes available when it has completed the tasks executed earlier, unless it supports concurrent execution.) If the underlying programming platform does not support dependencies, or if the application program chooses to manage it directly, it spawns a task only after its dependencies are satisfied. Similarly, if the platform does not support mapping tasks to devices, the application program explicitly executes the corresponding task on a specific device mapped by the program itself.

In case the platform supports task graphs, a common semantics of dependency edge is that a task may begin execution only after *all* its predecessor tasks have completed. This is not true for communication edges. Tasks with only communication edges leading to it may be started at any time. Both communication edges and dependency edges are used in mapping, but communication edges are more important in mapping. Two frequently communicating tasks are preferably mapped to the same device to reduce the communication latency. Similarly, if task $B$ is dependent on task $A$, it is useful to map $B$ to the same device that $A$ is mapped to. Such mapping reduces the latency in starting task $B$ after task $A$ completes, because the synchronization is local.

The main target of the task mapping step is to compute the best location for each task. One common solution for static tasks is to divide the task graph into components with a roughly equal number of nodes in each component and the minimal cut between components. This is similar to the algorithm for generating a task graph from a data graph. The task graph is subdivided, and each subgraph is allocated to a single device. Communication edges between subgraphs, that is, on the cut, imply inter-device communication. Edges between tasks in the same subgraph imply intra-device communication and hence impose a lower latency.

Algorithms that cut a static graph are generally not applicable for a dynamic task graph. However, if tasks are dynamically generated, they may be incrementally mapped in a greedy breadth-first fashion. In the greedy approach, the initial set of tasks that do not depend on any other task are mapped to devices in a round-robin fashion. Tasks that depend on this initial set are mapped next, and so on. In mapping each dependent task, edges leading to this task from already mapped tasks are used in assigning a device to this task. It is assigned to a device where most of its predecessors are – subject to load balance. We discuss this next.

## Task Scheduling Framework

There are two common designs for managing the scheduling. *Push* scheduling and *Pull* scheduling. In push scheduling, spawned tasks are sent – or pushed – to a target device for execution. In pull scheduling, devices themselves seek – or pull – tasks ready for execution from some task pool.

Task scheduling can be centralized or distributed. In centralized push scheduling, each task sends the basic information of the newly spawned tasks to a central task scheduler executing on some device. This *central scheduler* adds these tasks to a scheduling queue, and subsequently maps each task to a specific device for execution. A *device scheduler* on the target device may further maintain a list of tasks assigned to it and execute them in some order using a priority queue. The task scheduler and the device scheduler may be a part of the application program, but they are more commonly built into many parallel programming platforms.

In distributed push scheduling, the task spawner itself maps the generated task and sends it to the corresponding device. Again, it can be the application task itself that explicitly performs the mapping, but this role is often handled by the programming platform.

## Centralized Push Scheduling Strategy

If tasks are designed such that each task requires roughly the same time as others, push scheduling can be as simple as round-robin task distribution. On the other hand, tasks may have an affinity to certain devices, for example, if most input data for task $A$ is on device $i$, perhaps because its predecessor(s) executed on device $i$, it may have an affinity to device $i$. However, mapping task $A$ to $i$ may lead to load imbalance. Besides, all devices may not have the same speed or capacity. This is similar to packing different-sized items (tasks) into a set of different-sized bins (devices), such that the resulting packed-size of each bin is the same. This is an NP-complete problem.[5] If tasks are spawned dynamically, or have bin affinity, the problem is even harder. With dynamically spawned tasks, the scheduling is said to be "online." Round-robin distribution is not efficient in the presence of nonuniformity in task size, task affinity, task dependence, or dynamic creation. At the same time, in most situations, a large scheduling overhead defeats the main purpose: complete the application program as quickly as possible.

Several heuristics are used to perform task scheduling. In most, an estimate of the size of the task (the time it takes) and that of the speed of the device is required. Creating these estimates reliably is itself a major challenge. Nonetheless, variants of greedy algorithms are practical: they have low overhead and perform well on average. For example, always map the next ready task in the central task queue (a ready task is one whose predecessors have completed) to the device where it would complete the earliest.[6] This heuristic may be further enriched by modifying the order in which tasks in the central queue are mapped. For example, the order may be driven by the following heuristics:

1. a task on which a larger number of other tasks are dependent is mapped earlier

2. a task that has a longer chain of dependent tasks is mapped earlier

3. a task expected to take longer is mapped earlier

[5] Ullman, "NP-complete scheduling problems."

[6] Hall and Shmoys, "Approximation schemes."

These heuristics can be further augmented to account for device affinity. For example, if the data required by task $A$ is at, or close to, device $j$, $A$ would be likelier to finish quicker on device $j$ than on devices that do not have the data nearby. In other words, the estimate of when a task will finish on a particular device would include both the computation time and the time taken to fetch its input from other devices, where those may have been produced. (Generally, a task's output is produced at the device where it executes.)

It is also useful to realize that balancing load is easier when a large number of tasks (compared to the number of available devices) remain to be executed. Every time a device becomes idle, there are many waiting tasks that could be mapped to it. It is often toward the end of the application, when fewer tasks may remain to be executed, that load imbalance begins to impact the performance. Consequently, the following adjustments to the heuristics described above are sometimes useful:

1.  Reduce the size of tasks as some load imbalance metric increases, usually near the end of the application. This metric is based on the estimated execution times of the tasks already mapped but not yet completed.

2.  Map the next task simply to the device to which it has the highest affinity, when the load imbalance metric is below a threshold. On the other hand, if the load imbalance metric is above a threshold, map the next task to the device where it will complete the earliest (of course, after waiting for its turn to execute).

The *estimated* load imbalance may be defined as the ratio $\frac{t_e}{t_l}$, where $t_e$ is the earliest time when any device would complete its assignment and $t_l$ is the latest time when a device would complete its assignment. A simple example of the load imbalance metric $I$ is: $\frac{(t_l - t_e)}{t_{wait}}$, where $t_{wait}$ is the total time required by the waiting unmapped tasks. This allows the estimated imbalance to be weighted by the amount of unassigned work and works well for roughly equal-sized tasks.

More complex strategies may be required for highly skewed task sizes. For example, if there is extreme variance in the loads of tasks, two or three large tasks may take longer than all others combined. Subdividing large tasks is often the best way to achieve load balance in such cases. If subdivision is not feasible, such tasks must be started as early as possible.

Algorithms for load balancing can be applied in conjunction with task decomposition strategies. For example, in the case of block-cyclic domain decomposition, it is possible to create large initial tasks using larger blocks and smaller later blocks, as shown in Figure 5.6.

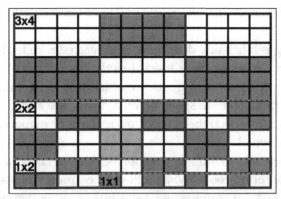

**Figure 5.6** Block-cyclic domain decomposition with reducing block size (different sizes are separated by dashed lines)

## Distributed Push Scheduling

A centralized scheduler quickly becomes the bottleneck; it does not scale well with an increasing number of tasks and devices. On the other hand, each device scheduler independently mapping each task spawned at that device, and then pushing that task to its mapped device is prohibitively complex. Each device is a map target of $n-1$ other device schedulers in an $n$-device system. Without a shared knowledge of the target's load state, $n-1$ independent scheduling decisions could not be expected to balance the full load. This requires extensive synchronization. An intermediate approach is to decompose the centralized scheduler into $k$ separate master schedulers, where $k \ll n$.

Each spawned task is then pushed to one of these master schedulers. This master assignment could be statically predetermined or may be decided on the fly, for example, by using a randomized algorithm. In general, the master schedulers together implement a distributed priority queue, and each task generator simply pushes to this distributed queue. Tasks from the distributed queue may then be removed and mapped by any of the master schedulers, albeit with proper synchronization. Alternatively, device schedulers may directly pull tasks from this distributed queue. We discuss pull scheduling next.

## Pull Scheduling

In pull scheduling, the target devices map tasks to themselves. They may fetch their tasks from a central queue or a distributed queue. Push scheduling often requires an accurate estimate of the time a task would take. Pull scheduling, on the other hand, reacts to the time that tasks actually take – including computation as well as memory and network access. This works well when the size or the number of tasks varies dynamically and cannot be predetermined. This also reacts well to unforeseen network bottlenecks or device slowdown.

Pull scheduling is inherently distributed since each device fetches tasks it must execute. The device scheduler seeks these tasks directly from some other device scheduler, or perhaps a central or distributed queue in which tasks accumulate. The more common approach is that tasks that are spawned on a device are added to a local queue by that device's scheduler. In effect, these tasks are tentatively mapped to the same device on which they are spawned.

The initial set of tasks that the application begins with may be mapped using a simple push strategy like round-robin. When a device completes its mapped tasks or nears the completion of its tasks, it requests new tasks from another device scheduler. If that other scheduler has a sufficient number of waiting tasks, it shares some of them with the requesting scheduler. If it does not, it rejects the request. This process is known as *work stealing*. If a request is rejected, the requester may choose another scheduler to make a new steal request.

Device schedulers do not generally monitor the status of other device schedulers. This means that when a device has no remaining tasks in its queue, it must guess which other device to request more tasks from. The usual approach is to iteratively select a random *victim* device to steal from, until it finds one that has sufficient remaining work to share. This implies that near the end of the application, all devices start to attempt to steal. On large clusters, this can lead to a significant loss of time before all device schedulers realize that there is no more work remaining. Early stopping heuristics are commonly used. For example, device schedulers may reduce the probability of subsequent steal attempts after each rejection, or wait for some time before the next attempt to steal. This assumes that each rejection indicates an increasing likelihood of further rejection, as a rejection implies a lack of waiting tasks at the victim scheduler. Each device scheduler may also monitor the number of steal requests it receives, and hence estimate the state of other devices.

## 5.4   Input/Output

Most parallel programs require input and produce output. Quite often, these input and output data are large in size. Reading and writing data to files is significantly slower than the instruction execution speed. Hence, file input and output adds a nontrivial time to the application makespan. This is true even if file IO is parallel. Files may be distributed across the computation nodes, in a central appliance, or some combination of the two. Even when files are all located on a central file server, these files are striped across multiple disks, allowing parallel disk IO. Further, such storage appliances support multiple access paths – they may have multiple controllers that can be reached through different network routes.

Thus there is a certain degree of parallelism, but this parallelism is usually not exposed to the client programs that read or write data.

True parallel file systems expose the parallel IO. They have each file potentially striped across multiple *storage targets* (ST). There may be a small number of dedicated STs, or there may be a separate target at every node in the cluster. Programs access the storage through *storage servers* (SS). A general architecture is shown in Figure 5.7(a). Programs executing on devices, that is, the clients, thus have multiple paths to the STs through the multiple SSs.

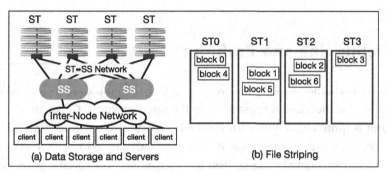

**Figure 5.7** Parallel IO

A file is divided into equal-sized blocks, with the blocks distributed round-robin to the STs (see Figure 5.7(b)). The size of the block may be specified for each file by the file creator. The application program is aware of this structure and knows which blocks of a file reside in which target. It can exploit this knowledge to effect parallel IO. If clients read blocks resident in different targets, the accesses can proceed completely in parallel. Similarly, writes are also parallel. If the output produced by different devices can be stored in a manner such that parallel write is possible, each thread can write its part of the output file (or files). Some programming platforms provide collective calls for efficient parallel reading and writing by multiple threads.

Note that the reading pattern is a bit different from the writing pattern. Two different threads usually write to different parts of a file, but two threads may need to read the same data. They may both read it on their own, or one can read and share the data with the other. A parallel file IO system supports both types of reads efficiently. In particular, parallel file systems use internal caching at the SSs as well as at the clients to reduce disk IO in case the same data is fetched multiple times. This involves a sequence of buffer copies just like network communication

An alternative is that programs explicitly share data among tasks. Different threads (possibly on different nodes) may read different parts of the file in parallel, and then interchange the data based on each thread's requirement. This can sometimes be more efficient than the file system caching, particularly if a parallel file system is not available or file caches are relatively small, and network bandwidth is significantly higher than disk IO bandwidth.

Note also that file read or write operations have high latency, and during these operations the compute load of the thread is generally low. A program may hide some file IO latency by overlapping two or more tasks on the same device. For example, the program's input may be divided into chunks. Task $A$ on device $i$ may read its input and then start processing it concurrently with task $B$'s read of the next chunk on that same device.

## 5.5   Debugging and Profiling

Regardless of whether a sequential version is initially employed as a parallel development tool, the core parallel design must address the same concerns. Correctness and performance debugging is quite challenging for parallel programs. Code line stepping is of some use, but it is hard to simultaneously maintain the mental map of the execution states of multiple threads. Moreover, many bugs manifest themselves due to a specific order between different threads and occur nondeterministically. Code-stepping creates determinism, thus obscuring such bugs. Tools to profile and debug should be used where available. With the help of such tools or without, effective debugging often requires writing programs in a way that aids debugging.

One way to debug is to log critical events and state parameters (variables) during the execution of the parallel program. After the execution, the log is analyzed for anomalous behavior and reasons for large waits and performance slowdowns. This analysis may be automated by scripts and programs that look for specific conditions, for example, large gaps in timestamp of certain events. This is also done by an inspection of the logged text, or with the help of a graphical visualization of timestamps or event counts. Note that multiple log files are often employed – possibly one per task. Tagging the logged events with a timestamp can help relate the approximate order of events recorded at different nodes, particularly for visualization. However, any such order must be taken as only a rough estimate because clocks are not synchronized.

The importance of interactive tools like *gdb* that can "attach" to a running process at any time and inspect its state cannot be overstated. This allows one to stop and start the execution at specific lines, events, or variable conditions. The program itself can be written in a way to maximize such debugging control. For example, special debugging variables may be introduced, which record complex conditions. Consider the following listing. The code waits in a loop when a certain inconsistent state is discovered. This is one way to ensure that the process waits on encountering suspicious condition.

```
if(idx1 > idx2 || num1 < idx1 && idx1 < num2)
      while(! debuggerReady);
```

Once the debugger attaches to this process, the related variables can be inspected. After the inspection is completed, the debugger may set the *debuggerReady* to true to step or continue beyond this point.

One of the most important arrows in the quiver of the parallel programmer, across design methodologies, is performance profiling. A profiler collects runtime statistics of an executing program and produces information like the number of times a function is called, the total time spent executing a block of code, the amount of data communicated, and so on. Profiling helps highlight an executing program's hotspots – the parts that take the most time. These are the parts that the programmer must focus on early in the development cycle. Parallel program performance has three broad components: compute performance, memory performance, and network performance. Computation-centric profiling tools are more common but separate memory and network profilers also exist.

Network and memory performance are ignored at the program's own peril. Even if only the computation profile is available, it can provide indirect hints about memory and network bottlenecks. In particular, one may measure the observed memory and network throughput and relate it to the peak throughput possible. If the obtained throughput is close to the peak, and the instruction throughput is not close to its peak, a redesign to reduce memory/network usage may help improve performance.

High-level performance analysis at the model level was discussed in Chapter 3. That must be a part of the initial algorithm design. Profiling confirms and augments that analysis. It helps uncover programming errors and provides a more detailed analysis of bottlenecks. Once the bottlenecks are understood, they may be accepted as necessary or ameliorated by refactoring the solution. One may subdivide the slow tasks or otherwise redesign the program. Sometimes, they also show the way to an improvement in the algorithm. Or, they may suggest that a given task or component requires a larger allocation of resources.

## 5.6 Summary

Design of parallel programs requires a delicate balance of many conflicting considerations, no matter what the programming model is. Besides eliminating sequentiality in the underlying algorithm, programs must reduce synchronization, communication, and processor idling. Good design is not about completely eliminating synchronization or communication. Rather, certain communication and synchronization events are often necessary. A careful design can still reduce the time spent in communication and synchronization by reducing their overhead, for example, by using high-level primitives or by overlapping waiting threads with other computing threads, keeping the processors busy. A careful decomposition of the problem into tasks goes a long way in controlling overheads.

Some general design principles introduced in this chapter include:

- Subdivide a solution into many sequential tasks, which may preferably be executed concurrently with each other.

- Reduce communication and synchronization, even if it means that the same computation is repeated in multiple threads sometimes.

- When communication or synchronization is necessary, try to overlap it with concurrent computation.

- Reduce the time spent in synchronized code fragments and prefer nonblocking synchronization.

- Well-designed and well-debugged parallel tools and libraries may be available for some components of the desired solution. It is helpful to decompose the solution such that some of the created tasks can be completed by these tools and libraries.

We have also discussed several techniques for domain decomposition and functional decomposition. Domain decomposition is generally employed for data-parallel algorithms, and is simpler when data is organized in a regular manner. Minding the design issues described above, block or cyclic domain decomposition, or a combination of the two, usually suffices. The key is to make units of data that are accessed together. Decomposing irregular data into tasks requires a deeper analysis. Some variant of graph cut is generally a useful tool in this situation. Where a good domain decomposition does not present itself, a functional decomposition may. Functional decomposition is mainly an artifact of the underlying algorithm. The algorithm may naturally provide ways to generate tasks in recursive, exploratory, or pipelined manners, for example.

Mapping tasks to computing devices in an equitable and efficient manner actually begins at the task design time. Tasks with too many predecessors would have to wait longer. This shows up clearly in the task graph. Long chains in a task graph inhibit parallelism. If a task graph is known in advance – whether or not it is provided explicitly – processors can be assigned to tasks in a manner such that tasks with closer interaction are allocated the same processor, or processors that can communicate efficiently with each other. At the same time, tasks should also be distributed equitably among processors, such that their loads remain balanced. If the workload of each task is uniform, or they can be estimated in advance, the load is easier to balance, particularly if all processors have the same capability.

Relative workloads are not always known in advance. In such cases, an initial allocation on the basis of estimated workloads may yet be useful. Load rebalancing algorithms are required to adjust the allocation when some processor completes its tasks well ahead of others. This is especially true when new work is created on the fly. In such situations, a work-queue or load-stealing algorithm is generally advisable.

The book by Foster[7] has a broad overview of parallel program design. The one by Xu and Lau[8] contains a broad coverage of load balancing strategies. A survey by Jiang[9] provides a good study of task mapping strategies. It is a good starting point for further reading. Tools like Metis[10] have been widely used for cutting large task graphs into subgraphs for mapping.

## Exercise

5.1. Compute the measures: (i) critical path length, (ii) average concurrency, and (iii) maximum concurrency (the maximum number of processors that can execute different tasks in parallel) for the following task graphs. Also work out a load-balanced mapping of these tasks on four processors.

(a)                                                              (b)

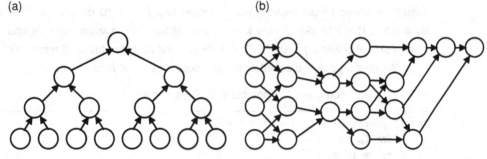

5.2. Devise a parallel version of merge-sort in terms of tasks that sequentially merge two sorted list, the size of the list may be as required. (Assume the time to merge is proportional to the length of the lists to merge).

   (a) Draw the task graph. Compute its critical path length and average concurrency.

   (b) Map the tasks to 16 processors, given that the initial list to sort has 128 elements.

5.3. Consider matrix multiplication $C = A \times B$, as described in Section 5.1. One task decomposition has $Task_i$ computing row $i$ of $C$ with $0 \le i < n$. $Task_i$ requires row $i$ of matrix $A$ and all columns of matrix $B$. $Task_{i+1}$ requires row $i + 1$ of $A$ and all columns of $B$, and so on. Distribution of $A$ among tasks is simple: one row to each task. However, all tasks require access to all columns.

---

[7] Foster, *Designing and Building Parallel Programs*.
[8] Xu and Lau, *Load Balancing*.
[9] Jiang, "A survey of task allocation."
[10] Karypis and Kumar, "A fast and high quality multilevel scheme."

(a) Compare the design where all tasks first receive all columns of $B$ (before starting their computation of $C$'s row) with the design where they fetch one column at a time in sequence, and compute one element of $C$ while fetching the next column of $B$ in parallel with it.

(b) If the tasks proceed in parallel at roughly similar speeds, they all require the same column of $B$ at roughly the same time. If $B$ is in a cache shared by all tasks, this can be helpful. However, suppose they do not, and $B$ is instead distributed columnwise among many nodes. All tasks fetch a column from the same node causing that node to become a bottleneck. Suggest a scheme to alleviate this contention.

5.4. In Exercise 5.3b, assume the matrices $A$ and $B$ are initially stored on the disk with a parallel file system – $A$ in the row-major layout and $B$ in the column-major layout. All processors can read from the same file in parallel using collective Read calls. (Collective Read allows nodes to efficiently fetch a contiguous block of rows from $A$ or a contiguous blocks of columns in an interleaved manner. For example, all node $i$ may receive columns $3i$ to $3i + 2$.)

How does this initial IO requirement impact the design in Exercise 5.3b?

5.5. Consider a 2D block decomposition for multiplying $n \times n$ matrices $A$ and $B$ on a message-passing system. Assume $P^2$ processors are organized in a $P \times P$ 2D grid, $n \gg P$. $A$ and $B$ are divided into $P \times P$ blocks (of size $\frac{n}{P} \times \frac{n}{P}$ each). Block $A_{ij}$ is a submatrix of $A$ and block $B_{ij}$ is a submatrix of $B$ with $i, j \in 0..P - 1$. Initially $A_{ij}$ and $B_{ij}$ are in the local memory of Processor $(i, j)$. We decompose and schedule the computation of $A \times B$ as follows.

Processor $(i, j)$ computes $C_{ij}$, one block of $C$, as follows:

```
forall processor i,j, 0 <= i,j < P
     Set Cij to all 0s
     for k in 0..P-1
          Cij = Cij + Aik * Bkj
```

Schedule the loop above so that different processors fetch different submatrices of $A$ and $B$ from different processors. (Hint: Rotate the submatrices as if on a 2D torus.)

5.6. We want to compute the transpose of matrix $A$ laid out in the row-major order in File1 of a parallel file system. This amounts to writing out $A$ in the column-major order into File2. Design tasks and map them to nodes. Assume collective reads and writes just as in Exercise 5.4.

5.7. LU-factorization algorithm (Listing 5.1) computes a lower triangular matrix L and an upper triangular matrix U given an $n \times n$ matrix A, such that A = L × U.

**Listing 5.1** LU Factorization

```
1 Initialize L = n×n identity matrix, and U = A.
2        for i = 0..n-1
```

```
3          for j = i+1..n-1
4              L[j,i] = U[j,i]/U[i,i]
5              for k = 0..n-1
6                  U[j,k] = U[j,k] - L[j,i]*U[i,k]
```

(a) Focussing on the computation of U, suppose U is divided into $B \times B$ blocks. Assume $\text{Task}_{lm}$ computes one $\frac{n}{B} \times \frac{n}{B}$ block of entries of U. Propose a domain decomposition for A. Accordingly, draw its task graph.

(b) Note that each task produces $\frac{n}{B} \times \frac{n}{B}$ sized block of U, but their blocks have varying number of nonzero entries. Given $p$ processors, devise a task mapping strategy, assuming all processors are equally capable.

5.8. Consider the task graph for reduction of $n$ items (review Exercise 2.12). There are $n - 1$ internal nodes (i.e. tasks) required to reduce $n$ elements. Suppose, we divide the $n$ items into $B$ blocks of size $\frac{n}{B}$ items each. Each block can be reduced sequentially within a single task. The single result of each task can then be reduced in a tree-like manner. This requires $B$ initial tasks, followed by $B - 1$ additional tasks in a tree-like graph. Assuming $B \ll n$, describe the trade-off between choosing different values of $B$.

5.9. Consider the problem of locating $m$ query items in a sorted list of $n$ data items. We may divide the $m$ query items into $B$ blocks of $\frac{m}{B}$ items each, and create $B$ tasks, with $\text{Task}_i$ performing a binary search for the $\frac{m}{B}$ query items in block $i$. Assume for simplicity that $m$ is divisible by $B$. Discuss the impact of task granularity, the value $B$, in comparison to $m$ and $n$.

Note that $B \leq m$ in the design above. Can you create finer-grained tasks such that multiple tasks may cooperate in locating each query item? Discuss the impact of this finer granularity.

5.10. Suppose our design calls for three kinds of tasks: $\text{Task}_a$, $\text{Task}_b$, and $\text{Task}_c$. We know that all tasks of type $\text{Task}_a$ take time $t_a$, $\text{Task}_b$ take time $t_b$, and $\text{Task}_c$ take time $t_c$. Say, $t_a = 2t_b = 4t_c$. Also given that tasks of each type interact heavily with other tasks of that type. Devise a static load-balanced way to map 16 tasks of each type to a total of 8 processors.

5.11. We need a centralized work-queue based dynamic "pull" mapping in a shared-memory program. Provide a lock-free synchronization scheme for each thread, taking items from this work-queue, if

(a) all tasks are known in advance and initially in the queue

(b) tasks can be generated on the fly and threads may be inserted into the queue

5.12. Consider a centralized work-queue based dynamic "pull" mapping in a distributed-memory program. The work-queue resides at one node, and the network latency is approximately 10 times the task computation time. In this case, pulling multiple work items at a time makes sense. Assume that tasks may also be generated on the fly and must be communicated to the node holding the work-queue. How many work items should a worker pull?

5.13. Consider a work-queue distributed among worker nodes on a network, and work-stealing based scheduler. Assume that all tasks are initially mapped (and no additional tasks are generated on the fly). The time taken by each task is 1 unit. The round-trip latency between any pair of nodes is 20 units. Devise an efficient strategy for each node's scheduler to steal work from other nodes' queues. The goal is to minimize the makespan. We focus on termination separately in Exercise 5.14.

5.14. Consider a work-queue distributed among worker nodes on a network and work-stealing based scheduling. Assume that all tasks are initially mapped. No additional tasks are generated on the fly, and all tasks are added to the local work-queue at the node at which the generator executes. Devise an efficient strategy for each node's scheduler to stop stealing. A node scheduler should not steal if it could increase the makespan. The goal is to minimize the time when the last worker stops stealing.

5.15. The following performance was observed when executing a shared-memory program on four similar processors:

| Processor | 0 | 1 | 2 | 3 |
|---|---|---|---|---|
| Time taken | 80 | 30 | 50 | 50 |

Four tasks executed the following pseudo-code with uniform domain decomposition over A$, and were mapped, one each, to the four processors. Postulate three reasons to which the difference in times can be attributed.

```
repeat N times:
        for all positions (i,j) in an n×n array A$
            temp = 0
            for all positions (k,l), i-5 < k < i+5, j-5 < l < j+5, (modulo n
                arithmetic)
                        temp = temp + A$[k,l]
            barrier
            A$[i][j] = temp / 36.0;
```

5.16. In Exercise 5.15, the code was changed to remove the barrier (the results were incorrect which we ignore). The performance was then recorded as follows:

| Processor | 0 | 1 | 2 | 3 |
|---|---|---|---|---|
| Time taken | 29 | 40 | 34 | 37 |

Postulate three reasons to which the difference in times can be attributed.

# CHAPTER 6

# Middleware: The Practice of Parallel Programming

We are now ready to start implementing parallel programs. This requires us to know:

*Question:* Where do I begin to program? What building blocks can I program on top of?

- How to create and manage fragments (and tasks).

- How to provide the code for the fragments.

- How to organize, initialize, and access shared memory.

- How to cause tasks to communicate.

- How to synchronize among tasks.

This chapter discusses popular software tools that provide answers to these questions. It offers a broad overview of these tools in order to familiarize the reader with the core concepts employed in tools like these, and their relative strengths. This discussion must be supplemented with detailed documentation and manuals that are available for these tools before one starts to program.

The minimal requirement from a parallel programming platform is that it supports the creation of multiple tasks or threads and allows data communication and synchronization among them. Modern programming languages, Java, Python, and so on, usually have these facilities – either as a part of language constructs or through standard library functions. We start with *OpenMP*, which is designed for parallel programming on a single computing system with memory shared across threads of a processor. It is supported by many C/C++ and Fortran compilers. We will use the C-style.

## 6.1  OpenMP

Language-based support for parallel programming is popular, especially for single node computing systems. Compiling such programs produces a single executable, which can be loaded into a process for execution, similar to sequential programs. The process then generates multiple threads for parallel execution. OpenMP is a compiler-directive-based shared-memory programming model, which allows sequential programmers to quickly graduate to parallel programming. In fact, an OpenMP program stripped off its directives is nothing but a sequential program. A compiler that does not support the directives could just ignore them. (For some things, OpenMP provides library functions – these are not ignored by the compiler.) Some compilers that support OpenMP pragmas still require a compile time flag to enable that support.

## Preliminaries

C/C++ employs `#pragma` directives to provide instructions to the compiler. OpenMP directives all are prefixed with `#pragma omp` followed by the name of the directive and possible further options for the directive as a sequence of clauses, as shown in Listing 6.1. Each pragma applies to the statement that follows it, which can be a structured block of code enclosed in {}.

**Listing 6.1** OpenMP Parallel Pragma

```
#pragma omp parallel num_threads(n)
{
      // This block of code is executed by each of n threads
}
// Only one thread executes here: the parent, also known as the master
```

The example shows the *parallel pragma* with one optional clause called *num_threads*, with a single argument *n*.

## OpenMP Thread Creation

Creating separate threads in OpenMP simply uses the parallel pragma shown in Listing 6.1. This pragma requests a fork of new children threads, all of which share the address space of the creating thread – the one that "encounters" the pragma. Each thread, including the parent thread, executes the pragma statement followed by an implicit barrier. Each thread has its own execution stack. The code block is called the parallel region. Each thread is identified by an ID between 0 and $n - 1$. The function `omp_get_thread_num()` returns this ID. The children threads are completed and deactivated at the barrier. The parent thread then continues execution of the code following the pragma statement. This is called the *fork-join model*. The argument *n* of the num_thread clause in Listing 6.1 specifies the number of threads in this group, including the parent. Thus $n - 1$ children threads are invoked. We may call this group a work-group or a barrier group.

Parallel pragmas can be nested by including another parallel pragma within the code block (but implementations require an explicit enabling of the nesting capability). If *n* different threads executing the parallel code encounter a parallel pragma each, they all independently fork their children threads (based on the arguments of the inner parallel pragma), and each subsequently joins with its children.

The scheduling of these threads on the available processors is performed automatically by the compiler runtime and the operating system. Some control is accorded to the programmer through the proc_bind clause, which allows certain threads to be assigned a scheduling affinity toward a subset of cores.

The parallel pragma supports other clauses. These include control over how the address space is shared and partitioned among the threads.

## OpenMP Memory Model

Even though OpenMP threads share the address space, making each variable visible to each thread increases the chance of inadvertent conflicts. Hence, OpenMP supports two levels of visibility. *Shared variables* are visible to an entire barrier group. *Private variables* are visible only to a single thread. Hiding private variables from others also allows the same name to be used in all threads. Otherwise, an array of variables – one per thread – would be required. This two-level visibility simplifies the design sometimes but also reduces the flexibility of allowing a variable to be shared between an arbitrary group of threads. This visibility is controlled by clauses to the parallel pragma: *shared* and *private* as shown in Listing 6.2.

**Listing 6.2** Memory Clauses for OpenMP Parallel Pragma

```
int i, k, l;
float j;
// Assume n is set
#pragma omp parallel num_threads(n) shared(i, j) private(k, l)
{
    int m, n;
}
```

In this example, variables *i* and *j* are declared as shared by all threads of the group. Both variables must be declared before the pragma. A variable that is declared before, but does not appear in either clause, is shared by default (this can be changed using the *default* clause). The clause shared(i, j) is redundant in this example, as *i* and *j* are shared by default anyway.

New variables declared within the parallel code block are private by default. Variables *k* and *l* are private to each thread. This effectively creates *n* new copies of variables *k* and *l*, respectively, in the process's address space at the fork time, each visible to a different thread. Similarly, there is a local $m$ and $n$, private to each thread. A natural question is what becomes of these copies at the join at the end of the parallel region. They are discarded (but see the *reduction* clause later in this section) and deallocated (but see *threadprivate pragma*). These copies may also be initialized by the value of the original using the *firstprivate* clause (in place of private). For example, in Listing 6.3, the value of $k$ is initially 11 in each thread; $l$ remains uninitialized.

**Listing 6.3** Memory Clauses for OpenMP Parallel Pragma

```
int l = 10, k = 11;
#pragma omp parallel firstprivate(k) private(l)
{
      // k is 11 but l is uninitialized
}
```

Operations on shared variables are not guaranteed to be sequentially consistent. Instead, OpenMP advances a thread-local view of each shared variables, which is allowed to diverge from other threads' views. Thus incoherence between two cache copies is allowed. Memory *flush* primitives (see Section 4.2) are provided for the programmer to control the consistency as required. OpenMP also allows flush to be limited to certain variables; in that case, it is no more a pure memory fence. The flush pragma, which may appear within the parallel region, is as follows:

**Listing 6.4** OpenMP Flush Pragma

```
#pragma omp flush (i, j, k)
```

In listing 6.4, $i, j$, and $k$ are names of shared variables and are together called the flush-set of this flush. OpenMP specifies that two flushes with an intersecting flush-set are seen in the same order by all members of the barrier group. Those flushes are sequentially consistent. Operations on variables in the flush-set cannot cross the flush in that order. In other words, any operation on variable $x$ that occurs in its program between two flushes that include $x$, must actually appear to start and complete between those flushes. When no variables are listed in the flush pragma, it is equivalent to a pure memory fence, meaning all shared variables are effectively flushed.

A flush is implied at all synchronization points. These include the entry and exit from the parallel region. Other synchronization constructs are discussed later in this section. This is a good time to bring up certain types of compiler optimization. Recall that instructions of a thread can be executed out of order. They may even complete their execution out of order if such reordered instructions do not contain a data race: read-write or write-write conflict. A compiler reorders instructions to increase both cache locality and instruction-level parallelism. However, a compiler analyzes only sequential sections of the code. In parallel execution, some other code executed by a different thread may cause conflicts undetected by the compiler. Recall the Peterson's algorithm (Listing 4.7). A few lines are reproduced below.

**Listing 6.5** Snippet of Peterson's Algorithm

```
1 // Assume shared ready and defer.
2 myID = omp_get_thread_num();
3 ready[myID] = true;
4 defer = myID;
```

Since there is no data race between lines 3 and 4, the compiler may think them independent and reorder them. We have already seen that the correctness depends critically on the correct order being maintained. Some languages use the keyword volatile to indicate such variables, instructing the compiler to keep them in order. OpenMP, in particular, specifies that a read of a volatile variable $v$ implies a *flush(v)* preceding the read and a write to a volatile variable $v$ is implicitly followed by *flush(v)*. If sequentializing all accesses to a variable is not necessary, an explicit flush is a better option. Listing 6.6 does so for the Peterson's algorithm.

**Listing 6.6** Snippet of Peterson's Algorithm With Flush

```
1 // Assume shared ready and defer.
2 myID = omp_get_thread_num();
3 ready[myID] = true;
4 #pragma omp flush(ready, defer)
5 defer = myID;
```

## OpenMP Reduction

Instead of allowing the final values of private variables to be discarded at the join, a reduction operation can combine their values. Parallel pragma accordingly has a reduction clause; arguments include the reduction operator and a list of private variables. The copies of each variable in the list are reduced, and the result accumulated into the original copy of that variable. This implies that each of the listed private variables must have an original, which must exist outside the parallel region.

**Listing 6.7** OpenMP Reduction

```
int k = 10;
#pragma omp parallel reduction(+:k) num_threads(2)
{
    k += omp_get_thread_num();
}
```

In Listing 6.7, the variable $k$ is reduced. Appearance in the reduction clause automatically declares $k$ to be private. Further, it is initialized to a value that is suitable for the reduction operation: 0 for addition, 1 for multiplication, a large value for *minima*, a small value for *maxima*, and so on. In Listing 6.7, all private copies of $k$ are initialized to 0. Each thread adds its ID to its private copy of $k$. Thread 0 thus leaves 0 in its copy of $k$, and thread 1 leaves 1. At the end of the parallel region, the values in the two copies of $k$ are reduced to $0 + 1 = 1$ in this example. Finally, the result is combined with the original $k$ using the same reduction function. Thus 1 is added to 10 leaving 11 in $k$ finally.

There are a few predefined reduction operations. OpenMP pragma to define new ones also exists. An example is shown in Listing 6.8.

**Listing 6.8** OpenMP Reduction Operation Definition

```
int max(int res,int val) { return (val>res)? val : res; }
#pragma omp declare reduction(mymax:int:omp_out = max(omp_out, omp_in)) \
                                        initializer(omp_priv = INT_MIN)
int k = 0;
#pragma omp parallel reduction(mymax:k)
{
      // Set k here
}
```

The declare pragma above sets up the reduction: both the operation as well the initialization of each private copy. This example names the reduction operator as *mymax*, which expects integer variables. The actual operation is accomplished by calling the function *max* on two partial results at a time. The function is called repetitively as per the binary tree structure described in Section 3.2; *omp_in* and *omp_out* are internal names. The clause syntax indicates that two variables are combined at a time, and the result is stored in one of them.

## OpenMP Synchronization

Low-level locks as well as higher-level critical sections and barriers are supported by OpenMP. Locks do not employ directives but are managed through function calls. This allows the program a bit more flexibility in creating and manipulating locks compared to pragmas.

```
omp_set_lock(omp_lock_t *lockname); // Acquire lock lockname
omp_unset_lock(omp_lock_t *lockname); // Release lock lockname
```

Before a lock can be used, it must be created by calling the function omp_init_lock. Its resources can be freed by calling omp_destroy_lock after the lock is no more needed.

`omp_set_lock` is a blocking lock. A nonblocking variant, `omp_test_lock`, exists, which returns `false` on failing to acquire the lock, and `true` on success. This allows the caller to go on to some other work without getting blocked. See Listing 6.9, for example.

**Listing 6.9** Threads Share Work Using Nonblocking Lock

```
omp_lock_t lock[N]
for (int i=0; i<N; i++) omp_init_lock(&lock[i]);
#pragma omp parallel // Each thread tries each lock in sequence
      for(int item=0; item<N; item++) {
            if(omp_test_lock(&lock[item])) {
                  workOnItem(item);
                  omp_unset_lock(&lock[item]);
            } // Otherwise some other thread has this lock; move on
      }
for (int i=0; i<N; i++) omp_destroy_lock(&lock[i]);
```

Each thread iterates over a list of items, seeking to process it. It attempts to acquire a lock corresponding to the item, and processes the item if it is able to. If it fails to acquire a lock, this means that some other thread was able to acquire it and process the item. We may assume that function `workOnItem` performs some type of processing on work item number `item`. Note that this code allows a slow thread to reacquire a lock that was released by an earlier thread. We leave the semantics of `workOnItem` to account for this. Note that this code is not the best way to share work between threads. We will discuss work sharing shortly. Locks, like all other OpenMP synchronization primitives, cause a memory flush and can be a reason for slowdown. Due to threads synchronizing at every iteration, this code is inefficient. Application of nonblocking locks does not reduce the synchronization function overhead itself. It only provides the flexibility to move on to another computation.

OpenMP also supports reentrant locks. In order to avoid confusion, they employ different functions: *omp_init_nest_lock, omp_set_nest_lock, omp_unset_nest_lock, omp_test_nest_lock,* and *omp_destroy_nest_lock.*

Higher-level primitives like *barrier* and *critical section* also exist. The barrier directive is straightforward and applies to the current barrier group (i.e. the inner-most parallel region).

```
#pragma omp barrier
```

It is important to ensure that all threads of the group reach the barrier pragma. Otherwise, the group deadlocks. This can happen if the pragma is, say, within an *if* statement, and some threads satisfy the condition while others don't. The critical section pragma provides a more fine-grained control.

```
// Inside a parallel region
#pragma omp critical(section1)
{ // Assume shared counter
    counter ++;
}
```

In this example, section1 is the name given to this section. A thread executing this code block has the guarantee that no thread executes any block also named section1. Two critical sections with different names are nonconflicting, meaning two threads are allowed to be in differently named critical sections at the same time. Critical section applies to all OpenMP threads within the process, not just the members of the current barrier group. A critical section without the name argument is globally critical. No two OpenMP threads may ever overlap their execution in any globally critical section.

Critical section is nothing but a wrapper using locks. The programmer does not need to explicitly manage locks; that's all. Locks and critical sections are both blocking and slow.

The *atomic pragma*, in comparison, is a limited critical section, that performs limited operations on a single shared-memory location. These can often be performed internally using Compare and Swap or other hardware-supported features and are more efficient than the regular critical section.

```
#pragma omp atomic
    x ++; // x is a shared variable
```

The atomic pragma has a few variants. It can be designated to be *read, write, update,* or *capture*. Reads and writes of a single memory location or a word are usually atomic in many architectures. However, atomic is a synchronization operation and ensures flush. Further, languages allow data types with multiple words. The entire variable can be read atomically using the read and write clauses. The update clause is typically a read-modify-write operation on a variable, as in the example above. The capture clause additionally allows capturing the updated variable (before or after the update) like so:

```
#pragma omp atomic capture
    v = x++; // Shared x. Atomically increment, capture old value in v
```

Further, the atomic pragma also has the option to force sequential consistency using the *seq_cst* clause:

```
#pragma omp atomic seq_cst capture
    v = x++; // Atomic increment and capture, sequentially consistent
```

*seq_cst* implies a flush pragma (without a variable list). Without the seq_cst clause, only the variable *x* would be flushed.

Thread creation and synchronization is the minimal facility a shared-memory parallel programming platform needs to support. However, it is useful for parallel programs to be designed in terms of tasks that share the overall work and threads that execute these tasks. The parallel pragmas discussed above do not provide a flexible interface to do so. We will next discuss general work sharing constructs and task management.

## Sharing a Loop's Work

Programs that loop through largely independent work items exhibit loop-level parallelism. They have a simple parallel adaptation. However, in the OpenMP parallel construct, that loop would have to be restructured so that each of the *n* threads gets a share of *N* work items, that is, get to perform a share of the loop's iterations. We have already seen one way to do this in Listing 6.9. Listing 6.10 is another, without any locks, but one that equally divides iteration. If some iterations take much longer than others, the early finishing threads wait at the join barrier, when they could have helped complete other iterations.

**Listing 6.10** Threads Share Work Using Parallel Pragma

```
int numPerThread = N/n; // Assume N is divisible by n
#pragma omp parallel num_threads(n)
{
      int start = numPerThread*omp_get_thread_num();
      for(int item=start; item<start+numPerThread; item++)
            workOnItem(item);
}
```

Such a subdivision can easily be generated by the compiler. The *for* work-sharing construct does precisely that:

**Listing 6.11** Threads Share Work Using *for* Pragma

```
#pragma omp parallel num_threads(n)
{
      #pragma omp for
      for(int item=0; item<N; item++)
            workOnItem(item);
}
```

The *for pragma* can appear anywhere within a parallel region and must be immediately followed by a *for* loop. This pragma distributes the iterations of the for loop among the threads of the barrier group. The loop needs to be in a form that the compiler can statically subdivide: a single clear initialization, single clear termination, and single clear increment. In case the loop is nested, only the outermost loop is subdivided, unless the *collapse* clause is used. The iteration variable for each loop is forced to be private, whether or not it is declared outside the parallel region.

The *for* pragma also has the clauses *private* and *firstprivate*, similar to the parallel pragma. Thus private copies can also be created at the beginning of the loop – one per thread sharing the loop. Again, copies are created per thread, not per iteration. Correspondingly, they are also discarded and deleted at the end of the loop, unless the *reduction* clause is included in the *for* pragma. Additionally, the *for* pragma also supports the *lastprivate* clause. If a variable appears in a lastprivate clause, the value in the last thread's private copy of this variable is saved into the master copy at the end of the loop. The last thread is the thread that happens to execute the last iteration of the loop. Thus, the lastprivate pragma allows the program to refer to a private variable after the parallel loop, just like it can after a sequential loop. Otherwise, the value of a private variable is undefined after the *for* loop. Note that threads other than the last thread have no direct influence on the value of a lastprivate variable at the end of the loop. One may use reduction instead to combine all the private copies into the master. Finally, the *linear* clause allows a more specialized initialization and update of private variables based on the iteration number.

Just as the parallel pragma has, the *for* pragma also has a barrier implied at its end. Each thread reaches this barrier after completing its share of the iterations. Unlike the parallel pragma, however, the *for* pragma allows the waiver of the final barrier with the use of the *nowait* clause. If the nowait clause is used, any thread that completes its assigned iterations may proceed with execution of the code after the loop. Note that a lastprivate update may not have yet happened in this case, and a thread after its exit from the loop must not expect it (unless it is the last thread).

The feature set for assignment of iterations to threads is also rich and is supported by the *schedule* clause. The assignment may be static or dynamic. It may be in blocks of iteration or interleaved.

One limitation of the *for* pragma is that we expect all iterations to be independent of each other so they may be executed in parallel. We are not always so lucky. Some dependencies can still be managed within the framework of the *for* pragma using the clause *ordered*. This clause is a declaration that the iterations of the loops are not entirely independent of each other, and the sequential order of iterations is important for certain parts. These parts are separately indicated using the ordered pragma as follows:

```
1  #pragma omp parallel for num_threads(n)
2      #pragma omp for ordered
3      for(int item=0; item<N; item++) {
```

```
4        orderInsensitivePart1(item); // Concurrent with other iterations
5        #pragma omp ordered
6            doThisInOrder(item); // Called with item = 0 to N-1, in that order
7        orderInsensitivePart2(item); // Concurrent with other iterations
8    }
```

A thread on reaching the ordered pragma (line 5 in the listing above) blocks until the execution of *all* ordered regions belonging to *all* previous iterations have completed. (There is no need to wait for the earlier iterations if the thread is executing the first iteration.) The *depend* clause of the ordered pragma provides a more fine-grained stipulation of dependency to some specific prior iterations.

In the following example, threads can work on their assigned items at their own pace, but their results need to be appended in the order of their iterations (on lines 11 and 13). Odd and even iterations append to different string accumulators. Hence, the odd and even ones can proceed independently of each other. In particular, iteration $i$ depends on iteration $i - 2$. This is enforced using the depend on line 8. The dependence is specifically on line 16, which has the source clause. That means that the source iteration must have reached line 16 for the dependent iteration to cross line 8. Since the ordered pragma itself is a serializer, no further atomic operation is needed by the append function or in the increment of the shared variable *completed*.

**Listing 6.12** Ordered Parallel Loop

```
1  int completed = 0;
2  string resultOdd, resultEven;
3  #pragma omp parallel
4  {
5      #pragma omp for ordered(1) // One level of loop ordering
6      for(int item=0; item<N; item++) {
7          string x = workOnItem(item);      // Concurrent with other iterations
8          #pragma omp ordered depend(sink:item-2) // Proceed if source-point of
9          {                                // iteration before previous is complete
10              if(item % 2)
11                  resultOdd.append(x); // append string to accumulator resultOdd
12              else
13                  resultEven.append(x); // append string to accumulator resultEven
14              completed ++;
15          }
16          #pragma omp ordered depend(source) // Point on which others depend
17      }
18 }
```

Since it is quite common for the *for* pragma to be the only statement in the parallel region, pragma *parallel for* is available as a shorthand combining the two.

```
#pragma omp parallel for
```

The parallel for pragma accepts both *parallel* and *for* clauses. Naturally, the *nowait* clause is not allowed on the combined pragma, as a barrier is essential at the end of the parallel region. Without the barrier, the master could proceed beyond the parallel region while other threads are computing, or may still be computing when other threads have reached their ends, and are deleted. That incurs a risk of race conditions and premature memory deallocation.

## Other Work-Sharing Pragmas

Looping over different tasks is one possible way to sequentially implement parallelizable work, but not the only way. A single-loop body usually indicates a data-parallel algorithm. More general task parallelisms may be required. If these tasks are statically known at the programming time, an alternative is to list a series of tasks, which may then be distributed to any number of threads for execution. The *sections* pragma is that alternative. Each static task is called a section in this terminology. The sections pragma is followed by a list of *section* pragmas, each indicating a different task. Their order is not important.

```
#pragma omp parallel
#pragma omp sections
{
#pragma omp section
      PerformTask1();
#pragma omp section
      PerformTask2();
#pragma omp section
      PerformTask3();
}
```

Sections allows independent task functions, instead of applying a case statement based on the iteration count of a manufactured loop. The sections pragma allows the private and reduction clauses. Threads have an implicit barrier at the end of sections, unless the nowait clause is used. Again, parallel and sections pragmas can be combined into a *parallel sections pragma*. The *section* pragma allows static tasks. We will see more flexible task specification later in this section.

```
#pragma omp parallel sections
```

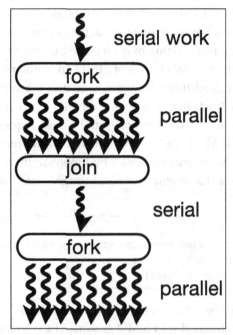

**Figure 6.1** Fork-join semantics

Sometimes, parallelization suffers because of certain steps that cannot be parallelized – a step that must be done serially. One way to manage this is a sequence of fork-join primitives, as shown in Figure 6.1. This imposes significant thread creation and deletion overhead. Instead, one may temporarily suspend the parallelism using the *single pragma* in a parallel region. This pragma is also considered a type of work-sharing pragma, one that forces all its work on one of the threads. Thus private and nowait clauses are available. In the absence of nowait, there is an implicit barrier at the end of the single block.

```
#pragma omp single
```

Note that work-sharing pragmas cannot be nested as the share of the work is determined once at the beginning of the pragma. This means that no work-sharing pragma may be directly inside another work-sharing pragma's code block, unless there is a nested *parallel* pragma creating new threads, which share the inner work-set among themselves.

## SIMD Pragma

OpenMP allows parallelization across multiple SIMD (Single instruction, multiple data) execution units on the same core. This is similar to a work-sharing construct, in that multiple execution units perform different iterations in parallel. However, no new threads are created. Rather, multiple iterations of the loop, each performing scalar operations are combined and *vectorized*. These sub-threads are called *SIMD lanes*, and they do not deviate from each other. They all execute one instruction in one clock cycle in the SIMD fashion (see Section 1.1). Thus *simd* pragma may be nested in the *for* pragma, and a combined *for simd* pragma also exists. Several clauses of SIMD are similar to work-sharing pragmas.

The simd pragma has additional clauses to control the vectorization itself. In particular, the *safelen(d)* clause instructs that iterations combined together in the same SIMD instruction must not be more than $d$ apart. The *simdlen(s)* clause requests that up to $s$ iterations be combined into a single SIMD instruction. The maximum number of SIMD lanes depends on the available hardware and is chosen by OpenMP implementations by default. The following listing shows one example of simd usage. Note that it uses a shorthand *parallel for simd* pragma.

```
float sum = 0;
#pragma omp parallel for simd reduction(+:sum) schedule(simd:static, 8)
      for(int item=0; item<N; item++)
            sum += workOnItem(item);
```

The *for* pragma assigns certain iterations to each thread. The iterations assigned to each thread may now be combined into SIMD groups. The *schedule* clause ensures that threads are assigned iterations in chunks of eight, so they may be vectorized. The kind of schedule, *simd:static*, ensures that if the chunk size (eight in this example) is not a multiple of simdlen, it is increased to make it a multiple to ensure that all available SIMD lanes are utilized.

Note that the function workOnItem is presumably not a SIMD instruction. Hence, it may not make sense to vectorize this function – unless it does, of course. A vectorizable function needs to be specially compiled using vector instructions. OpenMP has a *declare simd pragma* to accomplish this. This pragma instructs the compiler to generate vectorized code and is demonstrated in the following listing:

```
#pragma omp declare simd
float workOnItem(item)
{
      return In[item] * acos(item/N);
}
```

We assume that variables $N$ and $In$ are declared and initialized elsewhere. It is useful to note that vectorization is, in a sense, the domain of the compiler. A smart compiler will be able to vectorize many loops. On the other hand, compilers would not create threads as that is a higher-level decision left to the programmer. Threads together employ multiple cores at a time, whereas the SIMD lanes within a thread are occupied by the additional execution engines on the same core. The OpenMP *simd* pragma provides additional controls to help the programmer guide the vectorization when automatic vectorization may fail.

## Tasks

We have seen the allocation of a somewhat statically determined work tied to threads. This is not a convenient interface for dynamic tasks, particularly if the thread creation cost is high. We next discuss a more task-centric pragma, where explicit tasks are generated, allowing the OpenMP scheduler to assign them to any available thread. The *task pragma* allows the programmer to specify a complex task graph, with arbitrary dependency. These are particularly useful for irregular problems, including graph and tree processing.

```
#pragma omp task
{ // Code block
}
```

The *task pragma* creates tasks but does not create threads. Rather, tasks are created inside a parallel region, already under execution by multiple threads. Any thread encountering a *task* pragma generates a task with its code block according to its clauses. Depending on the clause conditions, the encountering thread may immediately execute the task's code block in-line, or fork it off. This forked task is scheduled at a later time to be executed by one of the threads in the creating thread's barrier group. The task creator asynchronously continues executing the code after the forked task's code block. There is no implicit barrier.

A task may share its creator's memory or it may request private memory. A copy of the encountering task's (or thread's) variable is created for the new task's private use. In addition to memory privacy clauses, there are scheduling hints: *priority(value)* and *untied*. The tasks with a higher priority value is scheduled before the one with a lower value if both are ready. A task may be suspended and resumed at scheduling events. An untied task may be resumed by any thread of the group. In contrast, a tied task is always resumed and executed by the same thread. Special pragmas also control the scheduling of tasks. The *taskyield pragma* suspends the task that encounters it, leaving the thread free to resume another task. The *taskwait pragma* allows the task creator to wait for its previously created tasks to complete, instead of continuing on asynchronously. Taskyield, taskwait, and barrier are scheduling events in addition to the creation and completion of tasks. When a thread encounters a scheduling event, it may switch the task it is executing.

Tasks can be nested, and the inner tasks follow the same semantics. Listing 6.13 shows an example:

**Listing 6.13** Concurrent Task Generation

```
#pragma omp parallel
    #pragma omp single nowait // Let one thread create tasks
    {
        while((taski = taskQ.dequeue()) != NULL) { // Get next task
```

```
#pragma omp task firstprivate(taski) // Private copy of taski
    workOnTask(taski);
    }
}
```

In this example, one of the threads in the barrier group dequeues items from a task queue and generates one task per item. Note the single pragma. It could sometimes be faster for all threads to participate in task generation. It may not be so in this case though, if the dequeue operation needs to be under mutual exclusion. The single version avoids any synchronization on the queue. No significant slowdown due to this sequential queue processing would be incurred if the number of threads available in the group is relatively small and the thread performing the *single* block is able to generate tasks for them quickly. Also note that the *for* pragma would not be suitable for a loop of the kind shown in Listing 6.13 because the number of iterations is not known in advance.

The task requires a private reference to the task, *taski*, because the task creator would go on to the next iteration of the while loop, updating the variable taski. The task, when scheduled, calls function workOnTask, listed below (Listing 6.14):

**Listing 6.14** workOnTask

```
1 void workOnTask(Tasktype taski)
2 {
3     Resulttype result = processTask(taski);
4
5     #pragma omp task shared(result) // Share the variable to avoid copy
6     {       // Forked child-task will safely queue result
7         #pragma omp critical(queueResult)
8         resultQ.enqueue(result);
9     }
10    if(analyzeResult(result) == EUREKA) { // If result is special, shout
11        consoleOutput(result);
12    }
13    // Now wait for the queuer child-task to complete, it shares 'result'
14    #pragma omp taskwait
15 }
```

workOnTask shows an example of tasks generating nested tasks. Each task executing workOnTask first processes its item, collecting the result in the variable result. It creates a new child-task on line 5 that would update the global results queue (line 8). Synchronization of resultQ is necessary, and the critical pragma ensures safe enqueuing. Concurrently with the child-task, the original task goes on to analyze the result, for example, looking for a singularity. It must wait, however, for its child-task to complete enqueueing the result, otherwise the variable result would be destroyed if the primary task exits. The taskwait pragma on line 14 ensures that.

Since forked tasks may be executed asynchronously, it is possible that the parent task is completed before the child task. In that case, its private variables are destroyed even if those are shared by the child task. It is up to the program to ensure that parents wait for the child in this case. Tasks also have a *depend* clause for explicit dependency enforcement. A task cannot be scheduled to begin until all other tasks that it depends on are completed. Both tasks and parallel constructs allow disabling of thread and task forks using the *if* clause. This allows, for example, recursive programs to stop creating too many fine-grained threads or tasks at the lower levels of the recursion tree, when each task becomes small enough to be processed sequentially. The overhead of creating too many tasks can impede speed-up.

As discussed above, OpenMP is designed for threads executing on a single node that share an address space. For a cluster of nodes, each with separate memory, OpenMP must be augmented by sharing of data across nodes. We discuss MPI next, which focuses primarily on the message-passing paradigm to share information across address spaces.

## 6.2   MPI

MPI is an interface for message-passing, and the de facto standard of the day for programs distributed across computing systems. MPI proposes a library-based implementation and does not add to the programming language itself. Just as many compilers support the OpenMP primitives, many library implementations of MPI exist, including for Java, Python, Fortran, and C/C++. We will examine a few important characteristics of message-passing in this section and see examples of message-passing primitives as well as the structure of programs that use them.

An MPI program can interact with any other MPI program if properly implemented. The other program needs to follow the standard and could use a different library and even a different language. The most common usage, however, is that several instances of the same program are started in their own processes, at multiple nodes in a cluster, and they interact with each other. This is the *SPMD* (single program, multiple data) style. It is not unusual for multiple processes to be started at one node, each running an instance of the same program. In such cases, employing one process per node with multiple threads occupying the different cores is often more efficient, even though MPI does facilitate memory sharing across processes on the same node. Both options complicate programming, however, as two separate layers of parallelism needs to be managed – the message-passing processors and the memory-sharing threads. In many cases, convenience trumps performance. We will later see an example of a programming platform, called *Chapel*, which better unifies the two.

As opposed to compiler-supported parallelization as in OpenMP, MPI entails somewhat lower-level structures. For example, a common template is:

```
forall process
      Read a section of the input
      iterate:
            Exchange additional data that is required
            Perform share of computation
            Collate and produce partial output
            barrier
      Collate and produce the final output
```

Let us next discuss specific components of MPI.

## MPI Send and Receive

MPI is process-centric; it allows processes to communicate. Of course, a process must be started before it can start to communicate. MPI implementations usually provide wrapper utilities like *mpiexec*, which can start these processes at any number of nodes. Any number of processes may execute on each participating node. All participating programs are required to call MPI_Init before starting to communicate and MPI_Finalize after no further MPI calls are needed. These calls are made once per process, even if the process employs multiple threads. MPI_Init is an opportunity for the library to initialize its data structures and ready the group of processes. MPI_Finalize allows the library to free unused memory. *MPI_Init_thread* must be called instead of MPI_Init if multiple threads are to be employed by a process. MPI uses an abstraction called *communicator* to refer to a group of communicating processes. The initial communicator is referred to by the constant *MPI_COMM_WORLD*. Once the programs start, new groups may be created and new communicators formed. MPI, like OpenMP, numbers the participating processes consecutively and the function *MPI_Comm_rank* returns the calling process's unique ID number in the context of a given communicator. This ID number is also called *rank*. Here is a bare skeleton MPI code:

**Listing 6.15** Basic MPI Snippet

```
MPI_Init(&argc, &argv); // MPI arguments are removed from argv
int numProcs, ID;
MPI_Comm_size (MPI_COMM_WORLD, &numProcs);// Number of processes in group
MPI_Comm_rank (MPI_COMM_WORLD, &ID);
// My ID
int vec[4] = {1, 2, 3, 4};
if(numProcs > 1) {
      if(ID == 1) {
            int destID = 0;
            int messagetag = 99;
            MPI_Send(vec, 4, MPI_INT, destID, messagetag, MPI_COMM_WORLD);
```

```
        // buffer, count, type, destination, tag, comm
    }
    if(ID == 0) {
        MPI_Status status;
        MPI_Recv(vec, 4, MPI_INT, MPI_ANY_SOURCE, MPI_ANY_TAG, MPI_COMM_WORLD,
            &status); // Return receipt information
        // buffer, count, type, source, tag, comm
    }
}
MPI_Finalize();
```

As a general rule, all MPI names are prefixed with *MPI_*. MPI functions return an integer code: *MPI_SUCCESS* on success, or an error code. We do not check the return values in our sample code for brevity.

Compare the *Send* and *Receive* functions to the primitives in Listing 4.14. A few additional arguments are used in the MPI functions. Notice the odd usage of the variable *vec*. It is used in both the send and receive. This is somewhat common with MPI programs. Remember, this program will be executed in separate processes, each with its own address space and, hence, its own instance of the variables. One process uses its memory allocated in vec as a send buffer, and another as receive buffer.

Instead of treating each buffer as a sequence of bytes, which is what network subsystems do, MPI allows the transfer of structured data. It defines base data types and allows user definition of derived data types, which may be used in its send/receive functions. This example passes four integers and employs the constant *MPI_INT*, which is a base type similar to "C" *int*. Indeed, the internal representation of an integer may be different on the recipient and the sender, but a well-defined MPI_INT is clearly interpreted on both ends.

The MPI communication functions apply to the specified communicator. In this case, the IDs *destID* and *MPI_ANY_SOURCE* refer to ranks with respect to the communicator MPI_COMM_WORLD. MPI_ANY_SOURCE is a special identifier to indicate that the recipient is willing to receive a message from any rank in the specified communicator. Further, a *tag* argument is included to allow messages to be classified into categories.

Given that each process may make multiple send and receive calls concurrently, a matching scheme is used to identify which send should pass its data to which receive. A send and a receive of a given communicator match if their IDs and tags match. In case of multiple possible match candidates, exactly one is selected. If two messages from the same sender and the same recipient match, the earlier send (in the sender's view) selects the earlier receive (in the recipient's view). MPI_ANY_SOURCE and MPI_ANY_TAG are wildcards that match any ID and any tag, respectively.

Note that the data types or size need not match. In fact, the recipient is free to reinterpret the data in terms of a different type; maybe, an array of four MPI_INTs in this case. The send's count parameter determines the actual size of the data to be sent. The receive's size argument indicates the maximum number of received data elements that would fit in its buffer. If the matching send passes more data than can fit, this is an error, which is reported in the *status* parameter of the receive call. The status indicates the actual number of data items received. It also includes the IDs and tags of the matched send, which may be initially unknown to the recipient if wildcard matching is used. See Listing 6.16, which is expanded from the example in Listing 6.15 for the recipient.

**Listing 6.16** MPI Receive Status

```
MPI_Status status;
MPI_Recv(vec, 4, MPI_INT, 1, 99, MPI_COMM_WORLD, &status);
int actualRecd;
MPI_Get_count(&status, MPI_INT, &actualRecd);
assert(actualRecd == 4);                        // We know 4 MPI_INTs were sent
assert(1 == status.MPI_SOURCE);// We know sender's rank: 1
assert(99 == status.MPI_TAG); // There was only one tag used
assert(MPI_SUCCESS == status.MPI_ERROR); // Better be
```

## Message-Passing Synchronization

We next turn to the synchronization implicit in the communication. As discussed in Section 4.5, because systems provide intermediate buffers, Send and Recv do not have to occur simultaneously, unless so mandated. Apart from asynchronous versions relying on buffers, MPI provides two variants of this synchronization:

1. *MPI_Ssend*: Synchronous send does not return until the matching receive has been called. This effectively provides a barrier. Synchronous send suffers from immediate synchronization overhead, and incurs a large latency.

2. *MPI_Rsend*: *Ready send* requires that the recipient is ready before the call to MPI_Rsend is made at the sender – possibly by employing additional synchronization. This allows the MPI implementation to bypass certain handshake initialization required for the synchrony. In principle, ready send can be more efficient than synchronous send, but not all MPI implementations exploit this possibility.

There is an explicit buffer based version called *MPI_Bsend*. MPI_Bsend uses buffers provided by the program before the send call. The functions MPI_Buffer_attach and MPI_Buffer_detach are available for buffer management. This allows the user to provide larger buffers than what MPI may allocate by default. If the buffer turns out to be insufficient to complete a MPI_Bsend, the send fails.

MPI_Send is a generic version of send, also called standard mode send. It is likely to incur lower latency than the other variants. It may employ the MPI's or OS's internal buffers, or wait for the receive to be called (and thus the receive buffer to become available). For example, it may eagerly send small messages but seek permission from the recipient before sending larger ones, allowing the recipient to provision buffers as required. MPI_Send does, in any case, guarantee that once it returns, the message has been extracted from the send buffer and is "on its way." This means that the sender is free to overwrite the send buffer any time after the return from MPI_Send, and the original message would still be received by a matching recipient. This property holds for all the four variants of Send. Hence, they are called blocking versions – the return is blocked until the send buffer can be saved.

There is only one MPI_Recv variant, as the synchronization semantics are driven by the sender. There also exist nonblocking variants for each of the four types of sends (and the one receive). These are, respectively, *MPI_Isend, MPI_Issend, MPI_Ibsend, MPI_Irsend*, and *MPI_Irecv*. These return immediately after a local setup, without guaranteeing any message progress. The sender may not modify the send buffer after these return, until a later assurance of buffer evacuation. Similarly, the recipient may not start to access the receive buffer after MPI_Irecv immediately after the call. It must wait for a later proof of receipt. These assurances and proofs are delivered via a *request* object, which is returned as a part of the send and receive calls, as follows:

```
MPI_Request request;
MPI_Irecv(vec, 4, MPI_INT, 1, 99, MPI_COMM_WORLD, &request);
// The recipient may proceed with code that does not require vec
MPI_Status status;
MPI_Wait(&request, &status);  // On return status has receipt info
// vec is ready to be used now.
```

MPI_Wait blocks in the code above until the receipt is complete, meaning that it follows the semantics of MPI_Recv – the blocking version of the operation that generated the request. Similarly, an MPI_Wait on a send request has the same semantics as the original blocking variant of send. In the following example, MPI_Wait has MPI_Ssend semantics: it does not return until the matching receive has been called. Like all versions of send, an MPI_Wait does not return until the values in the send buffer have been copied out and saved in an intermediate or the final buffer.

[1] *Defined*: Nonblocking communication, in addition to eliminating certain types of deadlocks (discussed later in this section), also allows processes to perform computation while waiting for communication to complete, as long as this computation is independent of the communication. This communication-computation overlap is an important technique to prevent long latency operations, as communication is, from creating idle periods and hence bottlenecks. This is called latency hiding and discussed further in Chapter 5.

```
MPI_Issend(vec, 4, MPI_INT, 0, 99, MPI_COMM_WORLD, &request);
// May not modify vec yet
MPI_Status status;
MPI_Wait(&request, &status); // returns after receive has been found
                 // AND data has been copied out; vec may be reused.
```

A side effect of the MPI_Wait call is that the request object is destroyed on completion. It cannot be and need not be waited upon again. There are other variants, like *MPI_Test*, which do not block but return with a flag indicating if the request is complete. This alternative supports busy-waiting, and requires that the request be explicitly destroyed using *MPI_Request_free*. There also exist convenience functions like *MPI_Wait_all*, *MPI_Wait_all*, and so on, that allow operation on an array of requests, in case many outstanding operations need to be completed. Generally, larger messages are more efficient to send than smaller ones, but buffer constraints or program logic can dictate that messages be subdivided and sent through multiple function calls. In such cases, the array-based wait or test functions can be useful.

If the message sizes vary significantly and dynamically, the recipient's pre-allocation of a large enough buffer to hold any sized message can be unreasonable. A peek at the incoming message allows the recipient to know what sized buffer to provision before actually reading the full message. There is a blocking variant, *MPI_Probe*, as well as a nonblocking one, *MPI_Iprobe*. They need to provide the source and tag information in order to perform the required matching. An example is shown below:

```
int flag;
MPI_Status status;
MPI_Probe(MPI_ANY_SOURCE, MPI_ANY_TAG, MPI_COMM_WORLD, &status)
int count;
MPI_Get_count(&status, MPI_INT, &count);
int *vec = allocateINTs(count);
MPI_Recv(vec, count, MPI_INT, status.MPI_SOURCE, status.MPI_TAG,
MPI_COMM_WORLD, MPI_STATUS_IGNORE);
performComputation(vec);
```

If *MPI_STATUS_IGNORE* is passed in the status parameter, no status information is returned. When a recipient uses a probe, the probe is matched with the send. A next matching receive by the *same* process is guaranteed to receive the message, whichever thread of the process the call may be made from. Note that the receive call includes the data's format. What if this is not known in advance? A recipient could determine the based on a probe of the incoming message, say, by using tag to specify the type. The recipient may receive using the appropriate type then.

Understand that sends and receives eventually require synchronization. Fairness is not guaranteed and deadlocks can occur. If, say, one receive matches two sends, either of those can be selected to provide its data. There is no guarantee that the unselected one would be selected at its next match. Latecoming matches could continually get selected ahead of it, causing that unselected match to starve. On the other hand, if two operations match, at least one of them is guaranteed to proceed. Apart from this, there is also a possibility of deadlock if the processes have both sends and receives. Both may depend on the other to complete, which neither may be able to do in the absence of intermediate buffers. For example, the following code could deadlock:

```
If (ID == 0) {
     MPI_Send(vec1, LargeCount, MPI_INT, 1, 99, MPI_COMM_WORLD);
     MPI_Recv(vec2, LargeCount, MPI_INT, 1, 99, MPI_COMM_WORLD, &status);
}
If (ID == 1) {
     MPI_Send(vec1, LargeCount, MPI_INT, 0, 99, MPI_COMM_WORLD);
     MPI_Recv(vec2, LargeCount, MPI_INT, 0, 99, MPI_COMM_WORLD, &status);
}
```

Both processes call MPI_Send first. It is possible neither can return because there is no buffer available to copy vec1 into. If either process could reach its MPI_Recv call, it would be able to provide the buffer into which the other process could transfer the data it sought to send. Since both processes wait for their sends to complete, MPI_Recv calls are not reached and receive buffers never become available. Even in cases where deadlock does not eventually occur, serialization could. For example, if A sends to B, and then receives from C – that receiving operation must wait until A can get past its send call, possibly blocking C's send until then. Nonblocking send and receive can ameliorate such a situation; the execution can proceed beyond the send even before its data is copied out, and reach the following receive.

## MPI Data Types

Data marshaling is an important component of message-passing. Each process normally maintains several data structure, a part of which it may need to share with a collaborating process. This part may or may not have a regular pattern in the sender's address space. Similarly, the recipient may also need to slot in the received data into various locations in its address space. On the other hand, the underlying communication is always in packets of contiguous bytes. This collation of data on the sender side from its data structures and then the distribution of incoming data into the recipient structure is a programming chore, and it would be a good idea for the programming platform to automate much of it.

The challenge here is to allow arbitrary data structures on the sender and programmer. This is somewhat easier for regular and semiregular data structures, which MPI facilitates. We will later see in Section 6.3 a more flexible approach, which supports irregular patterns better. Regardless, the programmer must not lose sight of the fact that this collation and distribution has a cost, even if it is performed by the platform. Programs with regular data structures that share large chunks of contiguous data are communication-friendly.

MPI allows defining of new types in terms of its built-in types and other user-defined types, in contiguous or noncontiguous arrangements. This allows specific noncontiguous parts of a buffer to be transferred and then stored noncontiguously at the recipient. We show a few illustrative examples.

**Listing 6.17** Derived Data Type: Array

```
MPI_Datatype intArray4;
MPI_Type_Contiguous(4, MPI_INT, &intArray4); // 4 contiguous ints
```

intArray4 in Listing 6.17 is the name given to four contiguous integers. Sending a single item of intArray4 type is equivalent to sending four items of MPI_INT type. A $100 \times 4$ matrix may be represented directly as 400 MPI_INTs in a row-major packing, or 100 intArray4 items; each intArray4 can be one row.

A column from a row-major 2D array is not contiguous, however. Sending an entire matrix just to share a column would take longer and would also require larger buffers. The entries in the column need to be collated and sent. These values would then be placed at appropriate entries at the destination. An example is shown in Figure 6.2. This operation is abstracted by noncontiguous data types, for example, MPI *vectors*, shown in Listing 6.18 – the sender collates and sends the last two columns of its matrix; the receiver distributes the arriving data into its first two columns.

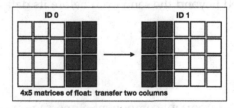

4x5 matrices of float: transfer two columns

**Figure 6.2** Transfer two columns

**Listing 6.18** MPI Data Type With Uniform Size and Stride

```
MPI_Datatype fColumn2x5;        // 4x, 2-float blocks, with stride 5
MPI_Type_Vector(4, 2, 5, MPI_FLOAT, &fColumn2x5 );
     // No. of blocks, No. of Items/block, block stride, type of items
MPI_Type_commit(&fColumn2x5);
If (ID == 0) // Matrix may be float*
```

```
    MPI_Send(&matrix[3], 1, fColumn2x5, 1, 99, MPI_COMM_WORLD);
If (ID == 1)
    MPI_Recv(matrix, 1, fColumn2x5, 0, 99, MPI_COMM_WORLD, &status);
```

MPI requires constructed types to be committed using *MPI_Type_Commit* before their use in data communication. This allows implementations to defer certain optimizations in the internal collation and distribution setup to final types and avoid it for the intermediate ones. In a linearized layout, vectors construct a data type with the following arrangement: $k$ blocks of $n$ items of the base type, with blocks separated by a gap of $m$ items each, implying a stride of $n + m$ items. The trailing "gap" at the end is not included in the type's definition (see Figure 6.3). This means that sending four elements of MPI_Type_Vector (1, 2, 5 ..) with $k = 1$, $n = 2$, and $n + m = 5$ is not the same as sending one element of type fColumn2x5, because the second (of four) element of MPI_Type_Vector(1, 2, 5 ..) starts right after the first two items, with no gap, as shown in Figure 6.4.

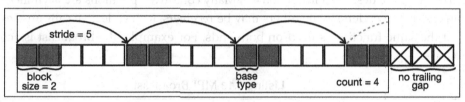

**Figure 6.3** MPI vector–type construction

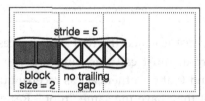

**Figure 6.4** Four contiguous elements of MPI_Type_Vector(1,2,5) delineated by dotted lines

There is a series of type constructors, with increasing flexibility, and also increasing complexity. The simplest type that suits the given requirement is likely to yield the best performance. The general constructor is *MPI_Type_create_struct*, which takes an array of types and their element counts, each of which can start at arbitrary offsets. In the following code, a new type tightly packs two ints, one float, and one fColumn2x5 (constructed earlier), leaving no gaps:

```
MPI_Datatype basetypes[] = {MPI_INT, MPI_FLOAT, fColumn2x5};
int blockCount[] = {2, 1, 1};
int byteOffset = {0, 0, 0};
for(int i=0; i<2; i++) {
```

```
    int typesize;
    MPI_Type_size(basetypes[i], &typesize);
    byteOffset[i+1] = byteOffset[i] + (blockCount[i] * typesize)
}
MPI_Datatype newtype;
MPI_Type_create_struct(3, blockCount, byteOffset, basetypes, &newtype);
// No. of blocks, No. of Items in blocks, start of blocks, type in blocks
```

The type constructors described earlier assemble old types to create new ones. The opposite, which subdivides composite types into smaller types, also exists, for example, *MPI_Type_create_subarray* and *MPI_Type_create_darray*.

## MPI Collective Communication

MPI also supports collective operations of the kind discussed in Section 4.5. Semantics are similar to those described in Section 4.5. Many collective operations are asymmetric – some ranks may be senders, while others may be receivers. MPI collective calls are designed so that the same function is used on both ends. For example, the broadcast is achieved as follows:

**Listing 6.19** MPI Broadcast

```
int root = 0;
MPI_Bcast(vec, 4, MPI_INT, root, MPI_COMM_WORLD); // All call
// sendbuffer, sendcount, sendtype, root, comm
```

The source of the broadcast is called the root – the process with rank 0 in this example. All members of the group must call this function. The buffer argument for the root acts as a send buffer, and that for others act as receive buffers. MPI_Bcasts on the same communicator match if they have the same "root." Recall that each process makes the MPI_Bcast call in its own address space. Not only do they provide their own buffers to the call, but they also indicate the data count and type. The two need not be the same in each member's call, but each member must expect the same total size of data. For example, some process may expect one data item of type intArray4 (as constructed in the previous section), while others expect four items of type MPI_INT.

MPI_Bcast is blocking, and care must be taken to avoid deadlocks. The following sequence may deadlock if, say, process A's first MPI_Bcast call matches process B's second call. and B's first call matches A's second call.

```
MPI_Bcast(vec, 4, MPI_INT, root1, comm1);
MPI_Bcast(vec, 4, MPI_INT, root2, comm2);
```

*MPI_Ibcast* is the nonblocking broadcast. That helps in the same manner non-blocking send and receive do. Other collectives also have nonblocking variants, but only blocking examples are provided in the listings here.

There is a difference of note between the noncollective nonblocking functions and the collective ones. The "blocking-ness" of a function is not considered in matching point-to-point primitives, but is considered for collective primitives. Nonblocking collective primitives only match other nonblocking collective primitives. Recall also that there is no tag in collective primitives to separate message streams. This means that collective primitives must be encountered in a consistent order across a group. In particular, for two consecutive collective primitives *A* and *B* encountered by a process for a communicator, all other processes in the group must encounter the one matching *B* after the one matching *A*, with *no other* collective primitive between them, blocking or nonblocking.

We demonstrate two collective primitives next. MPI_Gather is first. See Figure 6.5(d) for a pictorial illustration of this primitive. (Figure 6.5(a) illustrates broadcast, and Figure 6.5(c) illustrates scatter.)

**Listing 6.20** MPI Gather

```
int numProcs;
MPI_Comm_size (MPI_COMM_WORLD, &numProcs);
int allvecs[4*numProcs];
MPI_Gather(vec, 1, intArray4, allvecs, 4, MPI_INT, 0, MPI_COMM_WORLD);
    // send buffer, count & type; recv buffer, count & type; root; comm
```

The root in MPI_Gather (see Listing 6.20) is the gatherer. It gathers (i.e. receives) four MPI_INTs from each member of the group into allvecs. It must have enough space to accommodate them all. Every member, including the root, correspondingly sends vec, containing one intArray4 (defined in Listing 6.17), which carries four MPI_INTs. The receive buffer receives items in the order of rank. The ints sent by the process with rank *ID* is stored at the root starting at allvec[4 * *ID*]. Recall that the receive type and the send type can be different, for example, to allow four ints to be distributed into one column of a $4 \times 4$ row-major integer matrix on receipt.

MPI_Gather has separate parameters for the receiving type and the sending type to accommodate that the root is also a sender. On the other hand, if the root does not need its vec copied to its allvec, it may provide the constant *MPI_IN_PLACE* in place of vec in its call to MPI_Gather. Nonroots are not recipients, though. They may provide a NULL pointer for the receive buffer (allvec in this example). Their parameters for the receive type and the count are also unused.

If all processes require a copy of the gathered data, the root may broadcast it after gather. Or, they could all call *MPI_Allgather* instead of MPI_Gather, which can accomplish it more efficiently. Another variant, *MPI_Gatherv*, allows nonuniform gather: different senders may send different number of items. *MPI_Scatter* performs the reverse operation. *MPI_Alltoall*, as the name suggests, does both. It allows exchange from each process to each other process in one function. All processes scatter an array among the group and also gather from each member into an array. This effects a transpose of the distributed data in a way, as shown in Figure 6.5(b).

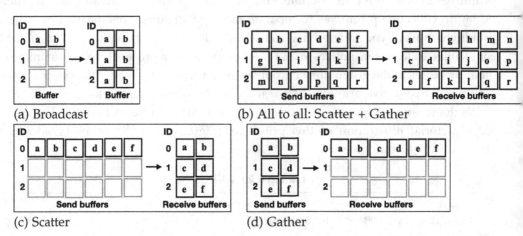

(a) Broadcast    (b) All to all: Scatter + Gather

(c) Scatter    (d) Gather

**Figure 6.5** Data broadcast gather and scatter

**Listing 6.21** All to All

```
const int sendcount = 2, recvcount = 2;
int vecin[sendcount*numProcs];
int vecout[sendcount*numProcs];
// Set values in vecout
MPI_Alltoall(vecout, sendcount, MPI_INT,
                              vecin, recvcount, MPI_INT, MPI_COMM_WORLD);
// send buffer, count & type; recv buffer, count & type; comm
```

In Listing 6.21, each sender distributes data from its send buffer, vecout, round-robin to the group, a block of sendcount items per recipient. Each recipient stores the received messages in the order of ranks of their sources. Like other collective communication, different processes may send different parameter values for type and count, but the total data sent must be equal to the total data received. MPI_Alltoall requires that all members have data to send in equal measure. If there are different sizes to send, *MPI_Alltoallv* or *MPI_Alltoallw* can be used. In these cases, the recipient may not immediately know where to store incoming data from process $i$ until it knows the sizes of data sent by all processes with ranks less than $i$. To remove this shortcoming, these functions also intake explicit starting location where each rank's data is stored in the receive buffer.

## MPI Barrier

All collective operations are semantically equivalent to a set of sends and receives, probably implemented in an optimized manner. Collective communication primitives do require that each member of the group call those functions. There is only loose synchronization – the calls do not need to overlap in time. Only the order among calls is enforced. For example, the root process for an MPI_Bcast call may return once its data is copied out. When the root returns, it has no guarantee that matching broadcasts, that is, matching receive events, have started. *MPI_Barrier* synchronizes. It has no arguments other than the communicator and applies to the communicator's group. A return from MPI_Barrier on any given process guarantees to it that matching MPI_Barrier function calls have been made on every other process.

```
// Perform partial computation and produce output
MPI_Barrier(MPI_COMM_WORLD);
// Next phase of computation
```

Odd as it may seem, there exists a nonblocking version of barrier as well MPI_Ibarrier. It is not actually a barrier, but a "notice" of barrier. Once MPI_Ibarrier on process $i$ is called, it is counted in. The corresponding wait function on that barrier's request is then the effective barrier. A successful return from MPI_Wait or MPI_Test implies that all processes have called MPI_Ibarrier. This separation of barrier into two steps can be useful to hide barrier latency. A late-arriving process blocks every other process in the group if a blocking barrier is used. With a nonblocking barrier, early-arriving processes can perform some independent computation in the interim, and perform post-barrier computation after MPI_Wait.

## MPI Reduction

Sometimes, partial computation is performed in parallel. Their results need to be combined. This may be done by gathering the partial results at one place, and then sequentially combining the partial results. However, recall from Section 3.2 that results could be combined in $O(\log n)$ steps in parallel, whereas the sequential combination takes $O(n)$ steps, to combine $n$ things. Similarly, collective operations can also be completed efficiently by using a binary tree structure. It makes sense then, that reduction can be completed like the gather. *MPI_Reduce* does that. Similarly, prefix-sum (see Sections 3.6 and 7.1) may also be performed efficiently in parallel using *MPI_Scan* and *MPI_Escan*.

```
// Perform partial computation and produce output
int root = 0;
// Compute partialSum
MPI_Reduce(partialSum, finalSum, 4, MPI_INT, MPI_SUM, root,
                                      MPI_COMM_WORLD);
    // send & recv buffers, number of reductions, datat type, operation ..
```

Any number of independent reductions may be performed together, if needed. This amortizes the overhead across multiple reductions. In the example above, four reductions are performed. Each process provides an array of four MPI_INTs. The first element of each array, at different processes, are reduced and the result stored in the first location of the receive buffer of the root. Similarly, the second, third, and fourth MPI_INTs are reduced and received in the corresponding slots in the root's receive buffer. *MPI_SUM* and several other constants refer to predefined operations. *MPI_SUM* implies addition. Users may define new operations – these are objects of type MPI_Op and encode binary operations, which must be associative. These operations are performed in parallel, but the rank order is preserved, that is, *rank0_data op rank1_data op rank2_data....* We will take an example below. Naturally, the operation must be well defined for the type of data, and the data type and count must be the same at all processes.

```
void reduceFunction(void *in1, void *in2_out, int *len,
                                      MPI_Datatype *type) {
// two input sequence, perform op per-item, leave result in 2nd array
        int left = (int*) in1, right = (int*) inout;
        for(int i=0; i<len; i++) {
                right[i] += left[i];
        }
}
MPI_Op myAdd;
int commute = 1; // Does my operation commute?
MPI_Op_create(reduceFunction, commute, &myAdd);
MPI_Reduce(partialSum, finalSum, 4, MPI_INT, myAdd, root,
                                      MPI_COMM_WORLD);
```

This illustration simply reimplements MPI_SUM. It expects the type of operands, which is passed in the MPI_Reduce call, to always be MPI_INT, and casts the pointers blindly. A more general function may do different things dynamically based on the specified type. The reduction function reduceFunction is written to perform multiple reduction operations at a time. This reduces the number of function calls, but note that the implementation of MPI_Reduce is not required to call reduceFunction on all four elements of partialSum and finalSum in a single call. Large vectors may be subdivided to overlap the reduction function with communication. Also, if the reduction operation is specified to be commutative, the MPI_Reduce implementation may switch the order of in and out buffers, that is, the rank order is not strictly preserved.

The reduction may be combined with other collectives. For example, *MPI_Allreduce* ensures that each member of the group receives the reduced data. Semantically, it is equivalent to reduction to a root followed by a broadcast. Similarly, *MPI_Reduce_scatter* scatters the reduced data among the group.

## One-Sided Communication

MPI also supports *one-sided communication*. It is one sided in the sense that there is no receive called by the program to match a send, or a send called by it to match a receive. This matching is effectively performed in the background by the MPI implementation, usually in a separate thread. As a result, in the user program's view, the send or receive does not even have a loose synchronization. Data in the address space of a recipient process gets modified asynchronously somewhat like shared memory programs. Similarly, another recipient may fetch data from a given process's address space asynchronously.

A natural question arises: How is the buffer management done? For example, if the recipient does not call the receive function, which buffer receives the data? This buffer ultimately is required to be in the recipient's address space. The solution is similar to a buffered send. This solution applies to both one-sided receive and one-sided send operations. A buffer is simply attached by each process to the collective *window*. Once attached, this block of its address space becomes *exposed* to other members of the group. It's a window through which any process in the group can "reach into" another process's address space – and read from it or write into it. This is known as *remote memory access*. The initiator of the operation is in charge of specifying the precise location within the exposed buffer, which is to be accessed through the window. The target, whose exposed part of the address space is accessed remotely, need not participate.

A group may create multiple windows, each process attaching a contiguous region of its address space to each window. Since the semantics of one-sided communication is different from the send–receive protocol, these are named differently: *put* to write into a remote address space and *get* to fetch from it. Listing 6.22 illustrates get and put.

**Listing 6.22** One-Sided Communication

```
1 MPI_Win win1;
2 MPI_Info info; // Provides hints to the MPI implementation. Unused here.
3 int *win1buffer;
4 // All members collectively create a window and attach a local buffer
```

```
 5 MPI_Win_allocate(numBytes, sizeof(int), info, MPI_COMM_WORLD,
 6          &win1buffer, &win1); // Allocate buffer, attach to window
 7      // buffer size, element size, info, comm, buffer pointer, window
 8 int sendable[4] = {0, 1, 2, 3};     // Private to this process's address space
 9 initializeBuffer(win1buffer); // The first integer will be used as a scale
10 MPI_Win_fence(0, win1); // Wait for all to initialize their win1buffer
11 int scale;
12 MPI_Get(&scale, 1,MPI_INT, (ID-1)%numProcs,0, 1,MPI_INT, win1); // Nonblock
13 // To buffer, to count, to type, from rank, from index, from count, from type, window
14 // Fetch into scale, one MPI_INT from previous rank
15 flag = 0;
16 MPI_Win_fence(flag, win1); // flag 0 implies no optimization
17 for(int i=1; i<SIZE; i++) {
18         sendable[i] *= scale;
19 }
20 MPI_Put(sendable, 4, MPI_INT, (ID+1)%numProcs, 1, 4, MPI_INT, win1);
21 // from buffer, from count, from type, to rank, to index, to count, to type, window
22 // More synchronization needed later to complete the put
```

The window is created at line 5 by allocating a block of address space at each process and attaching it to the window. This is a collective operation and all the matched MPI_Win_allocate calls expose their allocated buffers. All the blocks are associated with and are accessed through the returned MPI_Win variable at each process. Note that the buffer size need not be the same on all processes. It could be as low as 0 for some rank if there is no block to expose at that rank.

It is the responsibility of the user program to limit its access through a window to the sizes of the buffers exposed by other group members. Associating the element size with the exposed buffer facilitates the later use of array indexes directly as "addresses" into the window, as if structured arrays were exposed (e.g. see the index 1 on line 20). If the program needs to expose a preexisting buffer, MPI_Win_create may be used instead, but operations on buffers allocated through MPI_Win_allocate are often more efficient than those on buffers allocated using standard malloc routines. Both exposure methods require a static specification of the buffer. More dynamic attachment of buffer is also possible using MPI_Win_create_dynamic once followed by MPI_Win_attach and MPI_Win_detach any number of times.

In the listing above, line 12 on process $i$ asynchronously fetches the first element (which we know is an integer) from the window with the previous process $(i-1)$, modulo the group size. This fetched value, now in the variable scale, is used to scale all elements of the array sendable by all processes. This scaled sendable is next sent by every member of the group to the next process, $(i+1)$, modulo the group size, to be stored starting at offset 1, meaning the four integers are put at indexes 1 to 4 of the array win1buffer. Since there is no data race between the get and the put, no synchronization should be required between them.

Nonetheless, remote memory access functions are nonblocking. Since the get in line 12 is nonblocking, the variable scale may not actually have received the data until much after this line. MPI_Win_fence in line 16 ensures that the data is indeed available in the variable scale before it is used in line 18. Similarly, a return from put does not immediately mean that the data has been saved in the remote buffer. Like OpenMP, synchronization (e.g. by using a fence) ensures that the outstanding get and put operations are completed. Different from two-sided communication, one-sided communication functions do not use the "I" in their name to indicate nonblockingness because there is no blocking variant. There is no request argument, however, that could be later used to query about the completion of the get or put. Those variants do exist, and they use the letter "R" instead of "I" to indicate the request argument: MPI_Rput and MPI_Rget. The "R" variants also return the request object, which may later be queried using an MPI_Test or waited on using MPI_wait.

```
MPI_Rput(sendable, 4, MPI_INT, target, 1, 4, MPI_INT, win1, &request);
// No overwriting sendable here
MPI_Wait(&request, &status);
// sendable is 'free' to use
```

One-sided communication is similar to shared-memory programs: process $i$ may have a view of process $j$'s exposed address space that differs from the view of other processes of that same address space. Local caching is allowed. User-controlled synchronization is required to maintain consistency. This synchronization may be in the form of group-wide memory fence (as in the previous example), pair-wise synchronization, or locks on the target process's window.

Group-wide memory fences are similar to shared-memory fences and ensure that any earlier get and put operations on a window are completed and ordered before operations that appear after the fence. The flag parameter of the fence primitive is for the program to send hints that help improve the performance in certain cases. For example, the program may indicate that there is no put event between this fence and the subsequent one by specifying the flag MPI_MODE_NOPUT. Such hints allow the MPI implementation to forego certain synchronization steps. In all cases, outstanding get and put calls at a process complete before the fence returns on that process. In particular, an outstanding put must complete at the initiator before its fence returns, allowing it to reuse its buffer, but it may not have been written at the target yet. The matching fence on the target returns after the operation has completed there.

Synchronization may also be performed in smaller groups, particularly between a single initiator of one-sided communication and its target, using a protocol involving four events: *post, start, wait,* and *complete*. The corresponding functions are *MPI_Win_post*, *MPI_Win_start, MPI_Win_wait*, and *MPI_Win_Complete*. The initiator's post matches with the target's start. This handshake forms a mutual fence. Subsequent get or put events by the initiator are strictly ordered after these fences. Later, the initiator's complete matches the target's wait, marking the completion of all gets and puts since the poststart handshake. This is demonstrated in Figure 6.6. The target's local read from its exposed buffer, after a

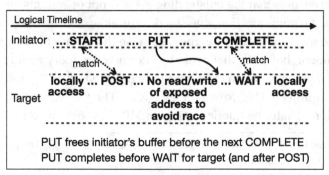

**Figure 6.6** Post, Start, Complete, and Wait synchronization

return from its wait, is guaranteed to observe the value put by the initiator between its matching start and complete. Similarly, the values that the target writes into its exposed buffer before it posts are guaranteed to be ready for the initiator to get between its start and complete. Unsurprisingly, MPI_Win_wait is blocking. The nonblocking variant MPI_Win_test also exists. On the initiator side, a return from MPI_Win_complete indicates that the buffer may be reused in case of a put, and the data has arrived in case of a get. Group-wide fences are often simpler to use than this four-event protocol, but also less efficient, particularly when no fence flag applies.

Lastly, MPI supports lock-based synchronization. This is mostly like shared-memory synchronization in that the lock is with respect to a window and can be controlled exclusively by the initiator; there is no event required on the target side, like a post, or a group-wide fence. An example is shown below. This is a coarse-grained lock – the entire exposed buffer on the given rank is locked at once. *MPI_Win_lock_all* locks all the ranks at once.

```
int flag = 0;
MPI_Win_lock(MPI_LOCK_EXCLUSIVE, targetRank, flag, win1);
          // lock_type, rank, flag, window
MPI_Put(sendable, 4, MPI_INT, targetRank, 1, 4, MPI_INT, win1);
MPI_Win_unlock(targetRank, win1);
```

When a full lock is not required, the *flush* primitive is also available. *MPI_Win_flush* does not return until the outstanding get and put for the corresponding window and rank return. Note that locking also implies a flush: at MPI_Win_lock all outstanding get and put are flushed.

```
MPI_Put(sendable, 4, MPI_INT, targetRank, 1, 4, MPI_INT, win1);
MPI_Win_flush(targetRank, win1);
```

Remote access is not just limited to get and put. As on other shared-memory platforms, read-modify-write operations are supported. For example, *MPI_Accumulate* operates (using MPI_Op) on a variable visible remotely through a window. This merges three messages – one requesting the data, another returning the original value, and the last to write back the updated value – into as few as one, reducing the latency significantly. Furthermore, *MPI_Accumulate* by two different processes through the same window to the same location exposed by a third process are serialized, meaning that the accumulation appears atomic with respect to competing accumulation primitives. Even so, accumulation does not implicitly cause a flush, unlike OpenMP. An explicit MPI_Win_flush or another synchronization method may be needed.

*MPI_Compare_and_swap* is also available as a special type of accumulation, which may be used to implement higher level or more fine-grained synchronization than the window-level locking of MPI_Win_lock. See Listing 6.23 for an example.

**Listing 6.23** MPI Compare and Swap

```
do {
        int oldval, expected = -1;
        // If Int at Index 1 on target's window == -1, write my ID, capture old value
        MPI_Compare_and_swap(&ID, &expected, &oldval, MPI_INT, target, 1, win1);
            // data, expected, old, type, target, index, window
        MPI_Win_flush(target, win1);
} while(oldval != expected)
// Limited to one item of certain types. There is no count parameter.
```

## MPI File IO

Any large parallel program is likely to read large input and write large output. Parallel file systems allow multiple clients to read and write simultaneously. It stands to reason, then, that MPI processes may benefit from reading and writing data in parallel. In principle, the storage may be considered akin to a process, which could broadcast, scatter, or gather data. MPI does not provide such interfaces. Instead, it supports a lower-level interface.

MPI allows processes to see a file as a sequence of structured data, that is, MPI_Datatype. The type that the file consists of is called its *etype*, short for elementary type. The file is effectively treated as an array of etypes.

Collective IO on this file provides an opportunity for parallel file access. Each process has its own view of a file. Although less common, it is possible for different processes to view the same file as an array of different etypes. MPI allows one level of indirection over etypes, meaning a process may, in fact, view a file as an array of *filetype*, which is an MPI_Datatype built from etype. The idea is to allow an arbitrary division of data between processes, and not only uniform interleaving or blocking of etypes across processes. The filetype would typically have holes to skip data relevant only to other processes. In addition to the filetype (and etype), the beginning of the data in the file is also a part of a process's individual view of the file. This beginning is specified as a byte-offset from the beginning of the file. This offset is not in terms of etype to allow an arbitrary length header that many files have.

Figure 6.7 shows a uniform interleaving. In this case, the filetype for all processes is the same; only their starting points are offset.

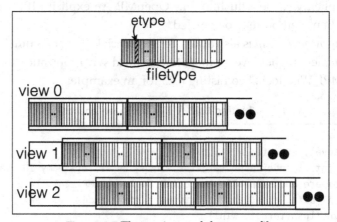

**Figure 6.7** Three views of the same file

Listing 6.24 illustrates a simple interleaved writing into a file – each process writes a section of the file.

**Listing 6.24** MPI IO

```
1 int byteBlock = 1024*sizeof(int);
2 int lower=0, extent=numProc*byteBlock;
3 MPI_Datatype filetype, int1K;
4 MPI_Type_contiguous(1024, MPI_INT, &int1K);
5 MPI_Type_create_resized(int1K, lower, extent, &filetype);
6        // Resize to artificially create holes
```

```
 7 MPI_Type_commit(&filetype);
 8
 9 MPI_File fh;
10 MPI_File_open(MPI_COMM_WORLD, filename, MPI_MODE_RDWR, MPI_INFO_NULL, &fh);
11       // Com, file name, access mode, implementation hint, file handle
12 MPI_File_set_view(fh, rank*byteBlock, MPI_INT, filetype, "native", MPI_INFO_NULL);
13       // file handle, start, etype, filetype, data rep, hint
14 MPI_File_write(fh, buf, 2*1024, MPI_INT, MPI_STATUS_IGNORE);
15 MPI_File_close(&fh);
```

All views use the same filetype on line 12 but different starting positions. *Native* data representation assumes that the byte layout in the file is the same as the byte layout in memory. If this is not the case, *external32* is more appropriate, which allows conversion between a platform-independent data layout and each process's memory layout. The *MPI_Info* type is a dictionary: a set of key-value pairs, which allows programs to pass on hints to the implementation. These hints are generally implementation dependent, and if no hints are useful, the constant *MPI_INFO_NULL* may be used. *MPI_File_open* and *MPI_File_set_view* are both collective. Each process on the communicator must open the same file in the same mode, but the info parameter may vary. The views are designed to be different across the group, but all processes must use identical data representation in their views, and their etypes must have the same size.

In Listing 6.24, each process reads 2,048 integers: two 1K blocks, based on its view. The view consists of blocks of 1,024 ints separated by the blocks of other processes. The starting point of the file is also offset according to the rank. In reading and writing (and seeking), the holes in the view are skipped. For example, if a process were to read 1,028 integers, its file handle would point to the fifth integer of the second block in its view, meaning the next read would continue from that point. Each process's file pointer is independent of other processes', and proceeds according to that process's reads or writes. MPI also supports global file pointers, that is, shared file pointers: one process's read advances the shared file pointer for everyone.

File read and write are analogous to receive and send. Unlike file open and set view, MPI_File_read and MPI_File_write are not collectives. Collective versions do exist: *MPI_File_read_all* and *MPI_File_write_all*. These allow the system to efficiently perform combined and parallel IO on behalf of multiple processors. The file access is sequentially consistent in this case. With separate file pointers, consistency can be demanded through the use of function *MPI_File_set_atomicity*, albeit at the cost of performance. The traditional weak consistency through the collective *MPI_File_sync* is also supported. IO completion does not cross sync boundaries, and syncs are seen in the same order by all processes. File open and close are sequentially consistent by default.

The IO primitives in Listing 6.24 are all blocking. Nonblocking IO is similar to nonblocking send/recv and is accessed through functions like *MPI_File_iwrite* and *MPI_File_iread*.

## MPI Groups and Communicators

A parallel programming platform naturally requires means to create parallelism: thread and processes, for example. So far, we have discussed only a rigid way to do so in MPI. An external tool like *mpiexec* creates a certain number of processes, all of which start with MPI_Init. In many situations, a more dynamic management of the degree of parallelism is required. Some parts of the program require more parallelism than others. There may also be a need to manage a task graph or to organize the processes into a hierarchy that allows them to perform multiple actions in parallel, each of which itself may be subdivided into other parallel activities.

We have seen how to create a single group of processes with a single communicator, using which they communicate. In this simple world, each process is identified by only its rank. MPI generalizes this to allow multiple, possibly overlapping, groups to exist. A process has a rank with respect to each group of which it is a member. To facilitate this, MPI defines an opaque type *MPI_Group*. Initially, a single group is associated with a single communicator MPI_COMM_WORLD. Set-like operations, like *MPI_Group_union*, are then used to create new groups from existing ones and to establish new communicators. Group creation is a local operation, and is done only on a per-process basis – the newly created group is known only on the creator. Here is an example:

```
MPI_Group allGrp, first3Grp;
MPI_Comm first3Com;
int incl_ranks[] = {0, 2, 4}; // Assume at least 5 members in MPI_WORLD_COMM.
MPI_Comm_group(MPI_WORLD_COMM, &allGrp);
MPI_Group_incl(allGrp, 3, incl_ranks, &first3Grp);
MPI_Comm_create(MPI_WORLD_COMM, first3Grp, &first3Com);
```

In this example, each member of the group of MPI_WORLD_COMM creates a new group. These groups' memberships coincide – ranks 0, 2, and 4 with respect to group allGrp. These members will have ranks 0, 1, and 2, respectively in each instance of first3Grp. Members of a group are always ranked. For new groups, these ranks are created by maintaining an order consistent with the constituent groups. For example, in case of union, the members of the first group are ordered before that of the second. For intersection, the ranks of the first group are inherited.

*MPI_Comm_create* in the listing above creates a communicator *first3Com*. Communication can then occur within the context of first3Com, which will involve members of the group *first3Grp*. Not all communicators have a single group. Communication may also be from one group to another. Such intergroup communicators, called intercommunicators, are particularly useful for client–server style work subdivision.

Group creation is a local activity. Each process may define its own groups. However, members of the group that may communicate on a communicator must all take cognizance. Communicator creation is a group-wide collective. All MPI_WORLD_COMM participants in the example above must call MPI_Comm_create. Their groups need not be identical, but each needs to be a subset of the group corresponding to the original communicator. In particular, different subsets of the original group may create their own communicators. For consistency, it is important that in

```
MPI_Comm_create(oldComm, newgroup, &newComm);
```

1. All processes of oldComm call MPI_Comm_create.
2. A process may specify an empty group.
3. If a process with rank $p$ on *oldComm* has rank $q$ in its *newgroup*, process $q$'s *newgroup* must be identical to $p$'s. This effectively divides the original group into disjoint subgroups.

It is not necessary to subdivide a communicator by first forming subgroups, and then creating new communicators for each subgroup. *MPI_Comm_split* can directly subdivide a communicator. Both are collective over the entire oldComm, which can be inefficient for large groups. If instead of subdividing the entire group into subgroups, only a few small subgroups need to be spun off; *MPI_Comm_create_group* is more efficient – it is collective with respect to only the new communicator. If $p$'s newgroup includes $q$, $q$ must also call MPI_Comm_create_group along with $p$.

## MPI Dynamic Parallelism

Instead of reorganizing already existing processes, MPI also supports dynamic creation of processes. *MPI_Comm_spawn* is a collective that creates children processes, but a single member of the parent group—the root—determines the spawn parameters. Other members must still call MPI_Comm_spawn to receive the handle to the intercommunicator, using which they may communicate with the child group.

```
int root = 0;
MPI_Info info;
MPI_Comm child_com;
int spawnerrors[numPROC];
MPI_Comm_spawn(command, argv, numPROC, info, root
          MPI_COMM_WORLD, &child_com, spawnerrors);
```

The location of the children processes is driven by the info argument and by the runtime environment, which generally uses a mechanism similar to the wrapper utility to start processes on various nodes. The children processes belong to a new group also called, somewhat confusingly, MPI_COMM_WORLD, but this is to unify the interface for starting groups of processes. For a given process, there is a unique MPI_COMM_WORLD, which consists of its siblings: the processes created along with it. This means that an executable may be run by a process started by an mpiexec-type tool or by MPI_Comm_spawn. If the program needs to know how it was launched, *MPI_Comm_get_parent* may be used:

```
MPI_Init(&argc, &argv);
MPI_Comm parent_com;
MPI_Comm_get_parent(&parent_com);
if (parent == MPI_COMM_NULL) {
    // This is a top level process
} // else, parent_com is the inter-communicator to the parent group.
// MPI_Comm_Spawn in the parents returns the same inter-communicator
```

The MPI_Init calls in the children processes and the MPI_Comm_spawn in the parents together form a collective primitive. All children must call MPI_Init before starting to communicate. The children's MPI_Init is necessarily later than the MPI_Init of the parent group. MPI_Finalize, on the other hand, is global. Every process must complete all outstanding MPI communications with every other process before its MPI_Finalize.

## MPI Process Topology

Point-to-point, and even collective, communication is somewhat low level. The program must keep track of explicit ranks to communicate. Sometimes it is easier to communicate directly in terms of data relationships. For example, if an $n \times n$ matrix is divided into $m \times m$ blocks and distributed block-wise among processors, one might want to receive the left-most columns from the right block, or the right-most columns from the left block (as shown in Figure 6.8). The basic idea is that instead of the program explicitly keeping track of neighbor process IDs, the MPI does it. Initially, the program defines the topology in terms of process IDs. Later, communication can refer to the so-created neighbors. The idea is to organize processes according to simple domain decomposition.

This is particularly useful for collective operations. A process can gather from or scatter to its neighbors, for example. Point-to-point communication is still in terms of rank IDs. However, query functions that return the IDs of the neighbors exist. Once the IDs of neighbors are known, standard send and recv can proceed as before.

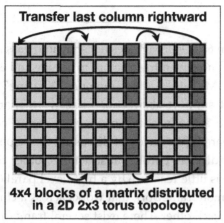

**Transfer last column rightward**

**4x4 blocks of a matrix distributed in a 2D 2x3 torus topology**

**Figure 6.8** Transfer according to process topology

MPI defines two types of topologies: *d*-dimensional grid and a general graph. The following listing imposes a 2D grid topology, using *MPI_Cart_create*, a collective primitive. All processes of a communicator must call this function with the same parameter values. Grids can wrap around in torus configuration, using the *periodic* Boolean flag, specified separately for each dimension. The topology creation functions return a new communicator, with which the new topology is associated. For optimization of the communication, MPI implementation may renumber the processes, providing a new ID in the new communicator, unless the caller requests that the processes retain their ranks.

**Listing 6.25** MPI Processes in a Grid Topology

```
int ID0;
MPI_Comm_rank(MPI_COMM_WORLD, &ID0);
MPI_Communicator newcomm;
int mxm = {m, m}, periodic = {true, true}, rerank = true;
MPI_Cart_create(MPI_COMM_WORLD, 2, mxm, periodic, rerank, &newcomm);
        // initial comm, dimension, Wrap-around?, rank rename?, new comm
int recv[4];
MPI_Neighbor_allgather(&ID0, 1, MPI_INT, recv, 4, MPI_INT, newcomm);
```

After Listing 6.25 creates the 2D torus, it performs a gather, so that each process receives the old IDs (i.e. the rank in the old communicator) of its four neighbors. Of course, the neighbors' new ranks can be directly given by a topology query function – *MPI_Cart_shift* in this case.

## 6.3   Chapel

As described in Section 6.2, OpenMP does not stray into passing messages explicitly to other threads, nor does it include the infrastructure to occupy and execute on multiple computing systems in a cluster. MPI does allow memory "sharing" across threads – processors really – but does not support abstractions like work sharing. It does allow processes on the same node to actually share memory in some cases, for example, by using MPI_Win_allocate_shared. (We have not discussed this aspect in Section 6.2).

Nonetheless, it hardly has parallel abstractions, other than the notion that multiple processes exist. There is little reason why a high-level parallel abstraction cannot be better integrated into a common framework that works across a cluster of nodes, each with cores sharing memory with each other. There exist several frameworks that do precisely that. We will discuss one briefly. It is called Chapel.[1]

### Partitioned Global Address Space

We begin by considering how Chapel extends the shared-memory programming style to a cluster of computing systems. Chapel is a language designed ab initio for task-based parallel programming.

Unlike MPI, a code distributor is not required to start copies of a Chapel program at multiple nodes, that is, *locales*. Rather, like sequential programs, Chapel executables start at the *main()* entry point, and then forks tasks to other locales as demanded by the program. Like MPI, these locales are set up by providing an argument when the execution begins. These locales are referred symbolically as an array *Locales* in the source code. Tasks are assigned to locales for execution.

Chapel also provides the illusion of a single monolithic address space across multiple processes and nodes. The actual data remains distributed among nodes under a layer of abstraction called *Partitioned Global Address Space* (PGAS, for short). The PGAS abstraction maps certain addresses to the local memory, or the given process's address space, and certain others to a different process's address space. Language support is required to do this seamlessly. Traditional languages only map variable names to local addresses. Library-based PGAS tools also exist; they provide function-based access to nonlocal memory like MPI does.

The Chapel compiler includes runtime support, so that message-passing code is automatically generated on behalf of the program, relieving the programmer from the

---

[1] Chamberlain et al., "Parallel programmability."
Burke, "Chapel."
Chapel, "The chapel parallel programming language."

nitty-gritty of message collation and communication. Chapel includes an inherent notion of *domains* – a set of indexes. Data arrays and structures are organized into domains. The following example declares an $n \times n$ 2D domain; assume $n$ is declared earlier as an integer. (0..#n indicates a range from 0 to $n - 1$, both inclusive.)

```
const TwoD = {0..#n, 0..#n}; // An nxn 2D domain
```

Additionally, locations are abstracted as *locales*, which contain native memory. It can be memory local to a node, or local to a central processing unit (CPU) slot on a nonuniform memory access (NUMA) node. Finally, a *domain map* maps or distributes domains to locales. This structure allows the program to be aware of the affinity between data in the same locale, and allows it to reduce cross-locale interaction, and thus data communication, without worrying about the actual data location or communication. Although programs can define complex and irregular mapping, some regular ones are built-in.

```
const TwoD = {0..#n, 0..#n}          // Constant declaration, 2D domain
                      dmapped BlockCyclic(startIdx=(0,0), blocksize=(8,8));
var distributedA: [TwoD] int; // Variable declaration, 2D array
```

The above listing, for example, declares a 2D domain along with its mapping. *BlockCyclic* is a built-in dmap distribution of a chosen block size. In this example, $8 \times 8$ blocks are distributed in a block cyclic fashion, round-robin to all available locales, starting at index $(0,0)$. The illustration on the right shows this for $n = 24$ and $numLocales = 4$. (numLocales is a built-in variable containing the number of locales in the current execution.) One may subsequently query the location of an

24x24
8x8

| locale | | |
|---|---|---|
| 0 | 1 | 2 |
| 3 | 0 | 1 |
| 2 | 3 | 0 |

index using distributedA[i][j].locale. There are other built-in distributions, analogous to MPI data types. Similarly, gather and scatter can be effected by reading from and writing to appropriate locations in the array distributed across locales. Separate from dmaps, scope-based allocation of variables on a certain locale is also supported. Before we take an example of that type, some understanding of the execution model is required. We discuss this first.

## Chapel Tasks

Chapel's syntax differs somewhat from C/C++. (Parts of it are similar to Python.) A study of Chapel's documentation would be required for readers trying to use Chapel. The goal of this section, apart from introducing the notion of PGAS, is to get a taste of a parallel programming language that seeks to let the programmer focus mainly on algorithm design and not on the low-level bookkeeping – hopefully, with little loss of performance. Some details about Chapel first (compare these to OpenMP):

1. Chapel uses a task-based model. Tasks can be forked off using the keyword *begin*. The forker may choose to wait for the forked task to complete or proceed asynchronously.

2. The *on* keyword is used to declare variables with its scope limited to a different locale, and to execute tasks on different locales. The location of tasks or variables are specified independently of each other. This lends significant flexibility to programs.

3. Work-sharing constructs exist, for example, *forall* and *coforall* loops.

4. Variables can be designated to be *synchronizing* variables or *atomic* variables, which allow certain synchronized operations. Furthermore, these operations act as memory fences, as regular accesses are not otherwise guaranteed to be sequentially consistent.

5. Variables (and constants) have static types, but they can be inferred and need not always be declared.

The task forker uses the keyword *sync* to wait for its tasks (and their nested tasks). We demonstrate the tasking, sync, and locales capabilities in the example below. The following code sequentially dequeues tasks from a queue, creating a task per item to be executed at one of the available locales. Compare Listing 6.26 to Listings 6.13 and 6.14, which accomplishes similar results with OpenMP.

**Listing 6.26** Task Queue Processing in Chapel

```
var loc = 0;
sync {
      while((taski = taskQ.dequeue()) != nil) {// Process next item on the queue
            begin { on Locales[loc] workOnTask(taski); } // Create task on a locale
            loc = (loc + 1)%numLocales     // Distribute Round-robin
      }
} // sync implies: wait for all tasks generated in the block
```

workOnTask is shown below. It does not specify a locale and forks a local task to enqueue the result – meaning it would be assigned to one of the local threads. The task proceeds asynchronously.

```
proc workOnTask(taski) // proc indicates a function. Types are inferred.
{
      var result = processTask(taski);
      begin resultQ.ATOMICenqueue(result); // Task on the same locale & Continue
      if(analyzeResult(result) == EUREKA) then { // If result is special, shout
```

```
            consoleOutput(result);
    }
}
```

There is no explicit thread management, other than instructing the Chapel runtime environment to use a certain number of threads. Local tasks are assigned to these threads, similar to OpenMP. Unlike OpenMP, there is no critical section construct. Hence, the queue must be synchronized separately using the function qvar.compareExchange, where qvar is an atomic variable, as shown below. All locales participating in the execution can see the same resultQ and the same qvar. (See the variable scoping illustration provided later.) This may not be efficient of course, and an aware program would try to reduce such implicit communication.

```
// Initialization
var qvar: atomic bool;
qvar.write(false); // Atomic variables cannot be directly assigned.

// Use
while(! qvar.compareExchange(false, true)); // Set to true, if false
do_criticalSection();
qvar.write(false);
```

## Chapel Variable Scope

Chapel does not include explicit private and shared variable designation. Other than the explicit location using domain dmaps described earlier, the location and scope of variable can also be implicit.

```
1 const OneD = {0..#n} dmapped BlockCyclic(startIdx=(0), blocksize=(8));
2 var distA: [D] int;              // Distributed array
3 on Locales[1] {                  // Codeblock for Locales[1]
4       var second = 2;            // This variable is on Locales[1]
5                       // The following loop executes on Locales[1]
6     coforall loc in Locales { // Create concurrent tasks, 1 per iteration
7           on loc {                      // On Locales[loc]
8               var local = distA[0] + distA[here.id*8] + second; // Fetch non-local
9           }
10      } // An implicit join with children tasks here.
11 }
12 on distA[local] do {computeSomething();} // Compute wherever the data is
```

In the listing above, a distributed array is declared initially. It is distributed in blocks of eight ints to all locales cyclically. The *on* primitive in line 3 sets the scope of its block as Locales[1]. The construction of variable *second* and the execution of *coforall* in line 6 happens at that location. The nested *on* primitive in line 7 requests one instance of task on each location, each executing line 8. The runtime fetches the variable values for *distA[0]* from location 0 and *second* from location 1 to compute the variable *local*. *distA[here.id\*8]* is guaranteed to be locally available at each location because of the blockcyclic distribution. *here* is a built-in variable referring to the current locale.

This method can simplify programming significantly, although possibly at the cost of performance. If it is aware of the location, a program can ensure that such remote accesses are rare. Note line 12, where the on primitive refers to a data item, not a locale. This allows the programmer to send some computation to whichever locale contains a given variable. This *on* primitive is encountered by whichever task started this code snippet – maybe, Locales[0], where the program execution might begin. Where it executes depends on the value of *local* at that location.

Sometimes, compilers can derive parallelization from a sequential program. Such efforts by themselves have proven to be insufficient in many cases. As argued in this book (see Introduction and Chapter 7 for example), the structure of parallel algorithms can be significantly different from that of sequential algorithms. While some predetermined sequential patterns can be converted into an efficient parallel program, it remains impractical in general. Chapel does not set out to derive such parallelism, but rather allows the programmer to devise the parallelism and then express it at a high level. It still has some way to go before its runtime is as efficient as hand-tuned MPI applications in communication. Not all of its main features have been included in this section. For example, it does have equivalents of reduction, single, barrier, and other synchronization primitives. It also has modern programming language features like iterators, zippering of iterations, promotion of functions from scalars to vectors, and so on.

## 6.4   Map-Reduce

OpenMP, MPI, and Chapel were all designed primarily with compute-intensive workloads in mind. They focus on ways for the program to distribute arbitrary computation. In contrast, the map-reduce paradigm was designed with more data-centered computation in mind. This paradigm focuses on the distribution and collation of data with a small number of primitives: *map* and *reduce*.

Map-reduce is built around the idea of large-scale data-parallel computation, where each data item is operated upon. This is the map operation. For generality, the map primitive is not one-in one-out – it may also generate data items. The program is nothing but a map function such that *map(item)* → *{item set}*. By itself, the map paradigm is quite limited; it is suitable only for purely data-parallel solutions. In data analysis, statistical properties of the data items are usually required. These are often computed used reduction. That forms the second step of the map-reduce paradigm. The program includes a reduce function such that *reduce({item set})* → *item*. The final item is the result.

Admittedly, mapping each data item and then reducing the entire map output is still restrictive. Analysis often requires classification and categorization of data, with sub-statistics about each class, possibly in addition to interclass statistics. Map-reduce allows this by imposing a structure on the data item: each item is a <key-value> pair. The key may be of any type that allows different keys to be distinguished. Additionally, keys should also be comparable, so that they may be sorted by the map-reduce framework. The value may be of any type. Values contain payloads that only the application program needs to analyze. Now we may define the map and reduce operations more comprehensively.

$$Map(K, V) \rightarrow list(K_i, V_i)$$

$$Reduce(K, list(V_i)) \rightarrow (K, list(V_j))$$

*Map* and *Reduce* are functions with fixed input and output patterns and user-provided implementation. Given a single <key-value> pair, the Map function generates a list of <key-value> pairs. This list is allowed to be empty. The keys in this list may be the same as the input keys, or different from them. For example, from a purchase history table, a list of <item, price> for all electronic goods may be produced. The framework collects all values with a common key and calls the program's Reduce function on these values. This Reduce function need not always produce a single reduced value. Like Map, it can produce a list of them. This may be thought of as Reduce performing multiple reductions. For example, it may produce the total, the average, and the variance of the prices associated with each electronic item $K$.

Given the two primitives, a rather complex analysis can be done by chaining together a series of map-reduce operations.

## Parallel Implementation

Map-reduce is a high-level programming model. The program needs no reference to hosts, locations, processes, or threads. While one can implement general solutions using map-reduce, it works best where underlying operations are naturally similar to map and reduce. The programmer does not need to provide parallel constructs as the parallelism is built into the map and reduce primitives. The input is expected to be a set of <key-value> pairs, with a Map operation to be performed on each. All these maps are independent of each other and may be performed in parallel. The results of the map have to be sorted by the Keys. Sorting, as we will see in Chapter 7, parallelizes well. Once the values are sorted into bins, one bin per key, different bins may be reduced in parallel. Thus the Map and Reduce functions need to be merely sequential. The parallelism comes from having a large number of map and reduce operations.

Since the parallelism is built into the framework itself, it is useful to consider the steps required:

1.  Set up the processes on all available nodes

2.  Locate and split the input list into batches. The input list is usually dispersed among multiple files.

3.  Assign the batches to a subset of the processes (call them *Mappers*) to execute Map on each <key-value> pair in the batch.

4.  Assign each unique key produced by Mappers to *Reducers*, the processes that execute the Reduce for each key, and "shuffle" the corresponding values to each Reducer from the Mappers.

5.  Let Reducers execute the Reduce function.

6.  Collate the lists produced by each Reducer. Generally, this is written to a file in a sorted order of Reducers' keys.

These steps can be executed in a pipelined fashion. A Reducer may begin to fetch the values for its assigned key before all mappers complete. This allows computation-communication overlap. The Reduce function is called only after all the values of a key are available, meaning all mappers must have completed (as any mapper may generate any key). In principle, certain types of reductions can also be performed incrementally.

Many programming platforms support map-reduce style computation and other associated utilities, including distributed file systems, job scheduling, structured data stores, machine learning frameworks, and so on. We will limit our discussion next to the basic map-reduce program structure as implemented in the Hadoop framework.[2] Hadoop is a library-based utility widely available with Java as the base language.

## Hadoop

Hadoop uses a distributed-memory setting and employs a distributed file system *HDFS* for input and output. The communication between Mappers and Reducers is also through files. This allows Hadoop-based systems to scale well, as long as sufficient disk space is available. Persistent storage also allows Hadoop to be resilient to processor failures. The

[2] White, *Hadoop*.
   Apache Software Foundation, "Hadoop project."

distributed controller for Hadoop, on realizing that a node has failed, simply hands its tasks afresh to a new processor by pointing it to the input and output file locations.

**Listing 6.27** Map and Reduce in Hadoop

```
public static class myMapper
        extends Mapper<inKeyType, inValueType, outKeyType, outValueType> {
    // Initialize variables used by one or all map instances

    public void map(inKeyType inkey, inValueType invalue, Context context)
            throws IOException, InterruptedException {
        // Possibly iterate over
                outKeyType outkey;
        outValueType outvalue;
        produce(&outkey, outvalue);
        context.write(outkey, outvalue);
    }
}

public static class myReducer
        extends Reducer<inKeyType, inValueType, outKeyType, outValueType> {
    // Initialize variables used by one or all reduce instances

    public void reduce(inKeyType inkey, Iterable<inValueType> invalues,
            Context context) throws IOException, InterruptedException {
            outKeyType outkey = inkey;
            outValueType outvalue;
            for (inValueType inval : invalues) { // Iterate over invalues
                accumulate(outvalue, inval);
            }
            // Possibly iterate producing multiple outvalues
                context.write(outkey, outvalue);
    }
}
```

Listing 6.27 is the template for most map-reduce stages. *produce* and *accumulate* are the only user functions required in a stage. An opaque Context handle is used to generate the output by both mapper and reducer. Two classes, *myMapper* and *myReducer* in this example, implement map and reduce, respectively. These classes are registered with the framework using a provided class *Job* before the job is launched.

An application may chain multiple map-reduce stages by using a sequence of jobs with input and output set accordingly. Hadoop also supports a two-step reduction. The keys emanating from a single mapper may be reduced at the mapper itself. Cross-mapper keys are then reduced at a reducer. This strategy of combining the values at a mapper first decreases the size of the data shuffled from mappers to reducers. Thus, Hadoop may well be called a map-combine-reduce framework. The program provides a Combiner class, just like it provides the Reducer class. For many applications, the Reducer class may also double as the Combiner class.

## 6.5   GPU Programming

The graphics processing unit (GPU) architecture (see Section 1.5) is logically similar to that of CPU. Yet, there are important differences, leading to a variance in their programming styles. These differences arise from the following:

1. GPUs have many more cores than CPUs do.

2. GPUs primarily have groups of SIMD style processors, whereas CPUs favor single instruction, single data (SISD) style. CPUs do have SIMD execution engines, but they require a more restrictive operand setup. Both SIMD units and GPUs need to be exposed through special programming constructs.

3. GPUs have significantly higher bandwidth to their attached memory than they have to the system memory (the ones attached to the CPUs). Similarly, CPUs have higher bandwidth to the system memory.

4. GPUs contain a relatively smaller cache. As a result, program-controlled cache management is often useful. The level of cache utilization does impact performance on CPUs, but the impact is much more substantial on GPUs. As a result, cache management on CPUs is not explicitly exposed to programs.

5. GPUs of the day, due to their relatively low memory size and indirect access to disk storage, are poor at context switching and virtual paging. This imposes significant limitations on the program.

### OpenMP GPU Off-Load

There is evolving support for GPU programming in OpenMP. It provides a simple programming model based on the computation off-load paradigm, which suits the clear separation between CPUs and GPUs at both architectural and OS levels. Programs start as a part of a CPU process, and specific functions are designated to be executed on the GPU. This may be thought of as a variant of a remote procedure call (RPC), as shown in Figure 6.9. We will refer to the GPU part of the code as the *device* part and the CPU part as the *host* part. Both belong to the same process. Hence, they can conceivably share a common address space. Sharing variables between the host and the device is not always efficient, however. A more common strategy is to treat the host and each GPU on a node as distributed-memory processors with explicit copying of shared data. In OpenMP terms, this is similar to the device code always using private variables. In some GPU architectures, inter-GPU sharing is efficient. Shared memory may sometimes be practicable for that part. OpenMP does not expose this shared style, though.

The OpenMP programming model directly exposes each GPU to the programmer, adding little further abstraction over it. Thus, unlike a CPU code, a GPU function is off-loaded to, and executes on, the specified GPU on the node at which the caller is executing. This GPU is identified by its rank. The rank is also called the device ID. Further, threads started on a device execute and finish on that same device.

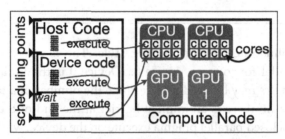

**Figure 6.9** GPU off-load

The OpenMP *target pragma* creates an off-loading task. This task executes on the device the structured block following the pragma. All variables used in this device code are "made available" to the device. Variables declared inside the block are created on the device. Variables used, but not declared inside the block, are declared outside, and hence exist on the host as well. Device versions of these host variables are created for device use. Thus, there is a device variable corresponding to each original host variable that appears in the target construct.

Unlike MPI_Win's explicit get and put primitives, the *map* clause of the target pragma is used to create the linkage between the device variables and their host counterparts. Map options allow original variables' values to be copied to the corresponding device variables at the beginning of the task. They also allow variables to be copied back from the device at the end of the task. Note that OpenMP implementations are allowed to omit physical device copies, and directly share the original copies instead, given that the device and the host functions share the same address space. Variables shared in this manner are copied to the device on access by a device instruction and may be cached on the device. The usual caveats about data races apply. It is, hence, useful to treat the host variables and their corresponding device variables as separate copies that are synchronized only before and after the task, depending on the map options. At other times, they may diverge from each other. Mapped variables generally should not be accessed in the host code concurrently with the device code. Traditional clauses *private* and *firstprivate* may be used instead of map. These variables are always copied to the device.

**Listing 6.28** OpenMP GPU Off-Load

```
// Initialize: int size; float *left, *right; Allocate float *result;
#pragma omp target device(0) map(to:left[0:size], right[0:size], size)\
                        map(from: result[0:size])
{// Device code:
     #pragma omp parallel for
         for (int i = 0; i < size; i++)
             result[i] = left[i] + right[i];
}
```

Listing 6.28 illustrates the off-loading style. The *target pragma* off-loads a task to execute the parallel for loop on device 0. (Device 0 is the initial default. The function *omp_get_num_devices* may be used to determine the number of attached devices.) The task is in-line by default; there is an implicit barrier at the end of the construct. The threads created by the enclosed parallel pragma execute on the device, while the host task or thread encountering the construct waits. If the *nowait* clause is specified in the target pragma, the target task is forked and scheduled for later asynchronous execution, while the parent task continues beyond the pragma. Note that separate pragmas must be used for each device – by using separate code, or by iterating over a block of code, using a different device ID in each iteration.

Arrays left, right, and result are originally accessible to the encountering host task. (Target tasks must not encounter target pragmas.) The *to* parameter in the map clause indicates that the device's private copies of arrays left and right are initialized from the original host values. The *from* parameter does the opposite: at the completion of the device code, the values in the result array are copied from the device variable back to the host variable. If both transfers are required, *map(tofrom: . . .)* may be used instead.

If a variable is used in the device code but is neither listed as a private (or firstprivate) nor in a map clause, implicit copy rules apply. Scalar values (int, float, etc.) are firstprivate by default, meaning they are copied from the host to the device for each target task they are used in. Nonscalars (arrays, structs, objects, etc.) are mapped *tofrom*, if not listed on any map, private, or firstprivate clauses. All scalars may also be mapped in both directions by using the *defaultmap(tofrom:scalar)* clause.

In addition to maps on the target pragma, a variable may also be persistently mapped, so it does not need to be recopied for each device task. We explore this next.

## Data and Function on Device

If any part of the target code-block includes a function call, that function is executed on the device. Like simd declarations, such functions should be declared to be a *target function* as shown in Listing 6.29.

**Listing 6.29** OpenMP Device Declaration

```
#pragma omp declare target
float scale = 0.1;
float shift(float dydx, float dist)
{
    return scale*dydx*dist;
}
#pragma omp end declare target
```

Notice that one may also declare variables to be device variables, for example, scale above. These variables act like static variables that reside on the device. No separate mapping is required; implicit map rules are applied. Once declared, these device variables may be available to the device code.

Sometimes, mapping – whether implicit or explicit – of each variable at each target task generation can be wasteful. Not all target tasks require every variable to be copied in or copied back. Rather, it may be possible that input variables are copied in before the first task in a sequence of tasks, and the output variables are copied out after the last task in the sequence. *Target data* pragma solves this problem. Map clauses on the target data pragma apply to its entire code block, which may contain target pragmas, as shown in Listing 6.30.

**Listing 6.30** OpenMP GPU Off-Load With Reduced Data Copying

```
1 // Initialize: int size; float X[size], Y[size]; Allocate: *diff
2 #pragma omp target data map(alloc:diff[0:size]) map(to:X[0:size])
3                         map(tofrom:Y[0:size])
4 {
5     #pragma omp target // size is firstprivate for task
6     {
7         #pragma omp parallel for
8             for (int i = 1; i < size-1; i++) // All GPU threads share size
9                 diff[i] = (Y[i+1] - Y[i-1]) / (X[i+1] - X[i]);
10    }
11    // host code can go here
12    #pragma omp target // size is again firstprivate
13    {
```

```
14          #pragma omp parallel for
15              for (int i = 1; i < size-1; i++) // All GPU threads share size
16                  Y[i] += shift(diff[i], X[i+1]-X[i]);
17          }
18  }
```

The code above processes a list of points {X, Y} on the GPU. diff is a local array that is used to compute the derivative on the device using the central difference method. Once all the derivatives are computed in the first target task (the pragma in line 5), the second task (the pragma in line 12) shifts each point up or down by modifying its Y coordinate. shift is the device function defined in Listing 6.29. The second task does not begin until the first task is complete, ensuring that there is no data race on the variable Y.

Both tasks use device-mapped variables X, Y, and diff, but not all need to be copied at each task. The first task only requires X and Y to be copied to the device, but not diff. All three must persist during the second task. Finally, only Y must be copied back to the host after the second task. This is controlled by the *target data* pragma (line 2) that contains the two tasks in its block.

Both tasks rely on the device data mapped by the target data pragma, which is the primary regulator for its listed maps. In this example, line 2 maps X *to* the device, ensuring that the device version of X is populated before any task begins. It maps Y *tofrom*, ensuring that Y is initialized on the device once before the first task and copied back once after the last. This avoids redundant transfers per task. The alloc clause for diff implies that diff is neither copied to the device nor copied back: the values are created temporarily on the device and are never required on the host. The two enclosed *target* pragmas may map additional variables. However, variables already mapped by the enclosing target data pragma are not recopied, unless the *always* parameter is explicitly specified in the map clause on the enclosed pragma like so:

```
#pragma omp target map(always, from: var1, var2, var3)
```

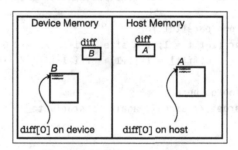

**Figure 6.10** Pointer mapping

It is worth noting that a pointer really has two aspects: the address value in the pointer variable itself and the data stored at that address. For example, in the code above, the pointer *diff* may contain the value $A$, meaning the floating-point array values are stored starting at address $A$. See Figure 6.10. Mapping diff to the device, and thus initializing the device copy of diff, also with the value $A$, would be incorrect, unless the device directly accesses the host memory. $A$ is the address of the data on the host. Hence, the data at $A$ must itself be mapped to the device. And the device's diff must be initialized with the address $B$, to which the host address $A$ is mapped. In OpenMP, mapping of diff maps both the pointer and its referred data. The pointer, being a scalar, maps as firstprivate and the array maps as per the map option specified, that is, *alloc* in the example above. This necessitates that the original $A$ must exist on the host and have a known size, even though it is never accessed there.

## Thread Blocks in OpenMP

Recall that GPUs contain a hierarchy of processors. The OpenMP constructs discussed above only create a single team of threads, meaning the entire target task is executed on a single streaming multi-processor (SM) (see Section 1.5). In order to let the threads be distributed onto all the SMs, OpenMP supports the creation of a set of teams, using the *teams* construct. We demonstrate in Listing 6.31 a shorthand pragma that combines *target, teams, parallel, for*, and *distribute* constructs.

**Listing 6.31** OpenMP GPU Off-Load Utilizing Multiple SMs

```
#pragma omp target teams distribute parallel for simd
                        map(to:X[0:size]) map(from:Y[0:size])
{
        for (int i = 1; i < size-1; i++)
            Y[i] = 0.5 * (X[i+1] + X[i]);
}
```

The teams pragma creates multiple teams of threads on the target. It may be enclosed within a target pragma or combined with it. The clause *num_teams(count)* requests count teams. Each team has the same number of threads. This number is limited by the GPU architecture, but clause *thread_limit(count)* may request smaller teams. There is no barrier synchronization possible between two teams executing on the device, except the implicit barrier at the end of the task. The *teams pragma*, by itself, replicates the entire task to the master thread of each team. The *distribute pragma* allows work sharing by the teams instead. The distribute pragma must be followed by a for loop; it distributes the iteration of the loop among the teams, quite like a *for* pragma does among the threads of a single team. The clause *dist_schedule* may be specified with the distribute pragma to control which iterations are allocated to which team. Still, only the master thread of each team gets that team's share of iterations. The *parallel for* allows the master thread of each team to further share its load with the threads of its team. Finally, the simd pragma ensures that each thread uses SIMD instructions. Recall that GPUs comprise SIMD processors.

A more explicit load distribution among the threads of the team is demonstrated below:

```
#pragma omp target teams distribute
      for(int i=0; ..) {
            #pragma parallel for
                  for( int j = 0 .. )
      }
```

In this case, the outer loop is distributed among the teams – which means the master thread of each team. Each master thread then encounters the parallel for construct, which is shared by its team of threads. A thread can query its rank within its team using the function *omp_get_thread_num* described earlier. *omp_get_team_num* returns the rank of the calling thread's team.

## CUDA

CUDA is a more mature GPU programming framework than OpenMP does. However, it focuses on lower-level constructs than OpenMP does. This finer program control is often able to extract higher performance. Like OpenMP, CUDA uses the off-load model – device functions are off-loaded to and executed on the specified GPU, identified by its rank, also known as the device ID.

CUDA has two main components. The first is a C-like programming language, called CUDA. It contains a small number of extensions to C/C++, but most of its functionality is exposed through functions. CUDA programs require a CUDA compiler, which may in turn leverage a C compiler for translating the standard C/C++ parts. Device functions are cross-compiled to be executed on the GPU. Host functions are compiled to the CPU. Both parts of the program are stored in a common executable, which includes instructions to load the device code on to the device as per need.

The second component is the CUDA runtime environment, which allows a CPU-executed code to interact with GPUs. It includes data communication, GPU code transmission, execution setup, thread launch, and so on. Like OpenMP runtime, CUDA runtime provides functionality that implements CUDA constructs and exposes functions that a program may use to query GPU information as well as control GPU behavior. Like MPI functions, CUDA functions return an error code on any error and the constant *cudaSuccess* on success. We will not check this returned code in our illustrations, but it is a good practice to do so.

## CUDA Programming Model

Unlike OpenMP, CUDA directly exposes the GPU core structure in a single construct. Listing 6.32 shows an example.

**Listing 6.32** CUDA GPU Off-Load

```
1 float *left, *right, *result;
2 cudaSetdevice(0); // We imply device 0, until reset to another device.
3 cudaMallocManaged(&left, sizeof(float)*size); // space visible on host & device
4 cudaMallocManaged(&right, sizeof(float)*size); // space visible on host & device
5 cudaMallocManaged(&result, sizeof(float)*size);// space visible on host & device
6 initialize_data(left, right, size); // On host
7 thread_func<<<num_teams, team_size>>>(left, right, result);
8 cudaDeviceSynchronize(); // Wait for thread_func to complete on device
9 Use(result);
```

The GPU task executes *thread_func*, as designated on line 7. In particular, each GPU thread executes this function, called a *kernel* in CUDA terminology. The kernel is an asynchronously launched GPU task. The function thread_func has the features of an RPC made by the host code but executed on the device. The host thread launches the kernel and proceeds to line 8 without waiting for its completion. Since it needs the results of the kernel execution in this case, it uses *cudaDeviceSynchronize* to wait for the asynchronously executing kernel to complete.

Thread creation is controlled by the "<<< >>>" construct, which includes the number of thread teams to create and the number of threads to create in each team, respectively. The function's parameters are passed by value to each thread, and each thread executes the function body. The team of threads is called a *block of threads* in CUDA. The block is further organized into groups of up to 32 threads; each group is called a *warp*. Threads of a warp execute together in SIMD fashion. It is useful to note that the thread terminology of CUDA differs from that of OpenMP. The entire CUDA warp is equivalent to one OpenMP device thread. In CUDA, the program directly controls each SIMD lane. The threads of the warp may diverge to execute different code-fragments.

The variables left, right, and result in Listing 6.32 are declared on the host, and point to memory allocated by the host code. Both the pointer and the address it points to are visible on both the host and the device. *cudaMallocManaged* is used instead of the standard C/C++ *malloc* or *new*. cudaMallocManaged allows the CUDA runtime to ensure that the allocated address is efficiently accessible on the device, but malloc and new are also available on both host and device. Thus, left, right, and result are truly shared between the host and the device in the example above. This means that any concurrent access must be properly synchronized. *cudaMalloc* may be used on the host to allocate private memory on the device, which is not accessible directly to the host code. Local variables in device functions as well as addresses returned by malloc or new called on the device are device-private.

The device function is written in a single instruction multiple threads (SIMT) style: every active device thread executes the function. Different threads executing this function may diverge to perform different instructions or process different sections of the data depending on the thread ID. The kernel function is indicated by the keyword _global_, and it cannot return a value.

```
__global__ void thread_func(float *left, float *right, float *result)
{
    i = threadIdx.x;
    result[i] = left[i] + right[i];
}
```

threadIdx is an in-built constant in each thread's memory, which stores the thread's ID. Note that it is a structure, allowing the threads to have a 1D, 2D, or 3D organization. For example, in a 3D array of threads, each thread has *threadIdx.x*, *threadIdx.y*, and *threadIdx.z* denoting the indices in three dimensions, $z$ being the most significant dimension and $x$ the least significant. This higher-dimensional thread organization is controlled by the variable *team_size*, which may be a positive integer or of type *dim3* as follows:

```
dim3 team_size(4, 8, 16); // 4x8x16, z dimension is 4, x is 16
```

This dimensionality is merely syntactic sugar. A row-major serialization of the indices provides a numeric rank for each thread. Blocks of threads with 32 contiguous ranks form warps. The serialized rank of a thread is:

$$threadIdx.z * (blockDim.y * blockDim.x) + threadIdx.y * blockDim.x + threadIdx.x,$$

where *blockDim* gives the number of threads in each dimension in a block.

The blocks may themselves be organized in 1D, 2D, or 3D manner, for example: *dim3 num_teams*(16, 16, 1). This higher-dimensional thread organization (as opposed to the integer rank we have seen before) makes it easier to process higher-dimensional arrays by simplifying the thread ID to array index mapping. The in-built variable *blockIdx* contains the rank of the thread's block, and blockDim contains the organization among the blocks. Each is of type *dim3* and can be accessed in a manner similar to threadIdx.

Since the entire block of threads is expected to be live and coresident on an SM, and shares its resources (without relinquishing them for a context switch), the capacity of SMs is explicitly exposed to CUDA programs. In current generation GPUs, no block may contain more than 1,024 threads.

## CPU–GPU Memory Transfer

One potential advantage of memory variables shared by the host and devices is that the data is fetched wherever it is accessed. However, recall that the memory bandwidth between the host and the GPU is relatively low. As a result, paging data into a GPU or back on demand may incur a long latency. Programs need to be cautious about how often the data is transferred back and forth. Sometimes providing hints using *cudaMemAdvise* to the CUDA runtime helps. Hints allow the program to indicate the preferred location for a given block of data, or that it is mostly accessed on a specific device. At other times, the long latency may be hidden by explicitly requesting that memory be prefetched into the device, concurrently with other computation that does not depend on that memory. This is accomplished by calling *cudaMemPrefetchAsync* on the host before the corresponding kernel is launched.

**Listing 6.33** Data Prefetching

```
cudaMemPrefetchAsync(left, size*sizeof(float), device, NULL);
cudaMemPrefetchAsync(right, size*sizeof(float), device, NULL);
```

The two function calls in Listing 6.33 schedule the transfer of *size*sizeof(float)* bytes of *left* and *right*, respectively, to the specified device. As an optimization, if the data is not initially written on the host, no actual transfer takes place. Once the data is prefetched to a device, access is local within a kernel and hence does not incur a long latency. To prefetch to the host, a special device ID *cudaCpuDeviceId* must be used. The last parameter (NULL) of the function *cudaMemPrefetchAsync* is a stream, which we will discuss shortly.

There also exist lower-level interfaces, where the transfer is performed explicitly by the host program, using one-sided communication. Refer to *cudaMemcpy* and *cudaMemcpyAsync*. Such explicit transfer may also become necessary for host variables not allocated using cudaMallocManaged. For global or static variables, one may declare them to be device variables, similar to the OpenMP declare target pragma.

**Listing 6.34** Device Declaration

```
__device__ int dev_var = 101;
__device__ int dev_func(int arg)
{
      return arg * dev_var;
}
```

The variable *dev_var* and the function *dev_func* in Listing 6.34 are both declared to be device entities. Device functions may be called from other device functions including the __global__ kernels. The __managed__ keyword is also available and indicates that a variable is shared between the devices and the host.

```
__managed__ int dev_var;
```

## Concurrent Kernels

Kernel launch is nonblocking on the host. The same CPU thread or different threads may each launch multiple kernels on to multiple GPU devices. However, each device may execute only one kernel at a time by default. The next kernel to that device waits until the previous completes. CUDA has an abstraction called *streams* that allows multiple kernels to execute concurrently, as long as the device can accommodate their combined resource requirements.

A device can execute streams concurrently. Kernels within a stream are in strict sequence. When no stream is specified, the default "Stream 0" is implied. This default stream cannot execute concurrently with other streams – this is required for legacy reasons. The stream is specified as follows.

**Listing 6.35** CUDA Streams

```
cudaStream_t stream1, stream2;
cudaStreamCreate(&stream1);
cudaStreamCreate(&stream2);
// Set up left, right, result, num_teams, team_size
thread_func1<<<32, 256, 0, stream1>>>();
thread_func<<<num_teams, team_size, 0, stream2>>>(left, right, result);
cudaStreamSynchronize(stream1); // Wait for events in stream1 to complete.
// May use result here
// Later, after streams are no more needed:
cudaStreamDestroy(stream1);
cudaStreamDestroy(stream2);
```

Both kernels in Listing 6.35 (thread_func and thread_func1) may execute concurrently, as they are in different streams. The third parameter in the <<<>>> construct requests an additional block of memory private to each block and shared by all threads of the block. We will discuss this shortly. *cudaStreamSynchronize* may be used on the host to wait for only a specific stream. *cudaDeviceSynchronize* waits for all outstanding executions on the device instead. Memory allocation and transfers may also be associated with specific streams.

**Listing 6.36** Hiding Communication Latency: Computation-Communication Overlap

```
thread_func1<<<32, 256, 0, stream1>>>(); // Execute in stream1
// Set up variables. Schedule following in stream2
cudaMemPrefetchAsync(left, size*sizeof(float), device, stream2);
cudaMemPrefetchAsync(right, size*sizeof(float), device, stream2);
thread_func<<<num_teams, team_size, 0, stream2>>>(left, right, result);
```

In Listing 6.36, the host thread first launches the kernel thread_func1 in stream1. This kernel may begin to execute immediately on the device. The host thread then associates the prefetch of memory areas *left and *right to a stream2 before launching thread_func in that stream. All three are nonblocking calls on the host. The prefetching can occur concurrently with the execution of thread_func1 as they are in different streams. The execution of the thread_func kernel follows the prefetch on stream2, thus ensuring that the access to *left and *right in the device function thread_func is local to the device. Note that it would be possible to launch the second kernel without the prefetch, potentially allowing it to run concurrently with the first kernel. However, if the data transfer takes significant time and the two kernels cannot both run together, overlapping the prefetching for a kernel, thread_func in this example, with the execution of another, thread_func1 in this example, would generally yield a higher performance.

An explicit copy of data may also be associated with a stream as follows:

```
cudaMemcpyAsync(dev_pointer, host_pointer, size, cudaMemcpyHostToDevice, stream);
```

*cudaMemcpyHostToDevice* indicates the direction in which the transfer is to take place. This parameter is required for legacy reasons. Contemporary CUDA runtime is able to infer the direction of transfer and *cudaMemcpyDefault* may be used instead.

Kernels may also be launched from within the device code, meaning any thread of a kernel may recursively launch a child kernel. Threads of the parent kernel may execute concurrently with the child threads but wait for the execution of the child kernel to complete before exiting themselves.

## CUDA Synchronization

CUDA supports atomic operations, memory fences, and execution barriers. Additionally, warps execute in synchrony, except when threads diverge due to the scheduler's decisions or due to conditional branches in the code. Note that no two threads of a warp may execute different instructions in the same clock. When threads of a warp diverge and start executing different parts of the code, they are no more in lock-step. Rather, subsets diverge.

Subsets take turn to execute their instruction, leaving some lanes in the warp unoccupied. For example, in Listing 6.37,

**Listing 6.37** Warps Can Diverge

```
if(threadIdx.x % 2) // Odd thread ID
      odd_work();
else
      even_work();
```

the odd-numbered thread IDs of a warp need to execute instructions of *odd_work*, while the even-numbered thread IDs must execute *even_work*. Both sets of instruction would be scheduled, but only half the threads of the warp would be active at one time.

Synchronization can be at various levels: among the threads of a warp, among those of a block, among all GPU threads, and so on. Different primitives exist at different levels for performance reasons. Intra-warp synchronization usually has a lower overhead than intra-block synchronization, for example.

Atomic operations are defined in one word, which may be 16-bit, 32-bit, or 64-bit. For example, *atomicAdd* allows the caller to add one word value to a memory word.

```
atomicAdd(&var, value);
```

Atomic operations like atomicAdd are atomic with respect to other threads on the same device. Variants exist that are atomic with respect to other devices and CPU, for example, *atomicAdd_system*. Variants also exist for atomic operations with respect to other threads of the block, for example, *atomicAdd_block*. The atomic operation is a powerful synchronization primitive, but it also serializes threads and does not scale well. GPU kernels commonly employ hundreds and thousands of actively executing threads. Performance impact can be significant if many of them perform an atomic operation on the same address at roughly the same time. Block-level synchronization is likely to have less slowdown. Warp-level operations are even more efficient, and several such synchronization primitives exist.

Relative to other atomic operation, Compare and Swap (*atomicCAS*) is more flexible and may be used to implement more complex synchronizations.

__syncthreads() is a block-wide barrier. There exist consensus-type variants as well, which perform a form of *voting*. For example, __syncthreads_count(predicate) allows each thread to also specify a Boolean value, and once all threads in the group have called the matching function, each function returns with a count of the number of threads that provided a true predicate in their calls. __syncwarp() is a warp-wide barrier, which is useful in bringing divergent warps back into lock-step. This can, in turn, help restore the efficiency of parallel memory operations.

Intra-warp synchronization instructions return statistics of the warp, like the number or the list of active threads. They also allow active warp threads to directly communicate without using shared memory. Threads may send or receive local scalar variables. Listing 6.38 uses this feature to reduce the values in the private variable val local to each thread of the warp, using the tree reduction algorithm shown in Section 3.2. After five iterations of the loop, the thread in lane 0 contains the reduced value in its val.

**Listing 6.38** Intra-Warp Reduction

```
1 // Possibly read val from a device array: val = left[index]
2 __syncwarp(0xffffffff);
3 for (int offset = 16; offset > 0; offset /= 2)
4     val += __shfl_down_sync(0xffffffff, val, offset);
```

The first parameter of all warp-wide sync primitives (e.g. __shfl_down_sync above) is a 32-bit mask indicating the lane IDs in the current warp (IDs go from 0 to 31), which are involved in that collective operation. 0xffffffff means all 32 lanes participate. __shfl_down_sync allows the executing thread in lane $i$ to fetch the private value val from lane $i+offset$, as long as $i+offset < 32$. For simplicity, Listing 6.38 uses the mask 0xffffffff at all iterations. The right half of the threads could be inactivated at each step, but changing the mask requires additional instructions. The warp-wide barrier in line 2 before the loop ensures that all warp threads are converged and start the loop in lock-step.

There is no kernel-wide barrier in CUDA, but there exists an abstraction called *cooperative groups*, which is an arbitrary group of threads. Threads within a group may barrier-synchronize, even if they are not in the same block, as long as the entire group is resident on the GPUs.

Recall that careful ordering of memory accesses is required if one thread reads the value written by another. Memory fences are required due to weak consistency semantics in CUDA, just like OpenMP and MPI one-sided communication. Warp-wide, block-wide, and system-wide memory fences are supported. For example, a __threadfence() function call by any thread $i$ ensures that its accesses to device memory before the fence are all ordered before its accesses after the fence. In particular, every memory write by device thread $i$ before its fence appears to all other device threads as having completed before any writes by thread $i$ after that fence (see Figure 6.11). __threadfence_block() orders memory accesses with respect to other threads in the block and __threadfence_system() with respect to all devices and the CPU. Note that unlike OpenMP, a cache flush is not implied in CUDA memory fences. Some implementations of CUDA do not provide complete cache coherence and variables must be declared *volatile* to disable caching. This can lead to performance degradation.

Synchronization primitives __syncthreads and __syncwarp include an implicit memory fence and (do not require the use of volatile).

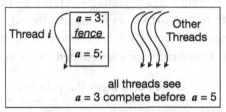

**Figure 6.11** GPU memory fence

## CUDA Shared Memory

As mentioned in Section 1.5, GPUs have relatively small caches. In order to maximize cache reuse, CUDA provides program control over cache behavior. But, rather than controlling the cache policy, CUDA allows the local fast memory to be subdivided into two components: the standard cache and a scratchpad, to which variables can be explicitly assigned. An expanded view of this local memory is shown in Figure 6.12. Each block of threads is

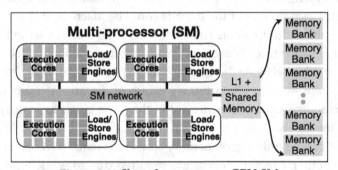

**Figure 6.12** Shared memory on GPU SM

mapped to one of the available SMs for execution. Since the scratchpad is local to the SM, CUDA exposes the scratchpad as a block-shared chunk of memory. The scratchpad memory is statically partitioned among all resident blocks executing on a given SM. As a result, the shared-memory requirement of each block determines, among other things, how many blocks of threads may execute concurrently. This SM–local memory is a scarce resource, and it is not virtualized for performance reasons. Hence, programs must use it wisely. This shared-memory allocation per block is requested in two different ways by a CUDA program. The first is by declaring variables with the __shared__ keyword, as shown below:

```
__shared__ int shtemp[1024]; // The size must be a constant
```

In the listing above, one instance of array shtemp[1024] is created per block and shared by all threads of the block. When all threads of the block exit, the array is freed. Since only these threads may access the variable, only these threads must initialize and consume its values. A common access paradigm may be as follows:

```
base = function_of(blockIdx, threadIdx, blockDim);
shtemp[threadIdx.x] = some_large_array[base+threadIdx.x];
__syncthreads(); // Ensure that all of shtemp is filled
// Now read any part of shtemp
```

The size of variables declared as __shared__, including array types, must be a constant known at the compile time.

The second, more dynamic, mechanism is that the host code requests at the kernel launch time a certain allocation of shared memory per thread block. The third argument of the kernel launch construct serves that purpose. For example, the following launch requests a dynamic allocation of 4,096 bytes per block if the size of int is 4 bytes.

```
thread_func<<<num_teams, team_size, 1024*sizeof(int)>>>(left, right, result);
```

The last parameter of the launch construct, the stream, is missing in this example and defaults to Stream 0. This dynamic allocation is accessed as an *extern* within the kernel function.

```
extern __shared__ int *shtemp;
shtemp[threadIdx.x] = some_array[base+threadIdx.x];
        // Launch ensures that this is not out of bounds
```

Since a single buffer is allocated at the kernel launch time, a single extern pointer should be used in the kernel. No dynamic shared-memory allocation by an executing device function is possible.

## CUDA Parallel Memory Access

Often memory access is also parallel in parallel programs. For example, a memory instruction is executed simultaneously for all threads in the warp. Variables reside in a common memory subsystem. Any thread may access any memory location at any clock-step. When multiple threads seek to access memory in the same clock-step, the memory subsystem may or may not be able to serve multiple disjoint locations simultaneously. Regardless, memory subsystems are commonly able to serve more than one integer, or one scalar at a time. We call the memory access granularity *memory atom*.

If the simultaneous access from parallel threads is a subset of one memory atom, the combined requirement can be satisfied by a single memory access.

This coalescing of accesses of multiple threads is performed transparently by the hardware. But given that CUDA exposes warp synchrony (modulo divergence), programs can be written to maximize coalescing.

The accesses to device memory and SM–local memory (aka block-shared memory) behave differently from each other. Device memory is accessed using the standard cache hierarchy, and device memory atoms are contiguous addresses. Thus, if threads of a warp access contiguous addresses, the coalescing efficiency is good: either all the accesses can be satisfied directly from one or two cache-lines, or from one or two memory atoms (which are brought into cache-lines).

Device memory atoms are aligned, meaning they begin at 32-, 64-, or 128-byte boundaries. Variable addresses in CUDA already begin at atom boundaries, courtesy of the compiler. Thus, indexes used in a warp may coalesce well if they are also aligned. For example, if the indexes used by a warp's threads are contiguous and thread 0 of the warp uses an address that is 128-byte aligned (meaning it is a multiple of 128), coalescing is effective. In other words, the following example is efficient because warp $i$ starts at offset $i \times 32 \times sizeof(int)$ for each array, and cumulatively accesses $32 \times sizeof(int)$ bytes. All these bytes belong to a single 128-byte aligned atom (if each array begins at an aligned address).

```
result[threadIdx.x] = left[threadIdx.x] + right[threadIdx.x];
```

Variables may be forced to be aligned as follows:

```
typedef struct __align__(16) {
    float x, y, z;
} PointType;
__managed__ PointType points[128];
```

Each element of points is aligned to 16 bytes using the __align__ keyword. Usually, such a struct would be 12 bytes long, but the alignment makes it 16 bytes long. Similarly, each row of a 2D array may be forced to start at aligned addresses, by aligning the array. Such an alignment leaves gaps in the representation but allows simultaneous accesses to coalesce when a part of a row is accessed by a warp as in the listing below:

```
A[blockIDx.x][threadIdx.x] *= B[blockIDx.x][threadIdx.x];
```

For any given row, the thread ID is used as the column number in warps 0..31, 32..63, and so on. They are aligned only if each row begins at an aligned address. See cudaMallocPitch to allocate an array with aligned rows.

SM–local scratchpad memory is a bit more elaborate and multiported. Not only is it able to service a 128-byte contiguous block of memory, but it can also service more complex patterns. To understand these patterns, let us consider the organization of SM memory. As shown in Figure 6.12, the SM memory consists of a number of memory banks, for example 32 banks are shown here. Addresses are distributed across these banks, and each bank is able to serve 4-byte atoms. Thus, if no more than one atom is required from any bank, the entire warp's memory access can be coalesced into a single cumulative access. If there are *bank conflicts*, however, accesses to the same bank must be serialized. The following accesses are conflict-free.

**Listing 6.39** Conflict-Free Block-shared Memory Access

```
__device__ M[10][32];
__shared__ shA[10][33]; // Last column is unused
int laneID = threadIdx.x; // Assume a 10x32 block
int column = threadIdx.y;
shA[laneID][column] = M[column][laneID];
__syncthreads();
// Operate on any part of shA
```

The loop iterates over columns of the matrix. A warp's threads all store values in column $i$ at iteration $i$. Array shA is stored row-major. Assuming shA$[0][0]$ resides in Bank 1, shA$[0][1] \in$ Bank 2, and so on, as shown in Figure 6.13. Assuming 32 banks, shA$[0][30] \in$ Bank 31 and shA$[1][0] \in$ Bank 2. Thus, each column is distributed across banks; column 0 is highlighted in the figure. This means that even for a row-major-ordered matrix, column order access is efficient. The example in Listing 6.39 also exhibits a common use of block memory. It

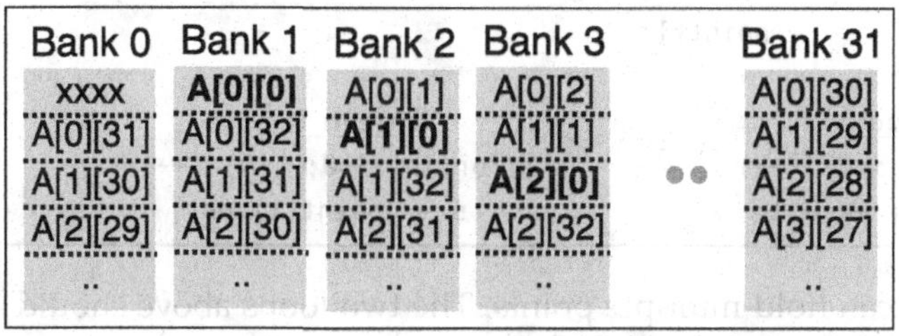

| Bank 0 | Bank 1 | Bank 2 | Bank 3 | | Bank 31 |
|--------|--------|--------|--------|--|---------|
| XXXX | A[0][0] | A[0][1] | A[0][2] | | A[0][30] |
| A[0][31] | A[0][32] | A[1][0] | A[1][1] | | A[1][29] |
| A[1][30] | A[1][31] | A[1][32] | A[2][0] | •• | A[2][28] |
| A[2][29] | A[2][30] | A[2][31] | A[2][32] | | A[3][27] |
| .. | .. | .. | .. | | .. |

**Figure 6.13** SM-memory bank addressing

uses block-shared memory as a user-controlled cache to make device memory accesses efficient. Suppose the device array M needs to be accessed column-wise, which does not coalesce well for row-major-ordered matrices. This code allows M to be first read row-wise in contiguous coalesced chunks. These chunks are written column-wise to the faster shared memory, without causing bank conflict. M can then be efficiently accessed column-wise from the shared memory. The __syncthreads() function call ensures that all required parts of M are brought in to the shared memory before the kernel starts to process it.

## False Sharing

We discussed how memory requests within a warp are coalesced for efficient operation. It is possible to arrange that each warp's accesses are contained, for example, in a single cache-line. Sometimes, however, cache-lines can create a hazard, and such a hazard is not limited to GPU threads, but also to CPU threads.

When two independently scheduled threads access different memory locations, which happen to map to the same cache-line, their accesses can interfere with each other, leading to a significant performance slowdown. This happens because, when thread $i$ writes variable $v$, which resides in some cache-line, that entire line is marked "dirty," in all caches. When thread $j$ executing on another core reads or writes variable $w$, which happens to map to the same dirty cache-line, a cache-coherent memory system delays the access until the line is "clean" again. The line is cleaned by writing thread $i$'s modified cache-line into the main memory and rereading the line into thread $j$'s cache. The two threads end up falsely, sharing variables $v$ and $w$ and impacting each other's performance. For example, consider Listing 6.40.

**Listing 6.40** False Sharing

```
struct Point {
    float x;
    float y;
    int nbr;
} point[];
```

| Thread 0 | Thread 1 |
|----------|----------|
| for(int i=0; i<N; i++) | for(int j=0; j<N; j++) |
|     point[i].y += 0.1; |     s += point[i].nbr; |

A cache-line can hold multiple points. The two loops above should be able to exploit the locality in their reference to service several access requests from the cache.

Threads 0 and 1 share no variables. Thread 0 updates the values in $y$, while thread 1 only reads the values in $nbr$. However, if structs are stored contiguously in memory, the two fields of struct Point are likely to map to the same cache-line. This means that the write to $y$ by thread 0 invalidates $nbr$ in thread 1. This would unnecessarily slow down thread 1 by refetching $nbr$ from the main memory, which might otherwise be found in its cache. If both threads write, the slowdown is more severe. There is no impact on read-only sharing. In general, it is a good practice to separate data structures that are repeatedly written by different unsynchronized threads.

## 6.6  Summary

This chapter introduces several programming tools – both language-based tools and library-based ones. For large clusters, MPI[3]-based programming is common. For GPUs, CUDA[4]-based programming is popular, but OpenMP[5] and OpenCL[6] alternatives are also increasingly used. While not as popular as the others, Chapel[7] is introduced here as an example of a programming language comprehensively designed for parallel programming. Some PGAS-based competitors include X10,[8] UPC,[9] and Global Arrays.[10] Intel's TBB[11] is optimized for shared-memory programming on single nodes, just like OpenMP. Julia[12] is somewhat more general in its support. However, its focus is on hiding parallel constructs to a large extent, which is useful for the ease of programming, but less so for learning parallel programming. Other than Hadoop, the Java ecosystem includes a number of programming abstractions like multi-threading, Parallel Streams to functionally hook sequences of parallel tasks using a fork-join framework, and Remote Method Invocation (RMI) to support RPC.

## Exercise

6.1. Use the SIMD construct of OpenMP for Jacobi iteration as follows. A is an $n \times n$ 2D array of floats.

```
1 forall i,j, 1 < i,j < n-1
2       A[i][j] = 0.25 *
3             ( A[i][j+1] + A[i][j-1]+ A[i-1][j] + A[i+1][j])
```

[3] Gropp et al., "A high-performance."
[4] CUDA Development Team, *CUDA Toolkit Documentation*.
[5] OpenMP Architecture Review Board, *OpenMP Application Program Interface*.
[6] Stone et al., "Opencl."
[7] Chamberlain et al., "Parallel programmability."
[8] Charles et al., "X10: An object-oriented."
[9] El-Ghazawi and Smith, "UPC: Unified parallel C."
[10] Nieplocha et al., "Global arrays."
[11] Voss et al., *Pro TBB*.
[12] Bezanson et al., "Julia: A fresh approach."

Note the apparent race condition in the code above. Make sure that the old values of A are added on line 3 always, never the new values.

6.2. Redo Exercise 6.1 with CUDA.

6.3. Implement the function

```
PrefixSum(Sum, A, n)
```

to compute the prefix sum of A in Sum. Use OpenMP. A is an integer array in the address space of the caller's process. Assume that up to 16 shared-memory processors are available. $n$ is the number of elements in A, and may be between 1 and $2^{30}$. Test your performance with values of $n$ equaling, respectively, $2^{10}, 2^{15}, 2^{20}, 2^{25}, 2^{30}$.

6.4. Redo Exercise 6.3 with MPI, with 2 to 24 nodes.

6.5. Given a matrix $A$ laid out in file $File1$ in row-major order, create file $File2$, where the transpose of $A$ is written in row-major order. Assume binary files with 4-byte floating point representation per number in the native format of the nodes. (Assume all nodes have the same native format.) Run the program on different square matrices of sizes $2^{20} \times 2^{10}$ to $2^{40} \times 2^{40}$ on 1 to 1,024 processors and analyze its scaling behavior. Does it scale strongly or weakly? Implement for the following scenarios:

(a) Processors are all on a single compute node with shared memory.

(b) Processors are across nodes, without any shared memory.

(c) Processor groups of size 4 each share memory within the group but not across groups.

(d) Processor groups of size 8 each share memory within the group but not across groups.

(e) Each processor group in Exercise (d) also shares a GPU.

Create tasks and map them to the devices. Be sure to consider the memory availability of devices in task sizing. You may use CUDA for GPU, OpenMP for shared-memory programming, and MPI for message-passing.

6.6. Redo Exercise 6.5(d) with Chapel.

6.7. Given a matrix $A$ laid out in file $File1$ in row-major order and $B$ laid out in file $File2$ in column-major order, write $A \times B$ in file $File3$ in row-major order. Run the program on different matrix sizes: $2^{10} \times 2^{10}$ to $2^{40} \times 2^{40}$ on 1 to 1,024 processors and analyze its scaling behavior. Implement for all five scenarios in Exercise 6.5.

6.8. Given matrices $A$ and $B$ laid out in row-major order in files $File1$ and $File2$, respectively, write $A \times B$ in file $File3$ in row-major order. Run the program on different matrix sizes: $2^{10} \times 2^{10}$ to $2^{40} \times 2^{40}$ on 1 to 1,024 processors and analyze its scaling behavior. Implement for all five scenarios in Exercise 6.5.

6.9. Given a list of 2D points *List* and a 2D upright rectangle $R$, find all points in *List* lying within or on $R$. The points are laid out in file *File1*, one after another with 4 bytes of $X$ coordinates in the native integer format followed by 4 bytes of $Y$. $R$ is specified on the command line with four integers: $X_1$, $Y_1$, $X_2$, and $Y_2$, the $X$ and $Y$ coordinates of the lower-left corner followed by those of the upper-right corner. Implement the OpenMP and MPI versions and analyze scaling with different-sized lists: $2^{20}$ to $2^{40}$. Implement the following algorithms.

(a) For each point, check if it is contained in $R$, and write into file *File2* if it is.

(b) Initially, sort all points by their $X$ coordinate. Given $R$ locate $X_1$ and $X_2$ in the sorted list. For all points between those two positions, check if its $Y$ coordinate is in the range $[Y_1, Y_2]$, and write into *File2* if it is.

Profile and compare the two algorithms. Suppose, instead of a single rectangle $R$, points contained within any of a list of nonoverlapping rectangles $\{R_i\}$ must be produced. Points may be written in any order. Discuss the conditions when the first algorithm should be used and when the second should be used.

6.10. In Exercise 6.9(b), given a list of possibly overlapping Rectangles $\{R_i\}$, produce file *File2* such that every contained point is listed only once no matter how many rectangles it may lie in.

6.11. Given a list of $2^{30}$ integer elements in an array *Elements* in the address space of one node $N_0$, implement MPI-based Quicksort using 8, 32, 128, 512, and 1,024 nodes, respectively. The sorted list should appear at $N_0$ on completion. The input array *Elements* does not need to be saved. Analyze the profile to check which parts take the most time and why. Analyze the efficiency and scaling.

6.12. Given a list of $2^{50}$ integer elements in a file *File1*, implement MPI-based Quicksort using 8, 32, 128, 512, and 1,024 nodes, respectively. Store the sorted list in file *File2*. Analyze your program's performance.

6.13. Given a list of $2^{50}$ integer elements in a file *File1*, implement hybrid OpenMP and MPI-based Quicksort using 8, 32, 128, and 512 nodes, respectively, with 8 processors, each sharing memory. Store the sorted list in file *File2*. Analyze performance.

6.14. Redo Exercise 6.13 but use Radix-Sort.

# CHAPTER 7

# Parallel Algorithms and Techniques

This chapter introduces some general principles of parallel algorithm design. We will consider a few case studies to illustrate broad approaches to parallel algorithms. As already discussed in Chapter 5, the underlying goal for these algorithms is to pose the solution into parcels of relatively independent computation, with occasional interaction. In order to abstract the details of synchronization, we will assume the parallel RAM (PRAM) or the bulk-synchronous parallel (BSP) model to describe and analyze these algorithms. It is a good time for the reminder that going from, say, a PRAM algorithm to one that is efficient on a particular architecture requires refinement and careful design for a particular platform. This is particularly true when "constant time" concurrent read and write operations are assumed. Concurrent reads and writes are particularly inefficient for distributed-memory platforms, and are inefficient for shared-memory platforms as well. It requires synchronization of the processors' views of the shared memory, which can be expensive.

Recall that PRAM models focus mainly on the computational aspect of algorithm, whereas practical algorithms also require *Question:* How do parallel algorithms differ from sequential algorithms? close attention to memory, communication, and synchronization overheads. PRAM algorithms may not always be practical, but they are easier to design than those for more general models. In reality, PRAM algorithms are only the first step toward more practical algorithms, particularly on distributed-memory systems.

Parallel algorithm design often seeks to maximize parallelism and minimize the time complexity. Even if the number of actually available processors is limited, higher parallelism translates to higher scalability in practice. Nonetheless, the work-time scheduling principle (Section 3.5) indicates that low work complexity is paramount for fast execution in practice. In general, if the best sequential complexity of solving the given problem is, say $T_0(n)$, we would like the parallel work complexity to be $O(T_0(n))$. It is a common algorithm design pattern to assume up to $T_0(n)$ processors and then try to minimize the time complexity. With maximal parallelism, the target time complexity using $T_0(n)$ processors is $O(1)$. This is not always achievable, and there is often a trade-off between time and work complexity. We then try to reduce the work complexity to $O(T_0(n))$, without significantly increasing the time complexity. Sometimes we start by assuming an even higher number of processors, which is not $O(T_o(n))$, for example, $T_o^2(n)$. This is not a practical algorithm on its own, but it can sometimes be useful as a subroutine executed on small subsets of the input in a recursive step.

Once the algorithm is ready, we rely on the work-time scheduling principle to manage its execution on the available hardware. A caveat: the work-time scheduling principle is designed for PRAM algorithms, and very much like PRAM algorithms, it focuses on the computational aspect of the solution. Directly applying this principle to map a PRAM algorithm onto a limited number of processors does not always exhibit the best performance. For example, in the context of the BSP model, communication overheads are lower if the virtual processors that inter-communicate substantially are mapped onto the same physical processor. For shared-memory machines, different PRAM algorithms can lead to different synchronization overheads. This can make an algorithm that is apparently faster on paper actually slower in practice. Hence, even though the theoretical algorithm may naturally suggest a task decomposition, it may need to be adjusted to account for the hardware architecture.

While the focus of this chapter is on parallel algorithmic style of thinking and ab initio design, it also presents a few cases of opportunistically finding inherently parallel steps in known sequential algorithms.

We have already discussed the reduction algorithm in Section 1.6, which is an example of a parallel algorithm organized as a binary tree of computations. This is an oft-occurring paradigm, where each processor performs some computation independently of others, creating a partial result. The processors then combine the partial results pair-wise into the final result, going up a tree. In its simplest form, this paradigm yields a work complexity of $O(n)$ and a time complexity of $O(\log n)$.[1] It works well for problems that have an $O(n)$ sequential solution. We begin with an example slightly more complex than the addition algorithm of Section 1.6. It demonstrates the common algorithmic technique called the *binary tree computation*, which is a special case of the well-known divide-and-conquer paradigm.

## 7.1  Divide and Conquer: Prefix-Sum

Formally, the prefix-sum of a list of data items: $d_i, i \in 0..n$ is another list $s_i, i \in 0..n$ such that

$$s_i = \sum_{j=0}^{i} d_j,$$

---

[1] At the risk of being repetitive, the base of log is assumed to be 2, unless explicitly listed.

where $a..b$ indicates the range from $a$ to $b$, both inclusive. A sequential algorithm to compute the prefix-sum is simply:

**Listing 7.1** Sequential Prefix-Sum

```
// Compute in s the prefix-sum of d
s[0] = d[0]
for(i=1; i<=n; i++) {
        s[i] = s[i-1] + d[i]
}
```

This is an efficient sequential algorithm – it takes $O(n)$ steps, and no algorithm may take fewer steps asymptotically. However, each step depends on the previous computation, precluding any meaningful parallelism.

Prefix-sum is a good example of problems where an efficient sequential algorithm does not admit parallelism, but a fresh parallel design affords significant parallelism. Trying to factor out and reuse common computation is an important tool in sequential algorithm design. That is precisely what causes the dependency, however. Instead, a parallel algorithm is designed to subdivide a problem into independent parts, even if those parts repeat some computation.

For the prefix-sum problem, the main question is how to compute $s[i]$ without the help of $s[i-1]$. An extreme way to break the dependency is as given in Listing 7.2.

**Listing 7.2** Trivial Parallel Prefix-Sum

```
// Compute in s the prefix-sum of d
forall processor i in 0..n
        s[i] = 0
        for(j=0; j<=i; j++) {
             s[i] += d[j]
        }
```

This method is not particularly useful. The slowest processor now takes the same time that the single-processor algorithm takes. The total time remains $O(n)$. The work complexity unnecessarily jumps to $O(n^2)$, well short of the optimal $O(n)$. This is not surprising, as there were too many dependencies broken above: $O(n^2)$, in fact. The computation at each iteration of the sequential algorithm depends transitively on all earlier iterations.

For some problems, it may be possible to break dependencies entirely at a small cost. For most, there is a trade-off between the parallelism obtained and the work complexity achieved. There are two general approaches to break such a chain of dependencies: top-down or bottom-up. The first subdivides a long dependency chain into smaller chains, breaking the dependency of each chain on other chains. For example, it may be possible to carry out a partial computation of $s[i]$ independently of $s[i-1]$, say, for some $i$. This is then followed by a subsequent step to compute the final $s[i]$ in parallel for different $i$. The second approach – bottom-up – computes in parallel partial results in small groups of $i$, followed by processing the dependency chain on these partial group-results. This yields a smaller version of the original problem, and hence a smaller chain. The following examples explain these approaches.

## Parallel Prefix-Sum: Method 1

We first break the dependency chain only between $s[\frac{n}{2}]$ and $s[\frac{n}{2}+1]$, allowing $s[\frac{n}{2}+1]$ to start to be computed before $s[\frac{n}{2}]$ is available. This, in turn, breaks the dependency of all $s[i], i > \frac{n}{2}$, on any $s[i], i \leq \frac{n}{2}$, as shown in the listing below.

**Listing 7.3** Partial Prefix-Sum: Breaking Dependency

```
// Compute in s the prefix-sum only of d[1+n/2..n]
s[1+n/2] = d[1+n/2]
for(i=2+n/2; i<=n; i++) {
    s[i] = s[i-1] + d[i]
}
```

Clearly, this does not compute the full prefix-sum, but a partial one. We will see that this works because it is simple to compute the full prefix-sums from this partial prefix-sum later. The partial computation above can proceed in parallel with the computation of the prefix-sum for values of $i \leq \frac{n}{2}$. It is clear that the work complexity of computing the prefix-sum of the first half of $s$ and that of the partial prefix-sum of the second half are equal to each other. Once both halves are computed, the full prefix-sum for $i > \frac{n}{2}$ remains to be computed. However, now that the correct value of $s[\frac{n}{2}]$ is known, the partial sums can be completed in a single parallel step in $O(1)$ time with $O(n)$ work as follows:

**Listing 7.4** Partial Prefix-Sum: Breaking Dependency

```
// Update prefix-sum of the second half of s
forall processor p in (1+n/2)..n
    s[p] += s[n/2]
```

as long as $s[\frac{n}{2}]$ is accessible in parallel to all processors (of Listing 7.4).

By itself, the trick above does not lead to an improved complexity, because the prefix-sum still needs to be computed for each half, within which the dependencies remain unbroken. One sequential problem has been subdivided into two sequential problems, each of a smaller size. Using the divide-and-conquer paradigm, one can divide the problem recursively until the size of the remaining problem reduces to 1 (or a constant number).

The recurrence relations for the time and work complexity, respectively, are then:

$$t(n) = t\left(\frac{n}{2}\right) + O(1)$$
$$W(n) = 2W\left(\frac{n}{2}\right) + O(n)$$

with $t(1) = O(1)$ and $W(1) = O(1)$. Hence, $t(n) = O(\log n)$ and $W(n) = O(n \log n)$, which is not optimal. This analysis assumes that $s[\frac{n}{2}]$ can be accessed by all processors concurrently. This holds for the CREW PRAM model and other models allowing concurrent read. Exclusive read, as in EREW PRAM, or a broadcast of $s[\frac{n}{2}]$ to all $\frac{n}{2}$ virtual processors, as in BSP, would require additional time. (See Exercise 7.2.)

## Parallel Prefix-Sum: Method 2

An alternate way to break the dependencies is to break many of them in one go. For example, we might break all dependencies between odd and even indexes.

**Listing 7.5** Partial Prefix-Sum: Odd-Even Separation

```
1 // Compute in s the prefix-sum of d
2 in parallel
3        Recursively Compute prefix-sum considering only even index i
4        Recursively Compute prefix-sum considering only odd index j
5 forall processor p in 1..n
6        s[p] += s[p-1]
```

Once the two partial prefixes are known, they can derive the full sum quickly from each other, as in line 6 in Listing 7.5. This variant of top-down interleaved decomposition has the same time and work complexity as the previous block decomposition. (See Exercise 7.3.) However, it does not suffer from the bottleneck of broadcasting $s[\frac{n}{2}]$ to the entire second half. Please note that the recursive structure of the overall algorithm (as of all the algorithms in this section) is similar to that of Method 1.

## Parallel Prefix-Sum: Method 3

Let us discuss the bottom-up approach next with the help of Listing 7.6.

**Listing 7.6** Partial Prefix-Sum: Odd-Even Separation

```
// Compute in s the prefix-sum of d
forall processor p, 0<p≤n and odd p
       s[p] = d[p]+d[p-1] // Pre sum pairs
Recursively compute prefix-sum on odd indexes of s
forall processor p, 0<p≤n and even p
       s[p] = d[p]+s[p-1]      // Post sum
```

The first *forall* sums the input values in pairs. The next step recursively computes the prefix-sum on these pair-wise sums, which are $\frac{n}{2}$ in number. This recursion will also proceed in the same bottom-up fashion. The second *forall* computes the final prefix-sum from the prefix-sum of the pairs. The structure of the algorithm is depicted in Figure 7.1. In Method 3, the dependencies are removed by reducing the input set first (in parallel, of course). The recurrence relations for time and work complexity for this algorithm are

$$t(n) = t\left(\frac{n}{2}\right) + O(1)$$

$$W(n) = W\left(\frac{n}{2}\right) + O(n)$$

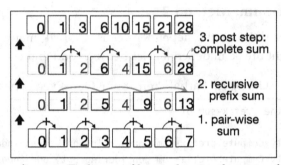

**Figure 7.1** Recursive prefix-sum. Each row of boxes denotes the state of the array *s* after each step. The numbers in the bottom row constitute the input values. The first and last steps are each fully parallel and completed in $O(1)$ by $O(n)$ processors.

This yields the optimal work complexity of $O(n)$, while retaining the time complexity of $O(\log n)$. An unrolling of the recursive statement shows that the structure of the solution is similar to the binary tree–based computation of Section 1.6: a reduction going up the tree followed by the completion step going down the tree, as shown in Listing 7.7 and Figure 7.2.

**Listing 7.7** Partial Prefix-Sum: Odd-Even Separation

```
// Compute in s the prefix-sum of d
for step = 0..(logn - 1)
        j = 2^step
        forall processor i in 1..(n/j)
                s[2*j*i-1] += s[j*(2*i-1)-1] // Reduce up the tree
for step = (logn - 1)..0
        j = 2^step
        forall processor i in 1..(j-1)
                s[j*(2*i+1)-1] += s[2*j*i-1] // Complete down the tree
```

Figure 7.2(a) shows the steps of the upward reduction pass, and Figure 7.2(b) shows the downward completion pass. Each level is shown as a row of boxes, which depict the values in the array after one step. In the upward pass, pairs are summed at each step, with the number of such sums halving at each step. The sum so produced at the last step of the upward pass is the sum of all values, which is also the prefix-sum $s[n]$. In the downward pass, the prefix-sum values are computed at each level from the prefix-sum evaluated at the level above. The bottommost level then computes the final prefix-sum.

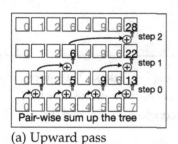

(a) Upward pass

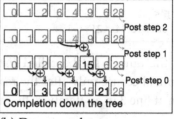

(b) Downward pass

**Figure 7.2** Prefix-sum algorithm in two passes up and down a binary tree. Each row of boxes indicates values at one step. The operations shown above the row in (a) generate the values in the row above. Operations shown below each row in (b) produce the values in the row below. The operations in each row can be performed in parallel.

Having found an efficient algorithm to reduce the dependency in the prefix-sum, we will soon see that the prefix-sum can, in turn, be used as a subroutine to break similar dependencies in other problems. Prefix-sum is more generically called a *Scan*, which has no connotation of adding. Rather, any associative binary operation can be used. *Exclusive scan* is defined as a scan where the $i$th element is not included in the $i$th result. For example, exclusive scan using addition is:

$$s_i = \sum_{j=0}^{i-1} d_j.$$

A scan algorithm can easily be modified to compute an exclusive scan. This is left as an exercise (Exercise 7.4).

## 7.2  Divide and Conquer: Merge Two Sorted Lists

We take another example of a divide-and-conquer algorithm. Merging of two sorted lists into a single sorted list is an important tool for sorting and other problems. (For this discussion, assume sorting is in increasing order, and all elements are unique.) The sequential algorithm to merge two lists, say, *list1* and *list2*, comprising $n$ elements each is as shown in Listing 7.8.

**Listing 7.8** Sequential Merge

```
1 i = j = 0
2 while(i < n and j < n)
3       if(list1[i] < list2[j])
4           output list1[i++]
5       else
6           output list2[i++]
7 while(i < n)
8       output list1[i++]
9 while(j < n)
10      output list2[j++]
```

Let the output list be called *list3*. This algorithm takes $O(n)$ steps. It is inherently sequential because only after the result of the comparison of the pair $list1[i]$ and $list2[j]$ is known at line 3 in an iteration, that the pair to compare in the next iteration is determined.

## Parallel Merge: Method 1

We first consider breaking this dependency like in the previous section. The standard binary subdivision of *list1* and *list2* into two halves each, followed by the merger of each pair does not yield two independent sub-problems. However, for each half, it is easy to determine the block of the other list that it needs to merge with, so that the recursive sub-problems do become independent.

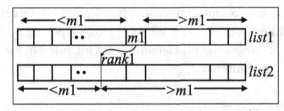

**Figure 7.3** Recursive parallel merge 1: $m1$ is the middle element of *list1*. $rank1$ is the positions of $m1$ in *list2*. Elements smaller than $m1$ in each list can be merged with each other, the remaining can be merged with each other. $m1$ need not participate in either merge.

Let the *rank* of element $x$ in *list*, denoted by $Rank(x, list)$, be the number of elements in *list* that are less than $x$.[2] Let us use the shorthand $rank1$ for $Rank(m1, list2)$, the rank of $m1$ in *list2*. Let $m1$ be the median element of *list1*. A single processor can find $rank1$ through binary search for $m1$ in *list2* in $O(\log n)$ time. This means, $rank1$ elements of *list2* are smaller than $m1$, just as $\frac{n}{2}$ elements of *list1* are smaller than $m1$. The remaining elements are greater than $m1$ (see Figure 7.3). Hence, the two smaller sets of elements

---

[2] Note that this usage of the term is slightly different from that in Chapter 6.

are the smallest $rank1 + \frac{n}{2}$ elements of $list3$. This implies that the first part of $list3$ can be obtained by merging the first $\frac{n}{2}$ elements of $list1$ with the first $rank1$ elements of $list2$. The second part of $list3$ can be obtained by merging the remaining elements of $list1$ with the remaining elements of $list2$. These are two independent merge sub-problems. The lists to be merged need not have the same length any more. In the Listing 7.9, we assume the lists to have $n1$ and $n2$ elements, respectively. The merged list is produced in $list3$.

**Listing 7.9** Parallel Merge 1: Top-Down Dependency Breaking

```
ni = max(n1, n2)
nj = min(n1, n2)
listi = longer of(list1, list2) // either if n1 == n2
listj = the other list
ranki = Search listi[n/2] in listj
in parallel
        list3[0..ni/2+ranki-1] =
                    Merge listi[0..ni/2-1] with listj[0..ranki-1]
        list3[n/2+rank..n1+n2] =
                    Merge listi[ni/2..ni] with listj[ranki..nj]
```

There is a shortcoming of the subdivision described above. If $ranki \ll \frac{ni}{2}$, the second merger possibly has too much work remaining – one list has $\frac{ni}{2}$ elements but the other may have as many as $nj$ elements of $listj$. The recurrence relations for the algorithm in Listing 7.9 for the EREW PRAM model are:

$$t(n) \le t\left(\frac{3n}{4}\right) + \log n$$

$$W(n) \le W\left(\frac{3n}{4}\right) + W\left(\frac{n}{4}\right) + \log n$$

This implies $t(n) = O(\log^2 n)$ and $W(n) = O(n)$. In practice, given a certain number of, say, shared-memory processors, one would allocate more processors to the larger sub-problem. Alternativey, one might consider subdividing into more balanced sub-problems. (See Exercise 7.12.)

## Parallel Merge: Method 2

The other manner of breaking dependency in the prefix-sum case can also be employed for merging. Note that merging is equivalent to finding the ranks of all elements of $list1$ in $list2$ and all elements of $list2$ in $list1$. The final rank in $list3$ of, say, element $list1[i]$ is $i + Rank(list1[i], list2)$.

Let $Ranklist(list_x, list_y)$ denote the list of the ranks $Rank(list_x[i], list_y)$ of all elements $list_x[i]$ of $list_x$. Suppose $Rank1 = Ranklist(list1, list2)$ and $Rank2 = Ranklist(list2, list1)$. Given $Rank1$ and $Rank2$, we can compute $list3$ as follows:

**Listing 7.10** Merge by Rank

```
in parallel
      forall processor p, 0 ≤ p < n
            list3[p+Rank1[p]] = list1[p]
      forall processor q, 0 ≤ q < n
            list3[q+Rank2[q]] = list2[q]
```

In the first step of the rank computation algorithm, we recursively merge only the even-positioned elements of $list1$ with the even-positioned elements of $list2$. In other words, we find the rank of $list1[i]$ for even values of $i$ in $list2_e$. We will use the shorthand $list_e$ to denote the even sublist, meaning $list_e[j] = list[2j]$, for $0 \leq j < \frac{n}{2}$. We do not need to create a separate $list_e$, but instead use the term to restrict consideration to the even indexes of $list$. Once $Ranklist(list1_e, list2_e)$ and $Ranklist(list2_e, list1_e)$ are known, we use them to find $Ranklist(list1, list2)$ and $Ranklist(list2, list1)$. We will use the shorthand $Rank_e1$ for the list of ranks of elements of $list1_e$ in $list2_e$, and $Rank_e2$ for those of elements of $list2_e$ in $list1_e$. Figure 7.4 demonstrates how to compute $Rank1$ and $Rank2$ from $Rank_e1$ and $Rank_e2$.

$Rank_e1$ and $Rank_e2$ can be computed recursively, like the bottom-up variant of the parallel prefix-sum algorithm. Say, $Rank_e1[i] = r_e$ is the rank of element $list1[2i]$ in $list2_e$. Figure 7.4 shows this element as $x_{2i}$. This implies that the $r_e$ elements of $list2_e$ are smaller than $x_i$, meaning $list2[0..2r_e - 1]$ are smaller than $x_i$ and $list2[2r_e] > x_i$. Hence, $Rank(x_i, list2)$ is also $2r_e$, if $x_i < list2[2r_e - 1]$, and $2r_e + 1$ otherwise. (Note that $list2[2r_e - 1]$ is not included in $list2_e$, and hence it was not compared in the recursive merging of $list1_e$ and $list2_e$.) Ranks of all elements of $list1_e$ in $list2$ and those of elements of $list2_e$ in $list1$ can be computed in this manner in parallel with each other, taking $O(1)$ time under CREW PRAM model. Thus, the work complexity to compute $Ranklist(list1_e, list2)$ and $Ranklist(list2_e, list1)$, given $Ranklist(list1_e, list2_e)$ and $Ranklist(list2_e, list1_e)$, is $O(n)$. Concurrent read is required because, say, $Rank(x_{i+1}, list2_e)$ may also be $r_e$. In that case, $list[2r_e - 1]$ would be required in the computation of both $Rank(x_{i+1}, list2)$ and $Rank(x_i, list2)$.

We next compute the ranks of the odd-index elements of $list1$ and $list2$. These are at $list1[2i + 1]$ for index $i$ of $list1_e$, and similarly for $list2$. (Note that $2i + 1$ may reach beyond the end of $list1$; these edge effects are easy to handle, but we ignore them here for simplicity of description. One may assume the value $\infty$ at such indexes.) $Rank1[2i + 1]$, which is a shorthand for $Rank(list1[2i + 1], list2)$, can be computed from $Rank1[2i]$ and $Rank1[2i + 2]$, ranks of even-index elements computed in the previous step. Recall that $list1$ is sorted,

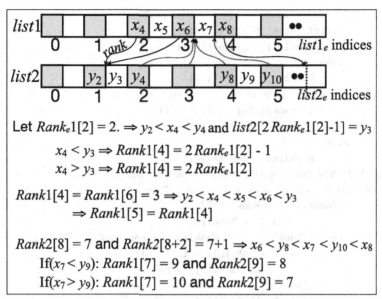

**Figure 7.4** Recursive parallel merge 2: The value of $list1[i]$ is $x_i$, and that of $list2[j]$ is $y_j$. $list1_e$ comprises the even positions of $list1$, and $list2_e$ comprises the even positions of $list2$. $Rank_e1$ and $Rank_e2$ are the rank lists with respect to $list1_e$ and $list2_e$.

and hence $list1[2i] < list1[2i+1] < list1[2i+2]$. Suppose $Rank1[2i]$ and $Rank1[2i+2]$ are equal; call them $r$. This means $Rank1[2i+1]$ must also be $r$, since $list2[r-1] < list1[2i]$ and $list2[r] > list1[2i+2]$ and hence $list2[r-1] < list1[2i+1] < list2[r]$. We may not always be so lucky though. For example, in Figure 7.4 $Rank(x_6, list2)$ is 3, and $Rank(x_8, list2)$ is much higher, say $n$. To find $Rank(x_7, list2)$, we must find which elements in the range $y_3..y_{n-1}$ are smaller than $x_7$. A binary search would find that index but would take too long; we seek an $O(1)$ algorithm.

Realize, however, that we already know the ranks $Rank(y_j, list1), y_j \in list2$, for all even $j$, $3 \le j < n$. These ranks are all either 7 or 8 in the example. We are looking for the index $k$ such that $Rank(y_j, list1) = 7$ for $j \le k$ and $Rank(y_j, list1) = 8$ for $j > k$. In this example, $k = 8$. $Rank(x_7, list2)$ is $k$ if $y_{k+1} > x_7$ and $k+1$ otherwise. $k$ can be computed in $O(1)$ time if processor $j$ for each even value of $j$ checks if $Rank(y_j, list1) + 1$ equals $Rank(y_{j+2}, list1)$. The processor – and there is exactly one – that finds it false may now compute $Rank(y_j + 1, list2)$ as well as $Rank(x_7, list2)$ in this example, and more generally $Rank(x_{r1}, list1)$, where $r1$ is $Rank(y_j, list1)$ and odd. This is detailed in Listing 7.11.

**Listing 7.11** Parallel Merge 2: "Bottom-Up" Dependency Breaking

```
Merge(list1ₑ, list2ₑ) // Create Rank1ₑ and Rank2ₑ
in parallel // First compute rank of even elements from Rankₑ
```

```
forall processor p, 0 <= p < n and p%2==0
    if(list2[Rank1[p]+1] < list1[p])
        Rank1[p] = 2*Rank1[p] + 1
    else
        Rank1[p] = 2*Rank1[p]
forall processor q, 0 <= q < n and q%2==0
    if(list1[Rank2[q]+1] < list1[q])
        Rank1[q] = 2*Rank1[q] + 1
    else
        Rank1[q] = 2*Rank1[q]
in parallel // Now compute the ranks of odd elements
    forall processor p, 0 <= p < n and p%2==0
        if(Rank1[p] == Rank1[p+2])
            Rank1[p+1] = Rank1[p]
        else if(Rank1[p]+1 == Rank1[p+2]) and Rank1[p]%2 == 1
            if(list2[Rank1[p]] > list1[p+1])
                Rank2[Rank1[p]] = p+2
            else
                Rank2[Rank1[p]] = p+1
    forall processor q, 0 <= q < n and q%2==0
        if(Rank2[q] == Rank2[q+2])
            Rank2[q+1] = Rank2[q]
        else if(Rank2[q]+1 == Rank2[q+2]) and Rank2[q]%2 == 1
            if(list1[Rank2[q]] > list2[q+1])
                Rank1[Rank2[q]] = q+2
            else
                Rank1[Rank2[q]] = q+1
```

The recurrence relations for the algorithm in Listing 7.11 for the CREW PRAM model is:

$$t(n) \le t\left(\frac{n}{2}\right) + O(1)$$
$$W(n) \le W\left(\frac{n}{2}\right) + O(n)$$

This implies $t(n) = O(\log n)$ and $W(n) = O(n)$. Work is optimal, but can time complexity be improved? Let us investigate.

## Parallel Merge: Method 3

Recall that the main task is to compute the ranks of every element of *list1* and *list2* in each other. Each rank can be potentially computed independently of the other ranks. One natural way to partition this task is to subdivide one of the lists, say *list1*, into its $n$ elements. Employing $n$ processors, each processor may complete its "merger" in $O(\log n)$ time by performing a binary search for its singleton element of *list1* in *list2*. *Partitioning* a problem into sub-problems is a common parallel algorithm design technique. This is demonstrated in Listing 7.12.

**Listing 7.12** Parallel Merge 3

```
forall processor p in 0..n-1
       Rank1[p] = find list1[p] in list2
forall processor q in 0..n-1
       Rank2[q] = find list2[q] in list1
```

This algorithm also performs concurrent reads, as all binary searches proceed in parallel. The time complexity remains $O(\log n)$, since the $2n$ rank computations are all independent of each other, and each performs a binary search through a list of $n$ elements. The work complexity, however, increases to $O(n \log n)$, which is sub-optimal. While this algorithm is simpler in structure than the previous one, the performance is worse. This suggests that processors replicate too much computation, and we should try to factor out some repeated computation.

A closer inspection indicates that $Rank(list1[m], list2) \leq Rank(list1[m+1], list2)$. Separate binary searches for $list1[m]$ and $list1[m+1]$ disregard this relationship, each proceeding independently of the other. On the other hand, we do not want the search for $list1[m+1]$ to wait until that for $list1[m]$ is complete. On the other side, trying to reduce the time complexity further by performing faster searches for $list1[m]$ may require multiple processors per search, leading to an even higher work complexity. We will see that such inexpensive algorithms may be usable on small sub-problems. Let us explore this further through the following digression.

As a sidetrack, consider searching for element $x$ in a sorted *list* using $P$ — *Aside: Parallel P-ary Search* — processors. Let's say we want to find $Rank(x, list)$. Extending the binary search, we subdivide *list* into $P+1$ blocks, with $n_P = \frac{n}{P}$ elements in each block. (The last block may have fewer elements.) Consider sublist $list_P[i] = list[n_P * i]$, $i < P$. Processor $p$ determines if $list_P[p-1] \leq x < list_P[p]$ $p = 1..P$. This condition is true for at most one value of $p$, given the assumption that elements in *list* are unique. If the condition does not hold for any processor $p$, it implies $x > list_P[P]$, that is, $x$ lies in the last block. In $O(1)$ time with $O(P)$ work, we thus determine the block of *list* in which $x$ may lie. We recursively employ all $P$ processors to find the rank of $x$ in that block next. This extends the sequential binary search into a $P$-ary search, as shown in Listing 7.13 below.

**Listing 7.13** $P$-ary Search

```
// Find rank of x in range L..R with P processors
if x < list[L]
       return Rank(x) = L
```

```
n_p = (R-L+1)/P
if(n_p <= 1) // Terminate recursion. No need to subdivide.
        if x > list[R]
                return Rank(x) = R
        forall processors p in 1..(R-L)
                if list[L+(p-1)] < x < list[L+p]
                        return Rank(x) = L+p
                return success // Some other processor will complete Rank
    if x > list[L+P*n_p]
        with P processors: Search in range {L+p*n_p}..R
    else
        forall processor p in 1..P-1
                if list[L+(p-1)*n_p] < x < list[L+p*n_p] // Test for equality
                        to find x with P processors: Search in range
                        {L+(p-1)*n_p}..{L+p*n_p}
                // x not in this processor's block. Return.
```

Each processor performs $O(1)$ comparisons per invocation of the function above. There are $O(\log_P n)$ invocations. Hence, the total time complexity is $O(\log_P n)$, and the work complexity is $O(P \log_P n)$. This means that the efficiency with $P$ processors is $O(\frac{\log P}{P})$. Nonetheless, this algorithm scales up to $P = n$, and takes time $O(1)$ with $n$ processors, which equals what brute-force search would take with $n$ processors.

The $P$-ary search algorithm above demonstrates one other algorithmic technique. It generalizes the binary tree computation structure that the parallel Merge Method 3 uses, which recursively considers the even indexes, reducing the problem size by half at each level. Some problems are amenable to partitioning into more than two sub-problems at a time, allocating an appropriate number of processors to each sub-problem. Many of these partitioning problems do not require any post-recursion operation – each sub-problem simply generates a known subset of the solution. The $P$-ary search is one such example.

Applying partitioning to the merging problem, we may select every $k$th element of $list1$ into $list1_k$, meaning $list1_k[i] = list1[ik]$. We merge $list1_k$ and $list2_k$ recursively, before deriving the ranks of the remaining elements. A large value of $k$ reduces the size of the recursive sub-problem. On the other hand, a large $k$ also leaves a large number of ranks remaining to be computed after the two sublists are merged.

Suppose $k = \sqrt{n}$. $list1_k$ and $list2_k$ are each of size $\sqrt{n}$. As a result, we can $P$-ary search to find the rank of each element of $list1_k$ in $list2$ using $\sqrt{n}$ processors for each search, as in Listing 7.14 below.

**Listing 7.14** Parallel Merge 4: $\sqrt{n}$ Subdivision

```
// Rank √n elements of list1 in list2
rootn = √n
```

```
forall processor p in 0..rootn-1
    with rootn processors P-ary Search list1[p*rootn] in list2[0..n-1]
```

$\sqrt{n}$ processors can find $Rank(list1_k[i], list2)$ for any $i$ in $O(1)$ time using $O(\sqrt{n})$ work. Since there are $\sqrt{n}$ elements in $list1_k$, $n$ processors can compute all of $Ranklist(list1_k, list2)$ in $O(1)$ time, with $O(n)$ work. We can similarly compute $Ranklist(list2_k, list1)$ in $O(1)$ time, with $O(n)$ work. This seems good; except much work remains – we do not yet know the ranks of $(n - \sqrt{n})$ elements of each list. We can compute these ranks by recursively solving smaller merge problems. See the illustration in Figure 7.5 to understand how.

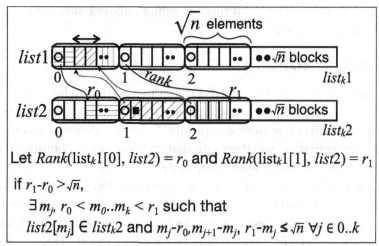

Let $Rank(list_k1[0], list2) = r_0$ and $Rank(list_k1[1], list2) = r_1$

if $r_1$-$r_0 > \sqrt{n}$,

$\exists m_j, r_0 < m_0..m_k < r_1$ such that

$list2[m_j] \in list_k2$ and $m_j$-$r_0, m_{j+1}$-$m_j, r_1$-$m_j \leq \sqrt{n}$ $\forall j \in 0..k$

**Figure 7.5** Recursive parallel merge 3: Each list is subdivided into blocks of $\sqrt{n}$ elements. The rank of the first element of each block, depicted as circles, is computed first. These ranks help subdivide the merging problem into up to $2\sqrt{n}$ smaller merging problems. Three of these sub-problems are highlighted – the first pair with horizontal hatching, the second with oblique, and the third with vertical hatching.

Consider two consecutive elements of $list1$ that are included in $list1_k$, say $list1[i\sqrt{n}]$ and $list1[(i + 1)\sqrt{n}]$. The ranks of these elements in $list2$ are known after the P-ary search. Call them $r_i$ and $r_{i+1}$. We know that ranks of all elements $list1[x]$, where $i\sqrt{n} < x < (i + 1)\sqrt{n}$, are also in the range $r_i..r_{i+1}$. This means that we can decompose the merger into smaller mergers: Merge $list1[i\sqrt{n}..(i + 1)\sqrt{n} - 1]$ with $list2[r_i..r_{i+1} - 1]$. This sub-problem can be large if $r_i \ll r_{i+1}$.

However, if $r_{i+1} - r_i > \sqrt{n}$, just as in parallel Merge Method 2, the range $list2[r_i..r_{i+1}]$ contains elements from $list2_k$ whose ranks in $list1$ are known. Those elements delineate blocks having no more than $\sqrt{n}$ elements each. Moreover, their ranks in $list1$ are not more than $\sqrt{n}$ apart, as they all lie in the range $(i\sqrt{n})..((i + 1)\sqrt{n} - 1)$. This ensures that we may now independently merge pairs of blocks of $list1$ and $list2$, respectively. The number of such pairs is at most $2\sqrt{n}$ as at least one block of each pair has $\sqrt{n}$ elements. The other can have fewer. Thus the recurrence relation for complexity is:

$$t(n) = t(\sqrt{n}) + O(1)$$
$$W(n) = \sqrt{n}W(\sqrt{n}) + O(n)$$

This means that $t(n) = O(\log \log n)$ and $W(n) = O(n \log \log n)$. This $W(n)$ is not optimal, even if the time complexity is now lower. A subtle point to note: each recursive sub-problem computes the ranks only with respect to its block of elements. For example, in Figure 7.5, the recursive sub-problem computes the rank of $list2[k+1]$, the element shown as ■, in the part of $list1$ marked by $\leftrightarrow$. If this computed rank is $srank$, $Rank(list2[k+1], list1)$ is $srank + Rank(list2[k], list1)$.

## Parallel Merge: Method 4

The last algorithmic technique we discuss in this section reduces the work complexity of an algorithm with high work complexity but low time complexity by combining it with another that has low work complexity. The main idea is to run the first algorithm on sub-problems that are small enough that its higher work complexity does not have a limiting effect on the overall work complexity.

Let us see how this works for the merging problem. Here, we use the faster algorithm to merge sublists $list1_k$ and $list2_k$, carefully selecting $k$. Note that algorithm Merge Method 3 merges two lists of size $n$ each using $O(n \log \log n)$ work. Since $list1_k$ and $list2_k$ have $\frac{n}{k}$ elements each, they can be merged using $O(\frac{n}{k} \log \log \frac{n}{k})$ work. This amounts to $O(n)$ if we choose $k = \log \log n$. In particular, it implies that if $list1$ and $list2$ have $n$ elements each, $list1_k$ and $list2_k$ can be merged in $O(\log \log n)$ time using $O(n)$ work.

Given $Ranklist(list1_k, list2_k)$ and $Ranklist(list2_k, list1_k)$ computed recursively, we can now compute $Ranklist(list1_k, list2)$ and $Ranklist(list2_k, list1)$, also in $O(\log \log n)$ time using $O(n)$ work ($k$ being $\log \log n$). Recall that if $Rank(list1_k[i], list2_k)$ is $r$, $list1_k[i] = list1[ik]$ lies between $list2_k[r-1]$ and $list2_k[r]$, that is, between $list2[(r-1)k]$ and $list2[rk]$. There are only $k-1$ elements between $list2[(r-1)k]$ and $list2[rk]$, and hence a single processor can locate $list1_k[i]$ in $O(k)$ steps. $\frac{n}{k}$ processors can, in parallel, compute the ranks of $\frac{n}{k}$ elements of $list1_k$ in $list2$ in $O(k)$ time. In parallel with these processors, $\frac{n}{k}$ processors can compute $Ranklist(list2_k, list1)$ in $O(k)$ time.

Similar to Merge Method 3, we now have $2\frac{n}{k}$ pairs of lists to merge, each with no more than $k$ elements. With $k = \log \log n$, each of these mergers can be completed by a single processor in $O(\log \log n)$ time, requiring $O(n)$ total work.

Thus the total time complexity of the optimal merge algorithm is $O(\log \log n)$, and its work complexity is $O(n)$ on CREW PRAM. This is work-time optimal. Time complexity of any work-optimal PRAM algorithm to merge two sorted lists with $n$ elements is

$\Omega(\log \log n)$. In fact, the lower bound to merge sorted lists on an EREW PRAM is $\Omega(\log n)$.[3] We generalize this idea in Section 7.3.

## 7.3 Accelerated Cascading: Find Minima

This section demonstrates a technique called *accelerated cascading*, which is designed to first reduce the depth of the computation tree, leading to an algorithm with lower time complexity at the cost of increased work complexity. That algorithm can then be combined with a work-efficient algorithm, which may have a slightly higher time complexity similar to Parallel Merge Method 4. We begin by recursively partitioning the problem into sub-problems. It is a generalization of the binary tree computation structure and partitioning, except the number of sub-problems is not two (or a fixed number), but a function of the problem size itself. For example, one may partition a problem of size $n$ equally into $\sqrt{n}$ sub-problems at each level.

We will use accelerated cascading to solve the problem of finding the minima of an unsorted list of values. (Assume these values are comparable to each other.) The regular binary tree structure works well for this problem as shown below.

**Listing 7.15** Parallel Minima

```
// Find the minima of list of n elements in O(log n) time
forall processor p in 0..(n-1)
        minima[p] = list[p]
for step in 1..log n
        forall processor p in 0..(n-1), p %(2^step) == 0
                minima[p] += minima[p+2^(step-1)]
```

Listing 7.15 requires $O(\log n)$ time and $O(n)$ work. Work complexity is optimal, as the best sequential algorithm is $O(n)$. Does there exist an algorithm with lower time complexity? Quite like the merge algorithms we discussed in Section 7.2, we can try to check for each element $list[i]$ if it is the minima. If constant time-common write is allowed (as in CRCW PRAM), $n - 1$ processors can in parallel determine in $O(1)$ time if $list[i]$ is the minima as shown in Listing 7.16.

**Listing 7.16** Fast Parallel Minima (Part 1)

```
// Find if list[i] is the minima
smallerthan[i] = false
forall processor p in 0..(n-1), p != i
        if(list[i] > list[p]) // Found a smaller element
                smallerthan[i] = true
```

---

[3] Hayashi et al., "Work-time optimal k-merge algorithms."

*smallerthan* is a variable that more than one processors may attempt to write simultaneously. All three versions of CRCW PRAM model support this operation – any writing processor writes true, and the algorithm is correct if any of the writes succeeds. Note that these writes cannot complete in $O(1)$ time in the EREW PRAM model, nor the BSP model.

*smallerthan*[i] is true if any element of *list* is smaller than *list*[i], and false otherwise. This implies that if *Smallerthan*[i] is false, *list*[i] is the minima. Computing *Smallerthan* in parallel on CRCW PRAM in $O(1)$ time requires $O(n^2)$ work. Listing 7.17 produces the minima value from *Smallerthan* in $O(1)$ time with $O(n)$ additional work.

**Listing 7.17** Fast Parallel Minima (Part 2)

```
// Produce the minima in smallerthan
forall processor p in 0..(n-1)
    if(smallerthan[i] == false)
        minima = index[i]
```

This algorithm, call it *Minima0*, works for Common-CRCW PRAM if the minima is unique, that is, only one element is strictly less than all others. Alternatively, we can break ties using list index in Listing 7.16.

Let us try applying the technique discussed in Section 7.2 to combine this nonoptimal $O(n^2)$ work algorithm with the optimal $O(n)$ algorithm of Listing 7.15, to improve the time complexity. Recall that Merge Method 3 has a work complexity of $O(n \log \log n)$, slightly higher than the optimal work complexity $O(n)$. The nonoptimal minima–finding algorithm is $O(n^2)$, which significantly higher than the optimal $O(n)$. To maintain the bound of $O(n)$ work, we might partition *list* into blocks of size $\sqrt{n}$. This two-step algorithm would find the minima of each block first, in parallel with other blocks. This requires $O(n)$ work per block on CRCW PRAM. With $\sqrt{n}$ blocks, the total work is $O(n\sqrt{n})$, with the time remaining at $O(1)$. In the second step, the minima of the $\sqrt{n}$ block minima can be computed by repeating the same algorithm. The second step also requires $O(1)$ time and performs $O(n)$ work. Let us call this $\sqrt{n}$-block algorithm *Minima1*.

*Minima1* computes the minima of a list containing $n$ elements in $O(1)$ time with $O(n^{1+\frac{1}{2}})$ work. *Minima1* was derived by employing the more work-expensive algorithm on smaller blocks of the data. Can we reduce this further by reapplying the same idea? The answer is yes. We look to increase parallelization and reduce time using more work.

Suppose we employ *Minima1* on blocks of size $\sqrt{n}$. The first step requires $n^{\frac{1}{2}}$ parallel invocations of *Minima1* on blocks of size $n^{\frac{1}{2}}$ each. The second step finds the minima of the $n^{\frac{1}{2}}$ block minima, again using *Minima1*. The resulting total work is $n^{\frac{1}{2}}n^{\frac{3}{4}} = n^{1+\frac{1}{4}}$. The time taken is that in two invocations of *Minima1*. Let's call this algorithm *Minima2*.

This could go on. After $k$ successive operations, the work complexity achieved is $n^{1+\frac{1}{2^k}}$. But, can this really go on indefinitely? If we use *Minima2* on the original problem, we require running $\sqrt{n}$ instances of *Minima1* in parallel, each on a block of $\sqrt{n}$ elements. Each instance of *Minima*1, in turn, divides its $\sqrt{n}$ elements into $\sqrt{\sqrt{n}}$ blocks of size $\sqrt{\sqrt{n}}$ each. This looks like the binary tree algorithm structure, except the number of sub-problems created at each level is not two. Rather, it is the square root of the size of the problem at that level. Each of those sub-problem's size is also the square root of the level's problem size. This is illustrated in Figure 7.6.

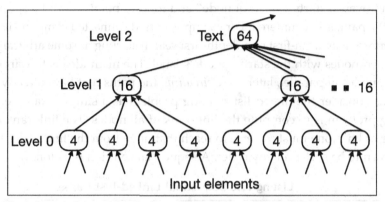

**Figure 7.6** Find the minima with accelerated cascading. The numbers in the boxes are the number of processors used to compute the minima of the output of the level below, one element per arrow.

We continue this recursion until the problem size reaches, say, two (or a higher termination constant). The number of levels in this recursion is $O(\log \log n)$. Since we can find the minima on Common-CRCW PRAM in $O(1)$ time, we know the $O(\log \log n)$ levels can each be computed in $O(1)$, given sufficient processors at each level. Note that there are $\frac{n}{2}$ computation nodes at step 0 (leaf level) and 1 node at the root. In general, there are $\frac{n}{2^{2^l}}$ computation nodes at level $l$, with $2^{2^l}$ elements processed per node. Given that $(n^2)$ work is required to find the minima of $n$ items, $(2^{2^l})^2$ work is required to find the minima of $(2^{2^l})$ items at each node on Common-CRCW PRAM. This adds up to $O(n)$ work at each level.

This leads to a total time complexity of $O(\log \log n)$ and a total work complexity of $O(n \log \log n)$. We will call this algorithm the fast minima method. Now that we have an algorithm requiring $O(n \log \log n)$ work, we can resort to the technique from Section 7.2 to obtain an $O(n)$ work algorithm.

Divide *list* into $\frac{n}{\log \log n}$ blocks with $\log \log n$ elements per block. We can compute the minima of each block in $O(\log \log n)$ time sequentially. One processor performs $O(\log \log n)$ work on one block in parallel with other processors working on other blocks. We next apply the fast minima algorithm on the $\frac{n}{\log \log n}$ block-minima, taking $O(\log \log n)$ time and $O(n)$ work. This combined algorithm is work-optimal and has a better time complexity than the algorithm with the basic binary tree structure.

## 7.4  Recursive Doubling: List Ranking

Solutions to list ranking in this section and Euler tour and connected components in sections 7.5 and 7.6 demonstrate the parallel algorithmic technique known variously as *pointer jumping* or *recursive doubling*. It is particularly useful for the traversal of paths in lists and graphs.

Such traversal starts at a "root node" and follows pointers until a specific node, or the end of the path, is encountered. For example, to find connected components in a graph, one may perform a breadth-first or a depth-first search starting at some arbitrary node, labeling all reached nodes with the starting node's label. The main idea is to start exploring paths from all nodes in parallel, later *short-circuiting* the paths that have already been explored.

Let us consider the linked-list ranking problem as a simple example. The linked-list ranking problem is to compute the link-rank of all nodes. The link-rank of a node is the number of links one must traverse to reach that node from the first node. The linked list is not known to be sorted in any order. A sequential solution is as follows:

**Listing 7.18** Sequential Linked-List Ranking

```
// Find the rank of all nodes. headnode is the first node of a linked list
current = headnode
rank = 0
while(current != NULL) {
        current.rank = currentrank
        current = current.next
        currentrank = currentrank + 1
}
```

If the only way to access the nodes is by following *next* references starting at *headnode*, no parallelism is available. Instead, a parallel algorithm requires a different data structure, one that allows direct access to different nodes. Consider *nodelist*, a list of references to nodes in an arbitrary order, that is, *nodelist*[$i$] for $i \in 0..n$ is a node in the liked list, and *nodelist*[$i$].*next* does not necessarily refer to *nodelist*[$i + 1$]. Now consider the following parallel algorithm:

**Listing 7.19** Parallel Linked-List Ranking

```
// Find the rank of all n nodes. headnode is the first node of a linked list
forall processor p in 0..n
        if(nodelist[p] == headnode)
                nodelist[p].rank[p] = 0
        else
                nodelist[p].rank[p] = 1
```

```
        skipnext[p] = nodelist[p].next
for step = 0..log(n+1)
      forall processor p in 0..n
            if(skipnext[p] != NULL)
                  nodelist[skipnext[p]].rank = nodelist[skipnext[p]].rank +
                                                nodelist[p].rank
                  skipnext[p] = skipnext[skipnext[p]]
```

*skipnext* is initially a copy of the next reference of each node. This copy is required because we later modify this reference to short-circuit certain nodes, and do not want to destroy the original linked list. There are $O(\log n)$ steps in the main loop of Listing 7.19. At each step, the processor assigned to a node updates the currently estimated rank of its next node with reference to its own estimate. Then, each processor short-circuits its *next* reference by "jumping" to its next node's *next* reference.

Figure 7.7 demonstrates this jumping algorithm. At step $i$, the ranks of nodes with ranks $0..2^i - 1$ are known. (Try proving this by induction on $i$.) Thus, there are $O(\log n)$ steps taken by each of the $n$ processors. The time complexity is $O(\log n)$, and the work complexity is $O(n \log n)$.

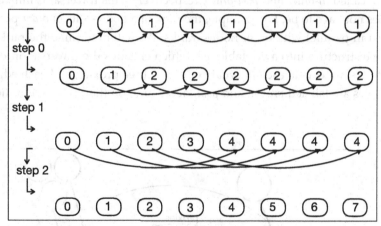

**Figure 7.7** Parallel linked-list ranking. *nextlist* is depicted by arrows, the values of *rank* are shown for every index after each step. These nodes are drawn in the order of the linked list and not the order of the indexes.

## 7.5  Recursive Doubling: Euler Tour

List ranking and pointer jumping are useful in graph traversal as well. Often graph traversal is simply a way to reach all graph vertices or edges. A parallel graph representation allows processors direct access to any vertex or any edge. Breadth-first or depth-first traversal is not necessary in such a context. In other settings, the path taken by graph traversal is meaningful. Such traversal may appear to be sequential by nature. However, they may not truly be sequential. For example, in breadth-first traversal, all children of a node may be traversed in parallel with each other.

In this section, we consider a depth-first traversal, particularly of a binary tree. This traversal is also called an Euler tour of the binary tree. It proceeds as follows:

**Listing 7.20** Euler Tour of a Binary Tree

```
// traverse a tree whose root is given
return if root == null
pre-visit(root)
traverse(left-subtree)
in-visit(root)
traverse(right-subtree)
post-visit(root)
```

The functions *pre-visit*, *in-visit*, and *post-visit* are application dependent. The order in which *pre-visit* is called on nodes is called the *pre-order*. Similarly, *in-visit*'s and *post-visit*'s orders are called *in-order* and *post-order*, respectively. This traversal is inherently sequential, but it does not have to be. For example, the rank of a node — its *in-order* position — may be computed in parallel with other nodes' ranks. We will determine the rank by turning the binary tree structure into a veritable list, which encodes the traversal order. As Figure 7.8 demonstrates, we divide each internal node into three proxies, and each edge into two. The node proxies are labeled *pre*, *in*, and *post*, depending on their position in the traversal. This

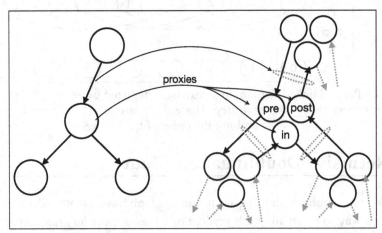

**Figure 7.8** Treating a binary tree (left) as a list (right). Proxies for a node and an edge are shown by the curved arrows.

need not be a physical separation of the data structure, it is simply a logical view of the same nodes. If "parent" references are maintained, those references can implicitly double as proxies. This transformation converts a tree into a list. The rank of (the proxy) nodes within this list is the Euler tour positions of each node. The time and work complexity are similar to that of list rankings – $O(\log n)$ and $O(n \log n)$, respectively.

If only the *in-order* rank is required, the list ranking algorithm does not count the proxies marked *pre* and *post* by simply setting the initial values of rank to 0 for these nodes (see Listing 7.19).

## 7.6 Recursive Doubling: Connected Components

Let us next see how to use pointer jumping to derive a simple algorithm to find connected components in an undirected graph. (The basic idea also applies to directed graphs.) Let us assume that graph $G$ is given as a list of edges *edgelist*, where the $i$th edge *edgelist*$[i]$ is a pair $(u, v)$, and $u$ and $v$ are integers identifying two vertices, respectively. Let us call the number of edges $m$, and the number of vertices $n$.

The goal of the problem to find connected components is to assign a label *label*$[u]$ to each vertex $u$, which identifies its connected component. If vertex $u$ has a path to vertex $v$, they are in the same connected component. If there is no such path, they are in different components. In other words, for all edges $(u, v)$, *label*$[u]$ = *label*$[v]$. Further, no such edge $(u, v)$ may exist such that *label*$[u]$ is different from *label*$[v]$. Vertices in different components have different labels. (Can you make labels be a component ID? See Exercise 7.19.)

Our first algorithm uses this property. It iteratively relabels each vertex until all the vertices of a connected component have the same label. For each edge $(u, v)$, it assigns the same label to $u$ and $v$. Of course, this must proceed in a controlled manner. Otherwise, labels may continue to change indefinitely. One way to control relabeling is to enforce asymmetry: a vertex's label is given to its neighbor only if that neighbor's label is larger.

**Listing 7.21** Compute Connected Components I

```
forall processor p in 0..n-1
        label[p] = p
Repeat until any label changes
        forall processor p in 0..m-1
                (u,v) = edgelist[p]
                if(label[u] > label[v])
                        label[u] = label[v]
```

Note that processors for two edges incident on a vertex $u$ may both write two different values to *label*$[u]$ in the same step. An Arbitrary-CRCW PRAM would allow any one of these writes to succeed. Listing 7.21 works under this model. It terminates with a correct labeling. The relabeling stops only when all edges have the same label on both its vertices. Since all vertices start with unique labels, and no edge exists between any pair of vertices in two different connected components, no such pair may have the same label. Also, if vertices $u$ and $v$ in the same component have different labels, it means at least two adjacent vertices on the path $u$ to $v$ have different labels. However, no two vertices connected by an edge are allowed to have different labels by the algorithm above.

How many steps are required before labels converge? At each edge where there is no convergence yet, the label of a higher-labeled vertex reduces by at least one. The initially smallest labeled vertex of each component never changes its label. Call that vertex the *root* of the component. The root's label is taken by its immediate neighbors first and then by their neighbors until it diffuses through the entire component. This process might suggest that the root's label reaches all the components in $O(\mathcal{P})$ steps , where $\mathcal{P}$ is the maximum length of the path from the root to any vertex in its component. This is not strictly true because the root's label does not necessarily reach its neighbor $u$ in one step, since another edge's processor may succeed writing its value in $label[u]$. Note, however, that the label of $u$ must strictly reduce everytime a neighbor updates it. Hence, in at most $d(u)$ steps, $label[u]$ changes to $label[root]$, where $d(u)$ is the degree of $u$. This is true for any vertex $v$ along the path from the root and the lable of the one with the highest degree can update last. Hence, the total complexity is $O(\mathcal{P} + d(G))$, where $d(G)$ is the degree of the graph. Since all $m$ processors may be active for all steps, the total work complexity is $O(m(\mathcal{P} + d(G)))$.

Ignoring the effect of the degree, the progress of labelling along different paths from the root appears to be similar to list ranking. It is reasonable to expect a similar pointer jumping would take time logarithmic in the length of the path. The difference here is that the graph is not a linear structure like a list, and we need to determine which way to jump. The labels we generate impose a direction to jump. Let the label-tree be formed by directed label-edge from vertex $u$ to vertex $label[u]$. This is a forest in general, and in the beginning, each vertex is isolated with the vertex's label set to itself.

In the next algorithm, processors are again associated with graph edges. For simplicity, we assign processors for both edges $(u,v)$ and $(v,u)$. Each processor attempts to merge two adjacent label-trees corresponding to its associated edge (if certain conditions are met) A label tree $T_1$ is said to be adjacent to label tree $T_2$ if there is an edge $(u,v)$ such that $u \in T_1$ and $v \in T_2$. In the label tree, we call vertex $v$ the parent of vertex $u$ if $label[u]$ is $v$ $u$ is a root if $label[u]$ equals $u$; the root is its own parent. Further, a label tree is called a star if all its vertices have the same label as that of its root. A star indicates a connected component. If no star is adjacent to any other, the algorithm terminates.

**Listing 7.22** Compute Connected Components of a Graph with $n$ Vertices and $m$ Edges

```
// Set label(u) == label(v), iff u and v are in the same component.
```

```
2 forall processor p in 0..n-1
3         label[p] = p
4 forall processor p in 0..m-1
5         active[p] = true
6 while(there is an active processor) {
7         forall p in 0..m-1, active[p] == true
8                 (u,v) = edgelist[p]
9                 if inStar(u) and label[u] > label[v]   // See Listing 7.23
10                        label[label[u]] = label[v] // Hook star's root to the smaller root
11                if inStar(u) and label[u] != label[v]
12                        label[label[u]] = label[v]   // Hook star's root to the other
                          if not hooked on line 10
13                if not inStar(u)
14                        label[u] = label[label[v]] // Pointer jumping
15                else
16                        active[p] = false
17 }
```

The processor for edge $(u, v)$ in Listing 7.22 first checks if $u$ is part of a star. If it is part of a star, it attempts to hook its parent, which is a root, to the parent of neighbor $v$. $v$ need not be in a star. The processor accomplishes hooking by relabeling $u$'s parent to that of $v$'s. This makes $u$'s root the child of $v$'s parent. Of course, if $v$ is also part of a star, processor $(w, u)$ may simultaneously hook $v$'s root to $u$'s root if $v$ and $w$ belong to the same star. Asymmetry must be imposed to prevent a cycle, just as in Listing 7.21. Hence, $u$ hooks its root to $v$'s root only if $v$'s label is smaller than $u$'s label.

Listing 7.22 ensures that all stars that can be hooked to another tree are indeed hooked, even if they fail to hook on line 9 due to symmetry breaking. The reason a star may fail to hook on line 9 is that all its adjacent stars may have roots with larger labels. If a star $S1$ remains a star at line 11, it may hook to any adjacent tree. That adjacent tree must not be a star at 11, because any star that is hooked on line 10 ceases to be a star. Further, any star $S2$ adjacent to $S1$ at line 9 could not remain unhooked on line 11 because $S2$ did have at least one adjacent star with a smaller root: $S1$.

If a star has no adjacent tree, it does not hook. In that case, that star is one of the graph's final connected components. See Figure 7.9 for an illustration. The vertex identifiers are shown in the ovals. Figure 7.9(a) shows the state of the algorithm at some step, when there are three label trees. The leftmost tree is not a star, and the other two are. Edges connect tree 2 to both tree 1 and tree 3; it is adjacent to both trees. The processor associated with edge $(7, 4)$ attempts to hook tree 2 to tree 3, while the one associated with edge $(6, 3)$ attempts to hook it to tree 1. In Arbitrary-CRCW PRAM, one of the writes succeeds in

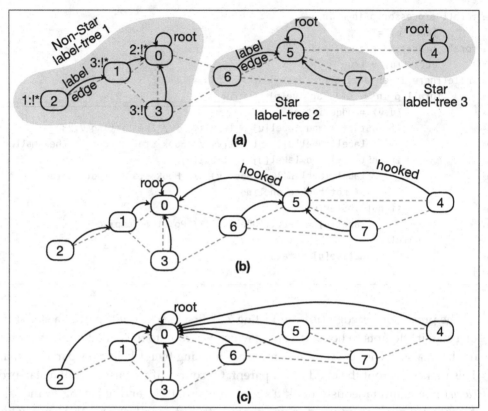

**Figure 7.9** Connected component computation. The number within the oval is the vertex identifier. Dark arcs indicate the labels. For example, *label*[2] is 1 in (a). This part shows three label trees, of which the first one is not a star, and the other two are stars. Graph edges are shown in lighter dashed lines. (b) shows the hooking of two stars. (c) shows one step of pointer jumping, which yields a single connected component with vertex 0 as the root.

line 9. Let's say the second one. In that line, tree 3 does not hook to tree 2 because tree 3 already has a smaller label. Instead, it hooks to tree 2 in line 11. Note that before that line, tree 2 becomes a part of tree 1. There is a single tree remaining after the two hooks, and it is not a star. A single step of the pointer jumping on line 14 turns the tree into a star, which is the final connected component. The algorithm terminates in the next iteration.

How does the algorithm know to terminate though? Since common write is allowed, processors may set a shared variable *anyactive*[4] to false at the beginning of every iteration on line 6. Every active processor then sets *anyactive* to true at the end of the iteration. If no processor sets *anyactive*, it remains false, and all processors terminate. The other step

---

[4] We dispense with the $ suffix for shared variables in this chapter; variables are shared by default in PRAM.

that is not detailed in Listing 7.22 is how to determine if vertex $u$ is part of a star. This step is described below.

**Listing 7.23** Compute if Vertex $w$ is Part of a Star

```
1 // inStar: True if all vertices in u's current component have the same label.
2 star[u] = true // All vertices are in lock-step
3 if label[u] != label[label[u]] // u's parent is not a root
4        star[u] = false
5        star[label[label[u]]] = false // u's grandparent is also not a star
6 star[u] = star[label[u]]          // If its parent was marked non-star, u is not star
```

We seek to determine in parallel for every node if it is a part of a star. A root that has any grandchild is not the root of a star. Hence, vertex $u$ whose parent is not the root (a root's label is its own identifier) is proof that the tree it belongs to is not a star. Such a vertex marks the grandparent as not a star. At the same time, a child-less child of root may incorrectly remain marked star because its star value is not reset on line 4 or 5. However, if the root has even a single grandchild, it is marked a non-star in line 5. This is the evidence for childless children of the root to be marked a star in line 6. Figure 7.9(a) demonstrates this. The processor for edge, say, $(2, 1)$ marks node 2 as a non-star first on line 4. This processor next marks the grandparent of node 2, which is node 0, a non-star on line 5. Finally, node 3 is marked a non-star by the processor for edge $(3, 0)$ on line 6.

The algorithm terminates in time $O(\log \mathcal{P})$. Until a node becomes part of a star, its distance to the root of its tree in a non-star tree halves in each iteration (unless that node is the root itself or its direct child). Once the tree becomes a star, it may hook to another tree with a new root, and the distances continue to halve. Since all $m$ processors may remain active until the end, the work complexity is $O(m \log \mathcal{P})$.

Sometimes it may be necessary to count the number of connected components and to assign contiguous identifiers instead of a root's label. This can be easily achieved by using a prefix-sum over differing labels in $O(\log n)$ time using $O(n)$ work as shown in Listing 7.24.

**Listing 7.24** Relabel Connected Components Contiguously

```
// Assign in id[p] the connected component identifier for each node p
forall p in 0..(n-1)
       if(label[p] == p)
              id[p] = 1
       else
              id[p] = 0
exclusive prefix-sum (id)
forall p in 0..(n-1)
       id[p] = id[label[p]]
```

## 7.7  Pipelining: Merge-Sort

We will next discuss several sorting algorithms, each of them designed to demonstrate an algorithmic technique. Parallel merge-sort derives directly from the parallel merge discussed earlier. Parallel radix-sort is efficient for sorting integer-based elements. Parallel quick-sort and sample-sort are also efficient for general cases.

We begin with an application of pipelining in merge-sort.

### Basic Merge-Sort

Recall from Section 7.2 that merge can be completed in $O(\log \log n)$ time with $O(n)$ work on CREW PRAM. Merge-sorting a list of $n$ comparable elements begins by merging $\frac{n}{2}$ pairs of singletons, followed by $\frac{n}{4}$ pairs of two-element lists, and so on, until the last step merges one pair of $\frac{n}{2}$-element lists. It proceeds as follows:

**Listing 7.25** Relabel Connected Components Contiguously

```
1 // Sequentially Merge-sort a list with n element
2 for step = 0 to ceil(log(n))-1   // Assume n is a power of 2
3        numpair = 2^(log(n)-step-1)
4        listlen = 2^step // Adjust last pair's len if n is not a power of 2
5        for pair = 0 to numpair-1
6             p0 = pair*2*listlen
7             merge list[p0..p0+listlen-1], list[p0+listlen..p0+2*listlen-1]
```

In Listing 7.25, the loop in line 5 can clearly be parallelized. This is demonstrated in Figure 7.10, where steps proceed upward from the bottom. Step $i$ computes level $i + 1$ from level $i$. Level 0 comprises one element per list. Merging different pairs at each step can proceed independently of each other. If we assume $\frac{n}{2}$ processors for the entire sort, these processors can all be allocated to one step at a time. At step $i$, $\frac{n}{2^{i+1}}$ pairs of lists are merged. The two lists in each pair at level $i$ have $2^i$ elements each. Using $2^i$ processors per pair-merge adds up to $\frac{n}{2}$ total processors at each step or, $O(n)$ work.

On the other hand, it appears that the steps of the loop in line 2 must proceed sequentially. After all, the lists at level $i$ are not available until step $i - 1$ is complete. That would imply that $\log n$ sequential iterations of line 2 are required. Step $i$ requires $O(\log i + 1)$ time and $O(n)$ work overall. This results in a total time complexity of $O(\log n \log \log n)$ and work complexity of $O(n \log n)$ to merge-sort on CREW PRAM. The time complexity on EREW PRAM is $O(\log^2 n)$. This is a work-optimal algorithm. Is it also time-optimal? Not so, it turns out. We introduce the algorithmic technique called *pipelining* that improves the parallelism, and hence the time complexity, without increasing the work complexity.

Pipelining amounts to incrementally performing otherwise sequential steps by decomposing them into sub-steps. Sub-steps can be performed on a part of the input, without waiting for the entire input. Such pipeline is possible if the steps also produce the output incrementally, one part at a time. Merging algorithms described in Section 7.2 satisfy this general requirement. Recall, for example, that Merge Method 2 merges two sorted lists by first ranking the even elements and then using the results to rank the odd elements. Thus it does not need the values of the odd elements at the start. Consequently, it produces the rank of the even elements first, and then the ranks of the odd elements later. Further, the entire algorithm is recursively applied, as illustrated in Figure 7.11 (for level 3 of Figure 7.10). The part of the list that is processed exponentially evolves to the entire list.

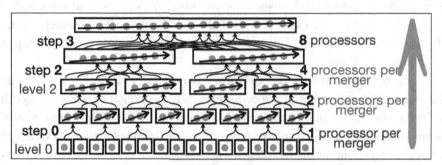

**Figure 7.10** Merge tree for merge-sort. steps proceed bottom-up. The number of merges halves at each level, the sizes of lists to merge (and produced) double at each level. The number of processors per merge operation also doubles at each step, ensuring that the total number of processors is constant across steps.

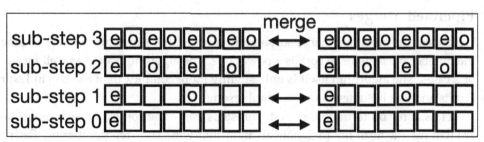

**Figure 7.11** Active sublists at each merger sub-step are marked. The even-positioned elements of the active sublist are marked $e$, and the odd-positioned ones are $o$. The odd ones are the newly activated elements at that sub-step. Thus, the number of active elements doubles at each sub-step. First, the ranks of the already active members are updated with respect to the other updated sublist. Then, the ranks of the newly active members are computed (see Listing 7.11).

In general, since the lists that merged at level $i$ comprise $2^i$ elements each, there are $\log 2^i$ sub-steps required at that level. At sub-step 0, only one element of each list is active: the 0th element. In sub-step 1, the first and the middle elements are active. They are, respectively, the even and odd elements at that sub-step. For each merger of two lists, a sub-step computes the ranks of each list's active elements with respect to the active elements of the other list. In sub-step $j$, $2^j$ elements are active, doubling with each sub-step. The rank of all active elements at sub-step $j$ can be computed in $O(1)$ from the ranks computed in sub-step $j - 1$ (see Merge Method 2).

That opens up the possibility of pipelining sub-steps. The newly active members required at sub-step $j$ of level $i$ may be produced by level $i - 1$ any time before sub-step $j$ of level $i$, and not necessarily before its sub-step 0. The pipeline would be perfect if those active members are produced by level $i - 1$ at sub-step $j - 1$. However, this is not quite how Merge Method 2 proceeds. It does not guarantee, for example, that the middle element of the merged list it produces for the level above is known after sub-step 1 (or, any earlier sub-step). On the other hand, it expects the middle elements of its two input lists to be available at its sub-step 1.

An adjustment to the merge algorithm is necessary to pipeline it. In particular, we relax the strict requirement of the order in which the elements of the merged list must be produced, and rather use them at the next level in the order they are actually produced. The main question we need to answer is: what partial results to produce at each sub-step and how to use them at the next level. The answer will also indicate when level $i + 1$ can begin after level $i$ has begun, and when it completes. Also note that pipelining implies that multiple levels have active computation simultaneously. Work complexity analysis and processor allocation must account for this. In the nonpipelined version of the merge-sort algorithm, only one level is active at a time, possibly simplifying processor allocation.

## Pipelined Merges

We discuss the pipelined merge-sort algorithm[5] next. For simplicity, we will assume that $n$, the number of elements to sort, is a power of 2. The algorithm works as well for nonpower of 2 cases. The algorithm itself is only slightly more complex than the one in Listing 7.25, but its analysis is somewhat more cumbersome.

Let us agree on terminology first. Sub-steps are in the context of each merge-sort step. We will use the term *tick* to denote an algorithm-wide sub-step numbering. Each node of the merge tree maintains an evolving list. This list is initially empty at all nodes except the leaves, and completes when it contains all elements in the subtree of that node (see Figure 7.10). At each tick, each active node incrementally merges some of the data produced

---

[5] Cole, "Parallel merge sort."

earlier by its children into its evolving list. A node becomes active and starts merging two ticks after elements start to appear in its children's lists. Three ticks after the children complete their lists, the parent also completes its merger and deactivates. The activation and deactivation happen level by level, from the leaf level to the root.

Thus level $i$ activates at tick $2i + 1$, and completes at tick $3i$. This means that three ticks after level $i$ is complete, level $i + 1$ also completes. Thus there are $O(\log n)$ ticks. We will see that the algorithm takes a constant time per tick. The incremental merger is similar to Merge Method 2, except a more general sublist is processed at each tick. We will refer to the final list produced by node $x$ by $L(x)$. The two children of a node at level $i$ are nodes at level $i - 1$. We call these children $x.left$ and $x.right$, respectively.

In a slight abuse of notation, we will use the level $i$ in place of node, that is, $L(i)$, $L(i.left)$, or $L(i.right)$. Since the operation at all nodes of a level is similar, our algorithmic description does not distinguish between them. Read $L(i)$ as the list produced by a generic node at level $i$. We do need to refer to a node's children; hence, $i.left$ and $i.right$. We also need to account for the evolution of the list at each node. We will denote the current list at any node at level $i$ at tick $t$ – meaning just before tick $t$ – by $L(i, t)$. $L(i, t + 1)$ is computed at tick $t$ by merging $L(i.left, t)$ and $L(i.right, t)$ with the help of $L(i, t)$. $L(i, t) = $ null for $t < 2i$ and $L(i, t) = L(i)$ for $t \geq 3i$. $L(0) = L(0,0)$ is the initial list at level 0. Each leaf node contains one element from the full list to be sorted (see Figure 7.10).

At tick $t$, the $2^{i-1}$ processors assigned to a node at an active level $i$ together compute

$$L(i, t + 1) = Merge(L_k(i.left, t), L_k(i.right, t)) \text{ using } L(i, t) \qquad (7.1)$$

where $L_k$ is the sublist of $L$, taking every $k$th element starting at $L[k - 1]$. The value of $k$ is 4 during the evolution of the children's lists. Once the children's lists are complete, $k$ is set to 4, 2, then 1 at the next three ticks. After that third tick, the parent's list is complete, since it produces a merger of the complete lists of its two children. Note that setting $k$ to 1 means that all elements of the children are included in $L_k$. Specifically, in Eq. (7.1):

$$k = 4 \text{ if } t < 3i - 1$$
$$k = 2 \text{ if } t = 3i - 1 \qquad (7.2)$$
$$k = 1 \text{ if } t > 3i - 1$$

The progression of ticks is demonstrated in Figure 7.12.

The important step of the actual merger at each tick at each level remains to be discussed. The Merge on Eq. (7.1) is completed in $O(1)$ time using $O(j)$ work, where $j$ is the number of elements in $L(i, t)$. This is due to the choice of $L_k$: old elements before the tick at a level are well interspersed among the new elements after the tick, even if they do not faithfully alternate like odd and even. We need another digression to explain this formally.

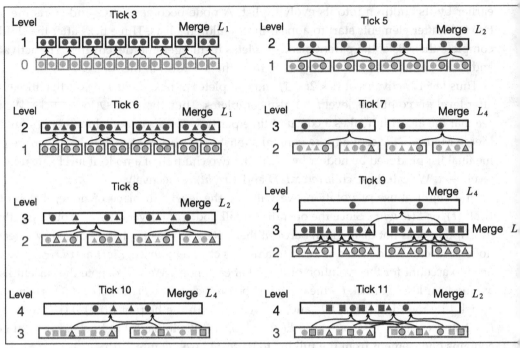

**Figure 7.12** Pipelined merge: ticks 3 to 11. Ticks 0–2 and 4 have no mergers and are skipped. The state of the active levels are shown. Inactive levels whose lists are used by active levels are also shown, but greyed out. The sublisting of the children is indicated with $L_1$, $L_2$, or $L_4$. Children's elements selected in the sublists are shown with a dark outline. The elements added to a level at successive ticks are shown as circles, triangles, and squares, respectively. At tick 9, both levels 3 and 4 are active. Note that the state of a level's lists is shown at the end of each tick. For example, at tick 9, the processors on level 4 merge $L_4(3,8)$, the sublists of the lists produced by level 3 at tick 8.

A sorted list $L'$ is called a *c-cover* of list $L$ if two consecutive elements $e_1$ 
> *Aside: c-cover Merging*

and $e_2$ of $L'$ have at most $c$ elements of $L$ between them. In other words, there are $c$ or fewer elements $e$ in $L$ such that $e_1 < e < e_2$. If $e_2$ is the first element of $L'$, we consider $e_1 = -\infty$, and if $e_1$ is the last element, we let $e_2 = \infty$.

Two sorted lists *list1* and *list2* with $n$ elements each may be merged in $O(1)$ time using $O(n)$ work on EREW PRAM if $Ranklist(X, list1)$ and $Ranklist(X, list2)$ are given and $X$ is a c-cover (for a constant $c$) for both *list1* and *list2*. We first "invert" $X$'s ranks by computing $Ranklist(list1, X)$ and $Ranklist(list2, X)$. Listing 7.26 shows how to compute $Ranklist(list, X)$, given $Ranklist(X, list)$. Since we know $r = Rank(X[i], list)$ for elements of $X$, that gives $Rank(list[r], X)$. We only need to derive the ranks of the other elements near $list[r]$ in *list*. An example is shown in Figure 7.13, explaining the steps of Listing 7.26, which computes those ranks. We use $c = 4$.

## Listing 7.26 $c$-Cover Merge

```
1  // Compute rankx = Ranklist(list, X) given xrank = Ranklist(X, list),
2  forall processor p in 0..(n-1) // n elements in list
3    rankx[p] = -1 // Unfilled value
4  forall processor p in 0..(|X|-1) // |X| is the number of elements in X
5    if(p == [x]-1 or xrank[p+1] != xrank[p])
6      if (list[xrank[p]] == X[p]) // Do not include X[p] in rank of list[xrank[p]]
7        rankx[xrank[p]] = p
8      else // Included X[p] is rank of list[xrank[p]]
9        rankx[xrank[p]] = p+1
10     if (p < n-1 and xrank[p+1] > xrank[p]+1) // Also rank the next element of list
11       rankx[xrank[p]+1] = p+1
12 forall processor p in 0..(n-1)
13   if (rankx[p] == -1) // Not filled yet
14     for i = p-1 to p-3 // Look up to 3 steps to the left for the first filled rank
15       if(xrank[i] != -1)
16         rankx[p] = rankx[i]
17         exitloop
18     if(i < 0) // No filled rank found (xrank[-1] is effectively 0)
19       xrank[p] = 0;
```

Like our prior assumption, the elements within each list remain unique. However, $X$ may have some elements that appear in *list* and others that don't. Since we define $r = Rank(x, list)$ as the number of elements in *list* that are strictly less than $x$, we must differentiate between these two cases. If $x == list[r]$, all elements to the left of $x$ in $X$ are less than $list[r]$, for example, $X[6] = 21$ in Figure 7.13. On the other hand, the rank of $X[1] = 9$ is 4. $list[4]$ is not equal to 9. This means that all the elements to the left of 9 in $X$, as well as 9, are less than $list[4]$. These cases are differentiated in line 6 of the listing. In either case, $list[r+1]$ is greater than $x$. $list[r+1]$ is also less than the element to the right of $x$ in $X$, as long as that element has a rank different from that of $x$. Hence, $Rank(list[r+1], X)$ is one more than the index of $x$ in $X$. Remember that two consecutive elements of $X$ may have the same rank, for they can have 0 elements of *list* between them. For example, the ranks of $X[2]$ and $X[3]$ are both 5. The listing lets the processor associated with the last of these equal elements of $X$ set the inverse rank (on line 5).

The processor associated with $x$ also sets the ranks of $list[r]$ and $list[r+1]$ in line 11. All the elements to the right of $list[r+1]$ that do not get a reverse rank in the previous step also have ranks equal to that of $list[r+1]$. For example, $r = 1$ for $X[0]$. $list[r+1] = list[2]$ has rank 1 (one more than the index of $X[0]$). The rank of the element to the right of $X[0]$ has rank $s = 4$ in *list*, meaning $list[s-1] = list[3]$ is definitely less

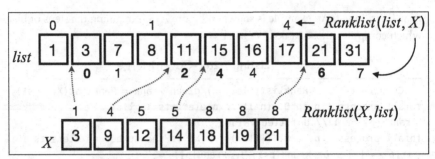

**Figure 7.13** Compute $Ranklist(list, X)$ given $Ranklist(X, list)$ in $O(c)$ time, if $X$ is a $c$-cover of *list*. The example shows integer-valued lists $X$ and *list*. The values $Ranklist(X, list)$ are shown above $X$. These ranks indicate the position of the corresponding elements of $X$ in *list*. The elements at those positions of *list* are ranked in $X$ at line 7 or 9 of Listing 7.26. These ranks are shown below *list* in bold font. The ranks computed on line 11 are shown in light font. Finally, the ranks of the remaining elements of *list* are computed at line 16 and are shown above *list*.

than $X[1]$. However, all such elements to the right of $list[r + 1]$, until index $s - 1$, are greater than $X[0]$. Hence, they all must have the same rank as that of $list[r + 1]$. This is completed in line 16 in Listing 7.26. This loop iterates at most $c$ steps if $X$ is a $c$-cover of *list*, as $s - r \leq c$.

$Ranklist(list1, X)$ and $Ranklist(list2, X)$ can be computed in parallel with each other. They both take $O(1)$ time and perform $O(n)$ work, given that $c$ is a constant. Recall that we are interested in computing $Ranklist(list1, list2)$ and $Ranklist(list2, list1)$. If the rank of element $i$ of $list1$, $Rank(list1[i], X)$ is $xrank1$, $X[xrank1 - 1] < list1[i]$ and $X[xrank1] \geq list1[i]$. All elements in $list2$ less than $X[xrank1 - 1]$ are definitely less than $list1[i]$. There are $Rank(X[xrank1[i - 1]], list2)$ of those. Additionally, some elements between the positions $Rank(X[xrank1[i - 1]], list2)$ and $Rank(X[xrank1[i]], list2)$ in $list2$ may also be less than $list[i]$. See Figure 7.14 for an example. $xrank1 = Rank(list1[3], X)$ is 1. $rankx2a = Rank(X[xrank1], list2)$ is 2. This means that the first two elements of $list2$ are all less than $list1[3]$. $rankx2b = Rank(X[rank1 + 1], list2) = 5$ implies that $list2[rankx2b] \geq list1[4]$. Some elements between index $rankx2a$ and $rankx2b$ may be smaller than $list1[3]$, but there may be at most $c$ such elements; 3 in this example.

Hence, one processor allocated to position 3 of $list1$ may compute its rank in $O(c)$ time. If $c$ is a constant, the work complexity is $O(n)$. This can be done in EREW PRAM with a bit of care. More than one element of $list1$, for example, $list1[2]$ and $list1[3]$, may have the same rank in $X$: $xrank1 = 1$. The processors assigned to find their respective ranks in $list2$, both read $Rank(X[1], list2)$. Since there are at most $c$ such elements in $list1$, they may be serialized to eliminate any need for concurrent read. This would require the processor assigned to every position to determine its serial order. One way is to count the number of elements to the left of its position in $list1$ that have the same rank as its own. We skip those details here. The following is a simpler CREW PRAM version.

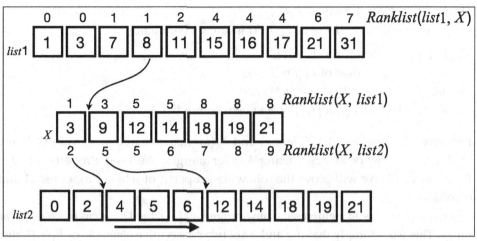

**Figure 7.14** Compute $Ranklist(list1, list2)$ given $Ranklist(list1, X)$ and $Ranklist(X, list2)$ in $O(c)$ time, if $X$ is a $c$-cover of $list2$. The example shows integer-valued lists $list1, X$ and $list2$. The values $Ranklist(X, list1)$ are shown above $X$, and $Ranklist(X, list2)$ below it. $Ranklist(list1, X)$ is shown above $list1$. $Rank(list[3], X)$ is 1. Given that $Rank(X[0], list2)$ is 2 and $Rank(X[1], list2)$ is 5, $2 \leq Rank(list1[3], list2) < 5$. Hence, $Rank(list1[4], list2)$ is 2+ the number of elements of $list2[2..4]$ that are less than $list1[3]$. There are at most $c$ such elements, in general

**Listing 7.27** Transitive $c$-Cover Merge

```
// Compute rank1 = Ranklist(list1, list2)
//    given rankx1 = Ranklist(list1,X), xrank2 = Ranklist(X, list2),
forall processor p in 0..(n-1) // n elements in list1
        i = xrank2[rankx1[p]-1]
        while(i < min(n, xrank2[rankx1[p]]))
            i = i+1
        rank1[p] = i
```

The listing above indicates that these ranks can be computed transitively: $Ranklist(L1, L3)$ can be computed from $Ranklist(L1, L2)$ and $Ranklist(L2, L3)$. Further, if $L1$ and $L2$ have a $c$-cover relationship, and so do $L2$ and $L3$, $Ranklist(L1, L3)$ can be computed in constant time with linear work. We say that two lists have a $c$-cover relationship if one of them is a $c$-cover of the other.

## 4-Cover Property Analysis

We can now discuss the pipelined merger of Eq. (7.1). The goal is to find and use 4 covers for each merger. We will see that the list in a node at the end of a tick is a 4-cover for the merger at its next tick. The following two properties hold.

◇1: $L_k(i, t-1)$ is a 4-cover of $L_k(i, t)$,
     and $Ranklist(L_k(i, t-1), L_k(i, t))$ is known before tick $t$.

◇2: $L(i, t)$ is a 4-cover of $L_k(i.left)$,
     $L(i, t)$ is a 4-cover of $L_k(i.right, t)$,
     and $Ranklist(L(i, t), L_k(i.left, t))$ and
     $Ranklist(L(i, t), L_k(i.left, t))$ are known before tick $t$.

Property ◇2 ensures that $L_k(i.left, t)$ and $L_k(i.right, t)$ can be merged in $O(1)$ time with $O(|L(i, t+1)|)$ work at tick $t$ using 4-cover merger. We need Property ◇1 to find the Ranklists of ◇2. We will prove the following property, of which Properties ◇1 and ◇2 are corollaries:

◇*: If $L_4(i, t)$ has $m$ elements in some range $l..r$, $L_4(i, t+1)$ has no more than $2m$ in that range. This would imply that if $a$ and $b$ are two consecutive elements of $L_4(i, t)$, meaning it has two elements in the range $a..b$, $L_4(i, t+1)$ has no more than four such elements. That would guarantee that $L_4(i, t)$ is the 4-cover of $L_4(i, t+1)$ for any $i$ and $t$.

The statement above can be proven by induction on $i$. Note that once the lists at a node's children are complete, the next three ticks at the parent are similar to the three steps of Merge Method 2. Every $2^2$th, then every $2^1$th, and finally every $2^0$th element of the children's final lists are merged. ◇* holds trivially in these cases. The following proof, hence, focusses on the ticks when the children lists are not yet complete when sublists are formed by selecting every fourth element meaning $k = 4$. We refer to the elements selected in $L_k$ (all $i$ and $t$) as samples. The other elements of $L$ will be called nonsamples.

By induction, if the statement holds at the children before tick $t$, it also holds at the parent after tick $t$ (i.e. before tick $t+1$). The base case is easy to prove, as it holds trivially at all levels whose children are complete. Figure 7.15 illustrates the inductive step of the proof. The figure takes two *consecutive* elements of $L_4(i, t)$: $a$ and $b$. (The same argument holds for nonconsecutive elements.)

Consider a node at level $i$. By the inductive hypothesis, if $L_4(i-1, t-1)$ has $\alpha$ elements in the range $a..b$, $L_4(i-1, t)$ has no more than $2\alpha$ in that range.

Since $L_4(i, t)$ has every fourth element of $L(i, t)$, if $L_4(i, t)$ has $m$ elements in the range $a..b$, $L(i, t)$ has $4m - 3$ elements in that range. Some of these $4m - 3$ come from the left child's sublist and the others from the right child's. Vertical bars in Figure 7.15 delineate the range $a..b$ in the children. There are fewer than $4m - 1$ elements in the two children's sublists in the range $a..b$, we include two additional samples that bound the nonsamples that may lie in the range $a..b$. Let $s_1$ samples come from the left sublist $L_4(i.left, t-1)$, and $s_2$ from $L_4(i.right, t-1)$. $s_1 + s_2 \leq 4m - 1$. By the inductive hypothesis, no more than $2s_1$ samples exist in $L(i.left, t)$ in the range $a..b$, and no more than $2s_2$ samples in $L(i.right, t)$. Since $L(i, t+1)$ is formed by merging $L_4(i.left, t)$ and $L_4(i.right, t)$, it cannot

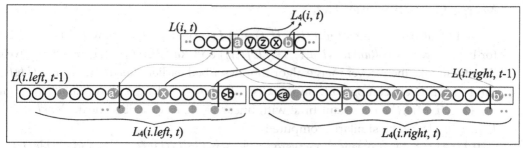

**Figure 7.15** Merging using cover: $L_4(i, t+1)$ is the 4-cover of $L_4(i, t)$. Node $i$ and its children are shown. Filled circles depict samples. Nonfilled ones are nonsamples. Elements $a$ and $b$ are two consecutive elements in $L_4(i, t)$. Hence, five elements of $L(i, t)$ are in the range $a..b$. Some of these five come from the left and the others from the right child's sublist. In these sublists, any sample in the range $a..b$ must be within the vertical bars. In particular, $a'$ is definitely less than $a$, and $b'$ is definitely greater than $b$. There are three samples in the left child in $a'..b'$, and four in the right. If no more than six and eight elements appear after tick $t$ in children's sublists, $L(i, t+1)$ may not contain more than 14 elements in $a..b$. Hence, at most four can be in $L_4(i, t+1)$.

contain more than $2(s_1 + s_2) = 8m - 2$ elements in the range $a..b$. This guarantees that its sublist $L_4(i, t+1)$ may not contain more than $2m$ elements in the range $a..b$, and $L_4(i, t+1)$ is the 4-cover of $L_4(i, t+1)$.

Thus, we can say that Property $\diamond 1$ holds, and $L_k(i, t)$ is the 4-cover of $L_k(i, t+1)$ for all $k$ in the pipelined merge progression. Since this applies to all levels, clearly $L_k(i.left, t-1)$ is the 4-cover of $L_k(i.left, t)$.

Further, considering that $L(i, t)$ was formed at tick $t-1$ by merging $L_k(i.left, t-1)$ and $L_k(i.right, t-1)$, we know that between any pair of consecutive elements of $L(i, t)$ there are no more than two elements of $L_k(i.left, t-1)$ and no more than two elements of $L_k(i.right, t-1)$. For example, consider consecutive elements $z$ and $x$ in $L(i, t)$ in Figure 7.15. There cannot be more than two elements in $L_k(i.left, t-1)$ in the range $z..x$. Were $z$ and $x$ both in $L_k(i.left, t-1)$, they would be its consecutive elements. If neither were in $L_k(i.left, t-1)$, it must not contain any element in the range $z..x$. If only one of $z$ and $x$ is in $L_k(i.left, t-1)$, it must be the only element in the range $z..x$. For example, in Figure 7.15, $x$ is in $L_k(i.left, t-1)$, and $z$ is not. In that case, the element immediately before $x$ in $L_k(i.left, t-1)$, $a'$ in this case, is definitely less than $z$, ensuring that there is only one element in $z..x$. Given, then, that the $L_k(i.left, t-1)$ contains no more than two elements in $z..x$, by Property $\diamond*$, $L_k(i.left, t)$ contains no more than four in that range. Hence, $L(i, t)$ is the 4-cover of $L_k(i.left, t)$. Similarly, $L(i, t)$ is the 4-cover of $L_k(i.right, t)$. That proves Property $\diamond 2$.

## Merge Operation per Tick

At node $i$, at tick $t$, we merge $L_k(i.left, t)$ and $L_k(i.right, t)$. We know $L(i, t)$ is a 4-cover for both. If we have $Ranklist(L(i, t), L_k(i.left, t))$ and $Ranklist(L(i, t), L_k(right, t))$, we can directly invoke the $c$-cover merge algorithm described earlier. $Ranklist(L(i, t), L_k(i.left, t))$ can be transitively computed from $Ranklist(L(i, t), L_k(i.left, t - 1))$ and $Ranklist(L_k(i.left, t - 1), L_k(i.left), t)$ in constant time with linear work, as described next. $Ranklist(L(i, t), L_k(i.right, t))$ can be similarly computed.

If $L(i, t)$ is null, it means there were no elements in $L_k(i.left, t - 1)$ and $L_k(i.left, t - 1)$, and this is the first time a child's list contains $k$ elements. Since $k \leq 4$, this merger can be done at each such node in $O(1)$ time with $O(1)$ work. In the general case, when $L(i, t)$ does exist, this means it was a merger of sublists $L_k(i.left, t - 1)$ and $L_k(i.right, t - 1)$, using $X = L(i, t - 1)$ as the 4-cover. This means we computed $Ranklist(L(i, t), L_k(i.left, t - 1))$ and $Ranklist(L(i, t), L_k(i.right, t - 1))$. We store them in lists $lrank$ and $rrank$, respectively, at node $i$. Also, since we use $L(i, t - 1)$ as a cover for computing $L(i, t)$, we compute $Ranklist(L(i, t - 1), L(i, t))$ (see $c$-cover merger algorithm earlier). This can provide, in $O(1)$ time with $O(L_k(i, t))$ work, ranks for their 4 covers: $Ranklist(L_k(i, t - 1), L_k(i, t))$. We store them in $erank$ at node $i$.

In Listing 7.28, $left.erank$ refers to the list $erank$ of the left child and $right.erank$ to that of the right child. Note that unlike Merge Method 2, the pipelined mergers cannot happen in-place. Multiple rank arrays are required. Some consolidation is possible, and the pipelined merger can be implemented on EREW PRAM. A 4-cover merge must be implemented in a way that the $lrank, rrank,$ and $erank$ are read by all active processors first and then updated at the end. We skip a detailed presentation of that.

**Listing 7.28** Pipelined $c$-Cover Merge

```
// Merge Lₖ(x.left), Lₖ4(x.right)), given lrank, rrank and erank
forall node x at level 2*tick+1..3*tick
     k = computek(level, tick) // See Eq. 7.2
     Using |L(x.left)/k| processors // assume |L(x.right)|==|L(x.right)|
          4-cover-merge(Lₖ(x.left), Lₖ(x.right, t), \
                              lrank, rrank, x.left.erank, x.right.erank)
     Update rankl, rankr, erank
```

Many mergers happen in parallel in the pipelined scheme, each completing in $O(1)$ time. The nodes at level $i$ of the merge-tree complete their processing at tick $3i$. This implies that all levels have completed after $3 \log n$ ticks, and the root node has the sorted result. The work at each level is also easy to count. Note that a level deactivates when complete. A level is complete when it receives all the elements of the list to be sorted. The lowest active level, call it $l$, receives all $n$ elements in a span of three next ticks. This means that up to $\frac{n}{2}$ processors remain active at this level, for we merge two lists of size $2^l$ each using $2^l$ processors at each node. No level below level $l$ is active. Levels above $l$ all use $k = 4$. Thus level $l + 1$ uses up to $\frac{n}{8}$ processors, and so on, up to the highest active level, $\frac{3l}{2}$. This adds up to $O(n)$ active processors at any tick. Thus the total work complexity is $O(n \log n)$.

## 7.8 Application of Prefix-Sum: Radix-Sort

Among sequential sorting algorithms, radix-sort is known to be particularly efficient for sorting small integers. The main idea of the algorithm is to divide each element, rather the sorting key, into small parts. The algorithm iterates over parts, the least significant part first. Each part takes a fixed number of values. For example, a 32-bit integer naturally consists of 32 1-bit parts.

Suppose, in general, there are $d$ parts, each taking $D$ values. For each part, the entire list is divided into $D$ buckets, which can be accomplished sequentially in $O(n)$ time for a list of size $n$. The sequential complexity to complete radix-sorting is $O(dn)$. Radix-sort relies on the different parts being sorted in a strict sequence. Hence, the only step that may be parallelized is the sorting of $n$ items into $D$ buckets.

Setting $d = 32$ for a 32-bit integer key, each of the $d$ sorts amounts to a single prefix-sum.

**Listing 7.29** Parallel Radix-Sort

```
1 // Radix-Sort list n-place
2 for i = 0 to 31
3         bsum = parallel prefix-sum bit[i] using $n$ processors // We count LSB as bit 0
4         forall processor p in 0..(n-1)
5             if(bit[i] of list[p] == 0)
6                     rank[p] = p - bsum[p]
7             else
8                     rank[p] = n - bsum[n-1] + bsum[p] - 1
9         list[rank[p]] = list[p]
```

This listing ensures that at iteration $i$, all elements with $bit[i] = 0$ move to the beginning of the list, and those with $bit[i] = 1$ move to the end. Additionally, they move in a stable way: two elements with $bit[i] = 0$ retain their order. Line 6 computes the ranks of the elements with bit 0. As seen in Section 7.9, bit 0 piggybacks on the prefix-sum of bit 1. The number of elements with $bit[i] = 0$ before $list[p]$ is the total number of all elements before it, that is, $p$, less those with $bit[i] = 1$, that is, $bsum[p]$. Similarly, the number of elements with $bit[i] = 1$ before an element itself with $bit[i] = 1$ is simply its prefix sum minus 1. Of course, the elements with $bit[i] = 1$ must all be ranked after all those with $bit[i] = 0$. The total number of elements with $bit[i] = 0$ is $n - bsum[n - 1]$. This is shown in line 8.

Since each prefix-sum takes $O(\log n)$ time with $O(n)$ work, the total time complexity for radix-sorting $d$-part keys is $(d \log n)$, and the total work complexity is $(dn)$.

Another version of radix-sort iterates over the bits in the reverse order, most significant part first. For certain platforms, that version would be more suitable. In the most significant part first scheme, the elements with $bit[i] = 0$ and $bit[i] = 1$ are recursively divided into two buckets. Thus the first bit subdivides *list* into two buckets, the next bit further subdivides each bucket into two, and so on. More importantly, each bucket can be sorted independently of the other buckets. Once a bucket becomes small enough, it may be sorted sequentially, while other processors continue to subdivide buckets. We leave those details as an exercise for the reader.

## 7.9   Exploiting Parallelism: Quick-Sort

The sequential quick-sort algorithm is organized quite like the sequential merge-sort algorithm, but there is no postpartition step. The quick-sort algorithm first partitions the given list *list1* into two lists *list1s* and *list1l* in a way that all elements of *list1l* are greater than every element of *list1s*. This generates two independent sub-problems that can be solved independently. This is top-down partitioning and follows a similar binary-tree structure as that of the merge-tree, but proceeds top to down. If we accept computing down the tree sequentially, the question that remains is: can we at least partition *list1* in parallel? Prefix-sum is the answer.

**Listing 7.30** Quick-Sort Partitioning

```
1 // Partition list1[a..b]
2 pivot = random value in a..b
3 forall processor p in 0..(n-1)
4         if(list1[p] < list1[pivot]) // Separate
5                 side[p] = 1
6         else
7                 side[p] = 0
8 index = Parallel Prefix--sum(side) using n processors
9 pdest = index[n-1]
10 forall processor p in 0..(n-1)
11        if(side[p] == 1)
12                index[p] = index[p]-1
13        else
14                if(p == pivot)
15                        index[p] = pdest
```

```
16          else if(p > pivot) // For large elements after the pivot position,
17                      index[p] = pdest + p - index[p]
18          else
19                      index[p] = pdest + p - index[p] + 1
20       list1[index[p]] = list1[p]
```

| final index 4 | 0 | 5 | 6 | 1 | 3 | 7 | 2 |
|---|---|---|---|---|---|---|---|
| prefix sum 0 | 1 | 1 | 1 | 2 | 2 | 2 | 3 |
| <pivot? 0 | 1 | 0 | 0 | 1 | 0 | 0 | 1 |
| list1 | 23 | 5 | 13 | 16 | 3 | ⑦ | 44 | 1 |

pivot

**Figure 7.16** Partition a list. Suppose index 5 is chosen as the pivot. Determine which side of the pivot each element lies on. Then, perform a prefix-sum on the small side. The large side prefix-sum can be derived from the small side, which is shown in final index.

Partition for quick-sort amounts to asking for each element of *list1*, if it is less than the pivot (call them *small*) or greater than it (call them *large*). The small and large sets are then sorted independently of each other. The pivot, if it is a part of *list1*, goes in the middle. Determining the set membership is trivially parallelizable with $O(1)$ time and $O(n)$ work. All processors must agree on the pivot. This requires concurrent read capability to complete in $O(1)$.

It is not sufficient to know which set an element belongs in. These sets must be constructed as well. Quick-sort separates the two sets in-place. We can do the same in parallel in the PRAM model. We need to find nonconflicting indexes for elements to transfer to, such that all the elements smaller than the pivot get smaller indexes than the rest. One can simply determine the position of each element within its set. Line 8 in Listing 7.30 computes the prefix-sum of the list *side* and stores it in *index*. The elements less than the pivot have a 1 in *side*. Thus, $index[p]$ contains the number of small elements to the left of position $p$, plus 1 for itself. *index* provides a contiguous numbering for all small elements starting at 1: a small element at position $p$ can be transferred to position $index[p] - 1$ without any conflict. This is demonstrated in Figure 7.16.

We similarly need to compute the prefix-sum for the large elements. A separate scan is not required because there are only two sets. The number of large elements to the left of position $p$ is $p$ minus the number of small elements to its left. However, the numbering for the large elements must start after the small elements and the pivot. An offset of *pdest* achieves that. This is computed in line 16.

The total complexity of partitioning is dominated by prefix-sum. Time complexity is $O(\log n)$ and work complexity is $O(n)$. Retaining the sequential quick-sort tree, there are $O(\log n)$ expected levels. (Please refer to a textbook on data structures or algorithms for an analysis of the number of expected levels.) The expected time complexity is $O(\log^2 n)$, and the expected work complexity is $(n \log n)$.

Note that the structure of the algorithm changes quite significantly in the BSP model. Processors cannot directly transfer an element to its proper side "in-place." Instead, each processor must send each element to the appropriate destination processor. Receiving processors may receive the elements in a location of their choice. (See Exercise 7.14.)

Back to the PRAM model, let us see if the time complexity can be reduced. Pipelining of prefix-sum could be an option, but no fast pipelined prefix-sum is known. Could we completely do without prefix-sum? We use it to physically separate the lists into small and large subsets. It may be possible to get by without such separation. By comparing with pivot $v$, each processor $p$ knows the subset its element $list1[p]$ is in. Suppose, we simply let it use that information to determine how to proceed. Depending on whether $list1[p]$ is in $list1s$ or $list1l$, if $p$ can determine its subset's next pivot, it can test again. For example, if $list1[p]$ is in $list1s$, and the pivot for $list1s$ is $v_s$, $p$ needs to compare $list1[p]$ with pivot $v_s$ next to determine which subset of $list1s$ $list1[p]$ lies in. It can go down the tree, comparing with a sequence of pivots. Thus, the initially *small* subset would be recursively divided into *small-small* and *small-large* subsets, and so on. If we can continue this process, labeling small as bit 0 and large as bit 1 at each test, the smallest element will see a sequence $0, 0, 0 \ldots$ and the largest would see $1, 1, 1 \ldots$. The bit for the first partition appearing first. This pivot itself is in neither set and may be assigned an *end* symbol indicating the termination of its bit sequence. Processor $p$ terminates when $list1[p]$ is chosen as the pivot. Questions remain:

- How does each process receive an appropriate pivot in each round?

- How is the final rank of each element determined?

In principle, one may use any pivot. The ideal pivot for any set is its median. We generally rely on "good" pivots by randomly choosing one of the elements in a set as its pivot. Pivots outside the range of values in a set are "bad," as they lead to up to $n$ levels in the quick-sort tree. If we can find the minimum value $m$ and the maximum value $M$ within a set, $\frac{M+m}{2}$ may be a good choice. Section 7.3 explains how to find the minima in (1) time with $O(n^2)$ work with the common write facility in CRCW PRAM. However, that algorithm requires the knowledge of the full set, as each element is compared with every other element of the set. Another possibility is to evolve a consensus. If processor $p$ knows the subset (and later sub-subset, etc.) its element $list1[p]$ is in and a prearranged address associated with that subset; it may write its own value as a proposal for the pivot of its subset. A concurrent write is required. In the Arbitrary CRCW-PRAM model, one of the proposers succeeds. In the next step, all members of the set read the winning pivot value and use it to classify themselves at the next level of the tree.

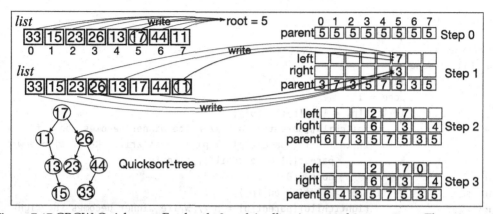

**Figure 7.17** CRCW Quick-sort. For levels 0 and 1, all writes are shown as arcs. The winner is shown in a dark color. In this example, processor 5 wins writing to root first. Hence $list[5]$ becomes pivot. Processors with elements less than $list[5]$ compete to write to $left[5]$. Processor 7 wins, and its element, 11, becomes the left child. Similarly, processor 3 wins on the large side. The losers on each side update their parents to 7 and 3, respectively. Processor 5, the parent processor, does not lie on either side and, hence, does not compete to write. The same process continues at other levels.

How to prearrange the address per subset? One way to designate a unique address for each subset is its position in the quick-sort tree itself. See Figure 7.17. We count the levels downward. The first partition is at level 0, which creates two sublists, one contains all elements in the left subtree of the parent (say, the *small* sublist) and the other in the right subtree. Let $parent[p]$, $left[p]$, and $right[p]$ contain the indexes, respectively, of the parent, the left child, and the right child for element $list1[p]$. $parent[p]$ doubles as the pivot for element $list1[p]$. Initially, all elements use the same pivot and $parent[p] = root$, one selected pivot. Once the sublists are partitioned, $parent[p]$ changes accordingly.

As described above, $parent[p]$ (i.e. pivot) is set by the arbitrary write of CRCW-PRAM by processors of each sublist. Processors $p$ with elements smaller than $list1[parent[p]]$ compete and write to $left[parent[p]]$. One succeeds. Processors with elements larger than the pivot compete to become the right child similarly. Again, one wins. All the writers read back to check if they won. The winner has the pivot. Losers need to continue the process. For simplicity, Listing 7.31 lets the chosen pivot also continue to process until the final termination. However, they are the only elements in their list – so they continue to repeat the same computation.

**Listing 7.31** Arbitrary CRCW Quick-Sort

```
1 //Quick-sort list
2 forall processor p in 0..(n-1)
```

```
3          root = p
4           parent[p] = root
5  done = 1
6  while(! done)
7       forall processor p in 0..(n-1)
8              done = 1
9              if(list[p] < list[parent[p])]
10                   leftchild[[parent[p] = p // Write winner becomes the left child
11                   if(leftchild[[parent[p] != p) // Lost write. Retry with new parent.
12                       parent[p] = leftchild[[parent[p]
13                       done = 0
14              if(list[p] > list[parent[p])]
15                   righttchild[[parent[p] = p // Write winner becomes the right child
16                   if(leftchild[[parent[p] != p)
17                       parent[p] = rightchild[[parent[p]] // Lost write.
   Retry with new parent.
18                       done = 0
```

The expected time complexity of Listing 7.31 is $O(\log n)$, as it takes $O(1)$ time per iteration, with $n$ processors active. The number of iterations is one more than the number of levels in the quick-sort tree. One last iteration is required to ensure that no processor sets *done* to 0. Thus, the expected work complexity is $O(n \log n)$. Recall that concurrent writes incur a cost even in the modern shared-memory platforms. Nonetheless, the algorithm described above is illustrative of a general application of leader election (which is a form of the consensus problem).

## 7.10  Fixing Processor Count: Sample-Sort

As mentioned earlier, concurrent PRAM operations do not translate well to practical programming platforms. In a more practical setting, $P$ processors, each, hold $\frac{n}{P}$ of the initial list that is to be sorted. As described in Chapter 5, a good parallel design attempts to maximize the number of relatively independent tasks, each performed sequentially at one of the processors. In the context of merge-sort, one would locally sort the $\frac{n}{P}$ elements at each processor, and follow that up with a $P$-way merge of the $P$ sorted lists. Similarly, in the quick-sort variant, it may be useful to partition the initial list into $P$ sublists, with each sublist getting elements larger than the previous sublist. Then, each sublist can be sorted by one of the $P$ processors independently of others. Both of these methods are facilitated by sample-sort.

Sample-sort is based on the creation of a smaller list of size $O(P)$, which is a cover for the initial list, not unlike the pipelined merge-sort. The main idea is to be able to find $P$

disjoint ranges of values $\{R_i, i \in 0..(P-1)\}$ so that the upper limit of range $i$ is less than the lower limit of range $i+1$, and the total number of elements in each range is roughly equal. Once $\{R_i\}$ is known, it is straightforward to determine the range in which each element $list[l]$ lies. One sequential binary search through $\{R_i\}$ for each $list[l]$ suffices. Thus, in $O(\log P)$ time and $O(n \log P)$ work, we can compute the $P$ lists $r[j], j \in 0..(P-1)$. $r[j][k]$ is the range number that element $k$ at processor $j$ lies in. Ranges are also called *buckets*.

Next, we collect all elements in bucket $i$ at processor $i$. This is the partition step of quick-sort. Each bucket can then be independently sorted. Alternatively, we can first reorganize the $\frac{n}{P}$ elements at each processor bucket-wise, sort each bucket, and then send the elements of bucket $i$ to processor $i$. The so-collected $P$ sorted sublists at each processor are merged to complete the sorting. Both schemes have similar communication requirements, and both rely on creating ranges in a way that the work is equitably distributed among all processors. This range creating follows the method of sampling as given in Listing 7.32.

### Listing 7.32 Parallel Sampling

```
1 // Find well distributed samples of list
2 forall processor p in 0..(P-1)
3         locally sort list[p] containing n/P elements available at processor p
4         sublist[p] = {list[p][i*n/(P*P)]} i in 1..(P-1) // Take P-1 separators
5 slist = sort(subllist[p], p in 0..P-1) using P processors // All separators
6 range = {slist[i*(P-1)]} i in 1..(P-1) // P-1 evenly sampled splitters
```

Listing 7.32 assumes that the input *list* is equally distributed among $P$ processors; $list[p]$ comprises the set of elements at processor $p$. Each processor initially sorts its list to find $P-1$ well-separated samples. Call them *separators*. These $P*(P-1)$ total separators are again sorted, possibly using all $P$ processors, in order to next find $P-1$ globally well-separated *splitters*. These splitters are put in the list $range[0..(P-2)]$. Two consecutive elements define a range. We may assume $range[-1] = -\infty$ and $range[P-1] = +\infty$ as default splitters. Thus, there are $P$ ranges. We also let each range be open at its upper end to ensure that there is no overlap among consecutive ranges.

*range* is a $\frac{2n}{P}$ cover of *list*, meaning there are no more than $\frac{2n}{P}$ elements in *list* between any consecutive elements of *range*. Figure 7.18 explains this. Note that between any two consecutive elements of *range*, say $a$ and $b$, there are $P$ elements of *slist*, each of which is a separator selected in line 4 of Listing 7.32. Suppose $n_i$ of these separators come from processor $i$. These $n_i$ separators are necessarily consecutive separators of processor $i$, and any separator just before or just after these $n_i$ separators in $list[p]$ (see $x$ and $y$ in Figure 7.18) are not in the range $a..b$. Up to $\frac{n}{P^2} - 1$ nonseparators just after $x$ and up to $\frac{n}{P^2} - 1$ nonseparators just before $y$, could be in the range $a..b$. Counting them in, no more than $(n_i + 1)\frac{n}{P^2} - 1$ elements of $list[i]$ may lie in the range $a..b$. That means there are never more than

$$\sum_{i=0}^{P-1} \left[ (n_i + 1)\frac{n}{P^2} - 1 \right] = \frac{n}{P^2} \sum_{i=0}^{P-1} (n_i + 1) - P \le \frac{2n}{P}$$

total elements of $list$ in the range $a..b$, since $\sum n_i = P$.

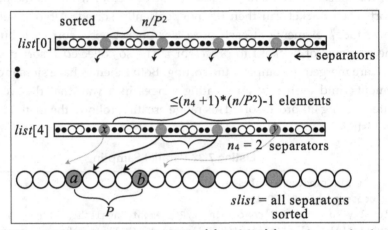

**Figure 7.18** Sampling a list. Assume $P = 5$. $list[0]$ and $list[4]$ are shown after local sorting. Filled circles stand for chosen separators, $P - 1$ per processor. $slist$ shows all separators of all processors. Again, filled circles in $slist$ show the chosen $P - 1$ splitters.

Local sequential sorting at line 3 requires $O(\frac{n}{P} \log \frac{n}{P})$ time and $O(n \log \frac{n}{P})$ work, with $P$ processors performing each sort. Forming $sublist$ takes $O(P)$ steps at each processor. The parallel sort of $P$-sorted lists, one at each processor, and each of size $P - 1$, appears to be similar to the original problem and may be performed recursively. However, this step is not the bottleneck for the entire algorithm if $P$ is small compared to $n$. Pair-wise merge, as in the merge-tree of Figure 7.10, suffices. The height of the tree is $\log P$. At level $i$, $\frac{P}{2^{i+1}}$ processors send $2^i(P - 1)$ elements each to their siblings, and those $\frac{P}{2^{i+1}}$ siblings merge two lists of size $2^i(P - 1)$ each.

The computation time at level $i$ is $O(2^i P)$ and work is $O(P^2)$. For the BSP model, $O(P^2)$ messages are sent at level $i$. Hence, the computational time complexity of merging at line 5 is $O(P^2)$, and work complexity is $O(P^2 \log P)$. $O(P^2 \log P)$ messages are sent. Sampling $slist$ into $range$ at one processor takes $O(P)$ time.

Finally, to complete sample-sort, the list $range$ is broadcast to all processors requiring $O(P^2)$ messages. After all the processors receive $range$, they form $P$ buckets each, taking $O(\frac{n}{P} \log P)$ time each. Then, each processor sends its elements of bucket $i$ (if any) to processor $i$. In the BSP model, upto $n$ elements are sent leading to a communication cost of

$O(n)$. After receiving its bucket from $P - 1$ other processors, processor $i$ merges them in time $O(\frac{n}{P})$, since no bucket has more than $\frac{2n}{P}$ elements.

Thus, the total time complexity is bounded by the initial local sorting: $O(\frac{n}{P} \log \frac{n}{P})$.

## 7.11  Exploiting Parallelism: Minimum Spanning Tree

We close this chapter with an example of discovering opportunities for parallelization in sequential graph algorithms. An oft-required task for weighted graphs is to find its skeleton – the minimum spanning tree. In this context, weighted graphs have weights associated with their edges. The spanning tree of a graph is a tree that includes all its vertices and a subset of its edges. The tree must be connected and without any cycles by definition. (A cycle is a path that does not repeat any vertex.) The weight of a spanning tree is the sum of the weights of all its edges. Many spanning trees may be formed in a graph. The minimum spanning tree (or MST) of a graph is one whose weight is no greater than the others. Figure 7.19 shows the edge-weights of an example graph with nodes numbered 0 to 7. The MST is shown in solid edges. Non-MST edges are in dashed lines.

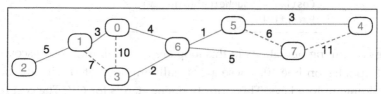

**Figure 7.19** Minimum spanning tree of a weighted graph

Prim's algorithm[6] is a greedy sequential algorithm to compute MST of a given weighted undirected graph $G$ with $n$ vertices and $m$ edges. It incrementally builds MST by adding one vertex and its connecting edge at a time, starting with an arbitrary vertex. At each step, it selects the edge with the least weight among those connecting any vertex $v \in$ MST constructed so far with any vertex $w \in G-$ MST.

In Listing 7.33, when vertex $minv$ is added to MST, its neighbor in the MST is specified by Parent[$minv$]. In other words, (Parent[$minv$], $minv$) is the connecting edge. The first vertex added to the MST has a null Parent. An auxiliary array Cost[$w$] maintains the weight of the least-weight edge connecting vertex $w$ to the evolving MST. Cost is not known in the beginning, and an overestimate is maintained. These estimates are lazily improved when a neighbor of $w$ is included in MST. When (Parent[$minv$], $minv$) is added to MST, the weight of that edge, which is Cost[$minv$], is smaller than the weights of all other edges connecting any vertex in MST with any vertex in $G-$ MST.

---

[6] Prim, "Shortest connection networks and some generalizations."

Inductively, if the current edges in MST are in the final **MST**, edge (Parent[*minv*], *minv*) must also be in the final **MST**. Otherwise, the path in the final **MST** from *minv* to Parent[*minv*] would have to go through another edge $(w, v)$ where $w \in G-$ MST and $v \in$ MST. However, then the cost of that final **MST** could be reduced by replacing edge $(w, v)$ with (Parent[*minv*], *minv*). That cannot be if **MST** is the minimum cost spanning tree.

**Listing 7.33** Prim's MST algorithm

```
1  for v in 1..n // n = Number of vertices in $G$. We are counting from 1 here.
2        Cost[v] = ∞
3        Parent[v] = null
4  MST = null
5  GV = {Vertices in G}
6  for i in 1..n
7        minv = vertex with min Cost[v] ∀ v ∈ GV // Break tie arbitrarily
8        GV = GV - minv
9        MST = MST ∪ (Parent[minv], minv)
10       for each vertex adjacent to minv
11            if Cost[v] > EdgeWeight(minv, v)
12                 Cost[v] = EdgeWeight(minv, v)
13                 Parent[v] = minv
```

The time-consuming operations in this loop are the minimum cost discovery on line 7 and the Cost updates on line 10. These are usually implemented with the help of a priority queue holding up to $n$ keys. This priority queue stands for $GV$. The cost reduction on line 12 requires up to $deg[minv]$ decrease-key operations in the priority queue, $deg[minv]$ being the degree of vertex *minv*. Of course, these $deg[minv]$ edges connected to *minv* are updated only once when *minv* is added to MST. Fibonacci Heaps[7] require $O(1)$ amortized time per decrease. Relaxed Heaps[8] can complete each decrease in $O(1)$ time in the worst case. Both require $O(\log n)$ time for each extraction of the minimum Cost vertex on line 7. This adds up to $O(m + n \log n)$ sequential time for the entire algorithm. Note that for dense graphs where, say, $m > n \log n$, this time is bounded by $O(m)$. For sparser graphs, $n \log n$ dominates.

Let's see how Prim's algorithm admits parallelism. The initialization on line 1 can be completed on EREW PRAM in $O(1)$ time and $O(n)$ work. The loop on line 6 is inherently sequential and requires $n$ iterations. Maybe, the priority queue operations can be parallelized: a single extract-min operation (line 7) and multiple decrease-key operations (line 10).

---

[7] Fredman and Tarjan, "Fibonacci heaps and their uses in improved network optimization algorithms."

[8] Driscoll et al., "Related heaps: An alternative to fibonacci heaps with applications to parallel computation."

One option is to subdivide the queue among many processors. Up to $n$ processors could be used, with processor $v$ associated with maintaining Cost$[v]$. Thus, the time to build this 'trivial' queue is $O(1)$ with $O(n)$ work. We can then resort to the minima-finding algorithms discussed in Section 7.3. That would require $O(\log n)$ time with $O(n)$ work on EREW PRAM to extract the minimum cost vertex. Decrease operations can be completed in $O(\log n)$ time with $O(n)$ work, with each processor $v$ updating Cost$[v]$ in parallel. Note that $O(\log n)$ time would be required for each processor to read the value of $minv$. If we allow CREW PRAM, the decrease operations would complete in $O(1)$ time. EdgeWeight$(minv, v)$ can be located in $O(1)$ time by processor $v$ with an adjacency matrix-based representation. This is demonstrated in Listing 7.34.

**Listing 7.34** Parallelized Prim's MST algorithm

```
1  forall v in 1..n // n = Number of vertices in G
2    Cost[v] = ∞
3    Parent[v] = null
4    inMST[v] = false
5  MST = null
6  GV = Build Priority Queue on Cost // Sequential time complexity is $O(n)$
7  for i in 1..n
8    minv = ExtractMin (GV) // Break tie arbitrarily
9    inMST[minv] = true
10   Append (Parent[minv], minv) to MST
11   forall v in 1..n
12     if inMST[v] == false && Cost[v] > EdgeWeight[minv][v] // EdgeWeight stored in
13                                          adjacency matrix
14       DecreaseKey(GV) for v from Cost[v] to EdgeWeight[minv][v]
15       Cost[v] = EdgeWeight[minv][v]
16       Parent[v] = minv
```

Listing 7.34 takes $O(n \log n)$ time, with line 8 taking $O(\log n)$ time per iteration, and $O(n^2)$ work, given that all $n$ processors are busy for all $n$ iterations. That is not efficient, particularly for sparse graphs. Maybe, a more specialized data structure can help: a parallel priority queue based on Binomial Heaps[9] allows $O(1)$-time $O(\log n)$-work extraction and decrease-key operations on CREW PRAM (see Section 7.11).

The total time on line 8 is then $O(n)$ with $O(n \log n)$ work. However, the inner loop on line 11 does not meet those bounds. We need to restructure this loop to focus on the actual number of edges incident on vertex $minv$, as in Listing 7.35. We assume that array $adj[v]$ (of size $deg[v]$) stores the identifier of every vertex $w$ adjacent to vertex $v$. Similarly, EdgeWeight$[v][j]$ stores the weight of edge $(v, adj[v][j])$.

[9] Brodal, "Priority queues on parallel machines."

**Listing 7.35** Restructuring the Cost update loop at line 11 of Listing 7.34 Prim's MST algorithm with Parallel Priority Queue

```
1   for j in 1..deg[minv]
2       v = adj[minv][j]
3       if inMST[v] == false && Cost[v] > EdgeWeight[minv][j]
4           DecreaseKey(GV) for v from Cost[v] to EdgeWeight[minv][j]
5           Cost[v] = EdgeWeight[minv][j]
6           Parent[v] = minv
```

The total number of decrease-key operations now is $O(m)$, leading to the total time $O(m+n)$ and work $O((m+n)\log n)$. This is a minor improvement over sequential time for sparse graphs. It is worth noting that other graph algorithms, e.g., Dijkstra's shortest path algorithm[10], also benefit from parallel priority queue operations similarly. That is left as an exercise. We discuss Priority Queues next.

## Parallel Priority Queue

*Binomial trees* of rank $r$ are defined recursively as follows:

1.  Binomial tree of rank 0 is a single node. Call it $B_0$.

2.  Binomial tree of rank $r$, $B_r$, is formed by two Binomial trees of rank $r-1$, $B1_{r-1}$ and $B2_{r-1}$ by making the root of one, say $B1$, a child of the other, $B2$. For example, in Figure 7.20(c), $B_2$ is constructed by making the root of $B2_1$ the second child of the root of $B1_1$.

In general, the children of the root of $B_r$ are respectively themselves roots of $B_0$, $B_1$, .. $B_{r-1}$, as seen in Figure 7.20(d). A simple induction on rank shows that a Binomial tree of rank $r$ has $2^r$ nodes and depth $r$. A Binomial heap stores keys at all nodes with the constraint that the key at every node is smaller (or larger for max-Heap) than the keys at its children. The parallel priority queue $Q$ is represented as a forest of Binomial heaps with the constraint that there are between 1 and 3 binomial heaps of every rank $r$, $r \leq Q_r$, the rank of the priority queue. In particular, let $n_i(Q)$ be the number of trees with rank $i$ in $Q$. $n_i(Q) = \{1,2,3\}$ for $i = 0..Q_r$. This ensures the $Q_r \leq (1+\log n)$ if $n$ items are stored in the queue. We associate the rank of a Binomial heap also with its root, meaning the root of a rank $r$ heap has rank $r$. Also, among a given set of nodes, the one with the minimum key is called the minimum node in short. The forest $Q$ has the following ordering property on the key values at its nodes.

---

[10] Dijkstra, "A note on two problems in connexion with graphs."

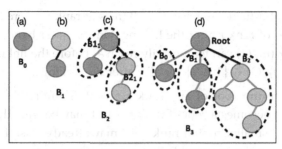

**Figure 7.20** Examples of Binomial trees of rank 0 to rank 4 from left to right

*Minimum Root*: The minimum root of rank $r$ in $Q$ is smaller than all roots of rank $r' \geq r$.

By this property, the minimum key of the queue is always at the minimum root among the roots of rank 0. For simplicity, we assume that the key values are unique, meaning all ties are broken. Let $Q.root[i]$ be the list of roots with rank $i$. Further, let node.child$[i]$ denote the $i^{th}$ child of any node. We refer to the key at a node by node.key. Two operations *Link* and *Unlink* are defined, which help maintain the heap property using multiple processors.

*Link*$(h1, h2)$ links the root $h2$ of heap $H2_r$ as a child of $h1$, the root of another heap $H1_r$. $H1_r$ and $H2_r$ are both of rank $r$. For the heap order property, $h1.key < h2.key$ for this operation. This forms a new heap of rank $r+1$ with root $h$. This linking is an $O(1)$-time operation by a single processor assuming $h2$ can be appended to $h1.child$ in $O(1)$ time. In addition, roots $h1$ and $h2$ must be removed from $Q.root[r]$ and $h$ appended to $Q.root[r+1]$. This can be accomplished by, say, using a linked list structure for *root* and *child*. (In principle, this requires $O(1)$-time memory allocation. This can be handled by allocating $P$ nodes per invocation of *Link* when using $P$ processors.)

*Unlink* is the inverse of *Link*. *Unlink*$(r)$ separates $H_{r+1}$, a heap of rank $r+1$ into two heaps of rank $r$ each. This is accomplished by nullifying the last child $h1$ of root $h$ of $H_{r+1}$. After this, $h$ is removed from $Q.roots[r+1]$, and $h$ and $h1$ are both added to $Q.roots[r]$. Again *Unlink*$(h)$ takes one processor $O(1)$ time.

The following conditions allow a set of parallel *Link* and *Unlink* operations to maintain the Priority queue properties.

1. One linking is done for the heaps of each rank, except the minimum root of any rank $r$ never participates in *Link*. This means that linking is only carried out if at least 3 roots of rank $r$ exist. This ensures that the Minimum Root Property is not perturbed by *Link*.

2. Condition 1 also means that at most one pair of nodes of rank $r$ may be linked together. If this holds for all ranks, up to two trees of each rank $r$ may be removed by linking, and at most one tree of rank $r$ may be added (when two rank $r-1$ trees are linked).

This means that if there are fewer than 3 trees of rank $r$ before the linkings, there can be at most 3 trees of rank $r$ after the linking. On the other hand, if there are more than 2 trees of rank $r$ ($n_r(Q)$ can temporarily reach 4) before the linkings, $n_r(Q)$ reduces by at least 1. Thus, $n_r(Q) \in \{1,2,3\}$ for all $r$ after the linkings.

3. Only the minimum root of any rank $r, r > 0$, is unlinked. After the unliking, that minimum root becomes a root of rank $r - 1$. It may become the new minimum root of rank $r - 1$, or a smaller root of rank $r - 1$ may already exist. Either way, the Minimum Root property continues to hold.

4. Condition 3 also means that a root at each rank is unlinked. This removes one root of rank $r$, but adds two roots of rank $r$, which were unlinked from the erstwhile minimum root of rank $r + 1$, unless $r$ was the maximum rank present in the priority queue. In that case, the maximum rank reduces by 1. Thus, the net increase in $n_r(Q)$ is 1 for $Q_r > r > 0$. Since the roots of rank 0 cannot be unlinked, $n_0(Q)$ increases by 2 after the unlinkings.

The parallel linking and unlinking are specified in Listing 7.36 and 7.37.

#### Listing 7.36 Parallel Link

```
forall r in 0..⌊1+log n⌋ - 2
  if(Q.root[r].size >= 3)
      (max, nextmax) = Two largest roots of rank r
    L = Link(Q.root[r][max], Q.root[r][nextmax])
    Remove(Q.root[r], max)
    Remove(Q.root[r], nextmax)
    Add(Q.root[r+1], L)
```

#### Listing 7.37 Parallel Unlink

```
forall r in 1..⌊1+log n⌋ - 1
  if(Q.root[r].size >= 1)
      min = Smallest roots of rank r
    (L1, L2) = Unink(Q.root[r][min])
    Remove(Q.root[r], min)
    Add(Q.root[r-1], L1)
    Add(Q.root[r-1], L2)
```

To insert an element to $Q$, a new singleton node $e$ is created with the element, and $e$ is inserted to $Q.root[0]$ and Parallel Link of Listing 7.36 is invoked on $Q$. The minimum element is always listed in $Q.root[0]$ (which can be kept sorted by the key). To remove the node with the minimum element, call it $Q.root[0][min]$, we simply remove that node from $Q.root[0]$. However, this may violate the Minimum Root property. The erstwhile second smallest root need not be in a rank 0 tree. In that case, the minimum root at rank 1 must be the new smallest, as it is guaranteed to be smaller than the smallest roots at higher ranks. One invocation of Parallel Unlink of Listing 7.37 can bring the new minima to rank 0. This can lead to 4 roots of rank 0, however. One invocation of Parallel Link (Listing 7.36) brings it down to 2 finally.

## MST with Parallel Priority Queue

Although it is possible to also decrease keys in $O(1)$ time using a pipelined version of *Link* and *Unlink*[11], for MST computation, it is sufficient to simply insert the new $Cost[v]$. This allows multiple entries for $v$ to co-exist, but the new cost is always lower, and it will be extracted first. On the other hand, those stale larger key values could be extracted later. We can use the $inMST[v]$ marker to discard such extraction, however. Since at most $m$ edges exist in the graph, up to $m$ entries may now exist in the priority queue, and up to $m$ extractions could occur on line 1 of Listing 7.34 (see Listing 7.38). That amounts to $O(m)$ total time to compute MST with $(m \log m)$ work. Note that $\log m$ is $O(\log n)$. As a result, the total work remains $O(m \log n)$. We assume $m \geq n - 1$. Otherwise, a spanning tree of $G$ does not exist.

**Listing 7.38** Parallelized Prim's MST algorithm with Parallel Priority Queue

```
1  forall v in 1..n // n = Number of vertices in G
2       Cost[v] = ∞
3       Parent[v] = null
4       inMST[v] = false
5  MST = null
6  GV = Build Priority Queue on Cost
7  for i in 1..n
8       repeat
9            minv = ExtractMin (GV) // Break tie arbitrarily
10      until inMST[minv] is false
11      inMST[minv] = true
12      Append (Parent[minv], minv) to MST
13      forall v in 1..degree[minv]
14           if inMST[v] == false && Cost[v] > EdgeWeight[minv][v]
15                Cost[v] = EdgeWeight[minv][v]
16                Parent[v] = minv
17                Insert(GV, (v , Cost[v]))
```

A shortcoming of all variants of the Prim's algorithm demonstrated above is the sequential loop (line 6 of Listing 7.33). This can only be addressed by an entirely different

---

[11] Brodal, "Priority queues on parallel machines."

structure. For example, Sollin's algorithm begins with each vertex of $G$ as an isolated tree. It merges these trees (not unlike the connected components algorithm of Section 7.6) by including the minimum-weight edge going out of each tree, progressively building larger trees. This affords an opportunity for multiple parallel mergers. Indeed, the number of trees remaining after each iteration is at most half of the number before the iteration. This is explored in Exercise 7.21.

## 7.12 Summary

This chapter presents several techniques useful for developing parallel algorithms. A model like PRAM often helps simplify thinking about the algorithm. Nonetheless, we need to evaluate the algorithms also in the context of practical architecture. For most shared-memory machines, CREW PRAM works well. Arbitrary-CRCW PRAM has some overhead but still works. On the other hand, only EREW PRAM is likely to translate well to message passing machines. For this environment, the BSP model provides avenues for a more careful accounting of overheads.

In either case, while designing parallel algorithms, we can either think in terms of the total number of operations required or the number of processors required. They are equivalent formulations of work complexity as a function of the problem size $n$. Hence, it is useful to think of the number of processors $p$ also as a parameter. The time taken by $p$ processors on the problem with size $n$ then becomes the way to measure complexity.

The task of designing an efficient algorithm often amounts to finding which sequential dependencies to break. This could be accomplished *e.g.*, by repeating a computation or deferring some computation, allowing them to proceed concurrently. Deferring works well in case the partial results of the originally dependent computation can be later retrofitted with the late-arriving results of that originally preceding computation, now turned concurrent.

Divide and conquer is among the most pervasive paradigms for parallel algorithm design, just as it is for sequential algorithm design. Division into two sub-problems at a time is quite standard in the sequential domain. That is often valuable in parallel algorithms as well and manifests as a binary computation tree. However, digging a bit deeper into the work-scheduling principle, subdivision into more than two problems at a time is useful in the parallel domain. Furthermore, in parallel algorithms, it may not always pay to carry out the recursion all the way to the top of the recursion tree, where increasingly fewer processors are employed. Nonetheless, if the total work remaining at the top of the tree is small, it matters little. Indeed, we can exploit that fact by using a less work-efficient and more time-efficient algorithm at the top levels.

Accelerated cascading is a powerful design pattern for parallel algorithms. It allows us to combine a divide and conquer solution with low time complexity but high work complexity with one that has a higher time complexity and a lower work complexity. Sometimes, the lower time complexity is obtained by subdividing the problem much more aggressively than into two each time. For example, if we subdivide a problem of size $n$ into $O(\sqrt{n})$ each time, the height of the tree shrinks to doubly-log in $n$: $O(\log \log n)$. If we subdivide into two (or a fixed number) at a time, the height is $O(\log n)$. However, the shrinkage in height can come at the cost of work complexity. By using the slower algorithm at the lower levels of the tree, we can quickly reduce the problem size. Employing the higher-work complexity algorithm on the smaller problems then adds up to lower total work.

Pointer jumping is another handy tool for graph and list traversal, where multiple processors can proceed with multiple traversals in parallel, exploiting each other's traversals. Pipelining is a useful tool when an algorithm is divisible into parts that need to be performed in sequence by a series of data items. Inserting multiple items into a tree is a good example. Many graph algorithms are based on processing edges or vertices in a certain order. This order can vary dynamically and can be updated each time the next vertex or edge is selected. Minimum spanning tree computation is an example. Parallel operation of priority queues can be a useful tool in such situations. The textbook by Jájá[12] is a good source for a more extensive study of parallel algorithms.

# Exercise

7.1. Give an $O(1)$ EREW PRAM algorithm to find the index of the single 1 in $BITS$, a list of $n$ bits. There is at most one 1 in $BITS$. If no 1 exists in $BITS$, the output must be $n$.

7.2. Analyze the time and work complexity of the recursive dependency-breaking parallel algorithm to compute the prefix-sum introduced as Method 1 in Section 7.1.

7.3. Prove that the algorithm in Listing 7.5 computes the prefix sum. Analyze its time and work complexity.

7.4. Modify the algorithm in Listing 7.7 computes the exclusive prefix sum. (Try not to first compute the prefix-sum before computing the exclusive sum from it).

7.5. Re-pose all the three methods for parallel prefix-sum computation discussed in Section 7.1 under the BSP model. Analyze their time and work complexity, and compare their performance.

7.6. Devise and algorithm to compute segmented prefix-sum $S$ of array $D$, where the segment markers are given in an array $F$, as shown below:

[12] Jájá, *Introduction to Parallel Algorithms*.

| 0 | 0 | 1 | 0 | 0 | 0 | 1 | 1 | .. | | | | $F$ |
| 2 | 4 | 1 | 0 | 3 | 5 | 2 | 1 | .. | | | | $D$ |
| 2 | 6 | 7 | 0 | 3 | 8 | 10 | 1 | .. | | | | $S$ |

Segment begins at index where $F$ does not have a 0 to its immediate left, and continues until a non-0 is discovered. We say a non-existent value like $F[-1]$ is non-0. Prefix-sum is computed for each segment.

7.7. Modify the segmented prefix-sum algorithm of Exerciseex:segscan to compute segmented prefix-minima $M$, given $D$ and $S$. $M[i]$ is the minimum element $D[j]$ among all $j < i$ within the segment of $i$.

7.8. Efficiently Compute the polynomial

$$\sum_{i=0}^{n} D[i]x^i,$$

given an array $D$, the integer $n$, and a real number $x$.

7.9. Given a list $BIT$ of $n$ 1-bit values, find the lowest such index $i$ that $B[i] = 1$. If no bit is 1, the answer is $n$. Find an $O(\log n)$ time algorithm with $O(n)$ work for EREW PRAM. Find an $O(1)$ time and $O(n)$ work algorithm for common-CRCW PRAM. (Hint: Subdivide $BIT$ into blocks of $\sqrt{n}$.)

7.10. Given a list $INT$ of $n$ integers, compute list $ANSV$ such that $ANSV[i]$ stores the value $INT[j]$ found at the largest index $j$ where $INT[j] < INT[i]$ and $j < i$. If no such $j$ exists, the answer is $n$. Find an $O(1)$ time algorithm with $O(n^2)$ work to compute ANSV on Common-CRCW PRAM. (Hint: Use Exercise 7.9.) Find an $O(\log n)$ time algorithm with $O(n)$ work to compute ANSV for EREW PRAM.

7.11. Compute Prefix-minima $M$ given input integer list $D$ with $n$ elements ($M[i]$ as the minimum of all $D[j]$ among $j < i$) in $O(\log \log n)$ time using $O(n \log \log n)$ work on Common-CRCW PRAM. (Hint: Use Exercise 7.10 to devise accelerated cascading.)

7.12. Recall Merge Method 1 in Section 7.2. There we subdivided the problem of merging two sorted lists into two unequal subproblems by finding the rank of the middle element of the larger list in the other list. This may not subdivide the smaller list equally. What if we also locate the middle element of the second list in the larger list. This will lead to three merger sub-problems none of them with more than half the elements from either list. Does that lead to an improved performance in time and work? Analyze.

7.13. Given a connected undirected graph $G$ with $n$ vertices and a list of $m$ edges $E$, where $i^{th}$ edge $E[i]$ is a pair of integers $(u, v), u < n, v < n$ indicating that vertex number $u$ and vertex number $v$ have an edge between them. Given $P$ PRAM processors, compute the list $RANK$ such that $RANK[j]$ is the level of vertex number $i$ in breadth-first search of $G$ starting at vertex 0. You may use any PRAM model.

7.14. Consider mapping the Quicksort partitioning algorithm on $P$ message passing processors. Revise the algorithm discussed in Section 7.9 to account for the given $P$ and provide the time complexity under the BSP model.

7.15. Reformulate the Sample sort algorithm in Section 7.10 for a CREW PRAM and analyze its time and work complexity.

7.16. A parallel strategy for sorting is to focus on finding the rank of each element. This is also called enumeration sort. With $n^2$ comparisons, ranks of each of $n$ element can be determined. Of course, we still need to find the rank of an element after comparing it to $n - 1$ other elements. How quickly can you enumeration-sort $n$ elements on

   (a) CREW PRAM

   (b) EREW PRAM

   Provide the time and work complexities.

7.17. The selection problem is to find the $k^{th}$ smallest element in a list $List$ of $n$ unsorted elements. Devise a parallel selection algorithm taking $O(\log^2 n)$ time and $O(n)$ work on CREW PRAM. (Hint: Consider recursively reducing the problem of selecting from $n_1$ unordered items to a problem of selecting from no more than $\frac{3n_1}{4}$ items in $\log n_1$ time with $O(n_1)$ work.)

7.18. Assume a sorting algorithm that runs in O(log n) time with O(n log n) work on CREW PRAM. Combine this sorting algorithm with the selection algorithm in Exercise 7.17 to accomplish parallel selection in $O(\log \log n)$ time with $O(n)$ work.

7.19. Consider the first algorithm in Section 7.6. Modify the algorithm to produce labels such that those labels double as the component number. All components must be sequentially numbered, but in any arbitrary order. Is there any change to the work complexity of the connected components algorithm due to this additional requirement?

7.20. Consider the CREW-PRAM minimum spanning tree algorithm described in Section 3.3. What changes could make it work on EREW-PRAM? What is the resulting time and work complexity?

7.21. Provide a CREW-PRAM algorithm with $O(\log^2 n)$ time and $O(n^2)$ work complexities to compute the minimum spanning tree of a graph with $n$ vertices. (Hint: Start with many small trees and merge them until a single tree remains.)

7.22. Provide an algorithm to compute the shortest path between two vertices $v_1$ and $v_2$ in an undirected weighted graph on EREW and CREW PRAM, respectively.

# Bibliography

Adve, S. V. and K. Gharachorloo, "Shared memory consistency models: A tutorial," *Computer*, 29, no. 12 (1996), 66–76, DOI: https://doi.org/10.1109/2.546611.

Adve, Vikram and Rizos Sakellariou, "Application representations for multiparadigm performance modeling of large-scale parallel scientific codes," *International Journal of High Performance Computing Applications*, 14, no. 4 (2000), 304–16.

Aggarwal, Alok, Ashok K. Chandra and Marc Snir, "Communication complexity of prams," *Theoretical Computer Science*, 71, no. 1 (1990), 3–28, ISSN 0304-3975.

Aggarwal, Alok, Ashok K. Chandra and Marc Snir, "Hierarchical memory with block transfer," in *Proceedings of the 28th Annual Symposium on Foundations of Computer Science*, SFCS '87 (Los Alamitos, CA: IEEE Computer Society, 1987), pp. 204–16, ISBN 0-818608-07-2.

Agrawal, D. and A. El Abbadi, "An efficient and fault-tolerant solution for distributed mutual exclusion," *ACM Transactions on Computer Systems*, 9, no. 1 (1991), 1–20.

Amdahl, Gene M., "Validity of the single processor approach to achieving large scale computing capabilities," in *Proceedings of the April 18-20, 1967, Spring Joint Computer Conference*, AFIPS '67 (Spring) (New York, NY: Association for Computing Machinery, 1967), pp. 483–5, ISBN 978-1-450378-95-6.

Apache Software Foundation, "Hadoop project" (2020), URL http://hadoop.apache.org.

Atchley, Scott, David Dillow, Galen Shipman, Patrick Geoffray, Jeffrey M. Squyres, George Bosilca and Ronald Minnich, "The common communication interface (cci)," in *2011 IEEE 19th Annual Symposium on High Performance Interconnects* (2011), pp. 51–60, DOI: https://doi.org/10.1109/HOTI.2011.17.

Benes, V. E., *Mathematical Theory of Connecting Networks and Telephone Traffic* (New York and London: Academic Press, 1965).

Beri, T., S. Bansal and S. Kumar, "The unicorn runtime: Efficient distributed shared memory programming for hybrid cpu-gpu clusters," *IEEE Transactions on Parallel and Distributed Systems*, 28, no. 5 (2017), 1518–34.

Bezanson, Jeff, Alan Edelman, Stefan Karpinski and Viral B. Shah, "Julia: A fresh approach to numerical computing," *SIAM Review*, 59, no. 1 (2017), 65–98, DOI: https://doi.org/10.1137/141000671.

Bichot, Charles-Edmond and Patrick Siarry, *Graph Partitioning: Optimisation and Applications* (Hoboken, NJ: Wiley, 2011), ISBN 978-1-848212-33-6.

Brodal, Gerth Stølting, "Priority queues on parallel machines," *Parallel Computing*, 25, no. 8 (1999), 987–1011.

Brodal, Gerth Stølting, Jesper Larsson Träff, and Christos D. Zaroliagis, "A parallel priority queue with constant time operations," *Journal of Parallel and Distributed Computing*, 49, no. 1 (February 1998), 4–21.

Burke, Kyle, "Chapel: A versatile language for teaching parallel programming: Conference workshop," *Journal of Computing Sciences in Colleges*, 30, no. 6 (June 2015), 16, ISSN 1937-4771.

Chamberlain, B. L., D. Callahan and H. P. Zima, "Parallel programmability and the chapel language," *International Journal of High Performance Computing Applications*, 21, no. 3 (August 2007), 291–312, ISSN 1094-3420.

Chapel, "The chapel parallel programming language" (2019), URL https://chapel-lang.org/.

Charles, Philippe, Christian Grothoff, Vijay Saraswat, Christopher Donawa, Allan Kielstra, Kemal Ebcioglu, Christoph von Praun and Vivek Sarkar, "X10: An object-oriented approach to non-uniform cluster computing," in *Proceedings of the 20th Annual ACM SIGPLAN Conference on Object-Oriented Programming, Systems, Languages, and Applications*, OOPSLA '05 (New York, NY: Association for Computing Machinery, 2005), pp. 519–38.

Chlebus, Bogdan S., Krzysztof Diks, Torben Hagerup and Tomasz Radzik, "New simulations between crcw prams," in J. Csirik, J. Demetrovics and F. Gécseg (eds.), *Fundamentals of Computation Theory* (Berlin, Heidelberg: Springer, 1989), pp. 95–104, ISBN 978-3-540481-80-5.

Cho, Sangyeun and Rami Melhem, "On the interplay of parallelization, program performance, and energy consumption," *IEEE Transactions on Parallel and Distributed Systems*, 21 (April 2010), 342–53.

Clos, Charles, "A study of non-blocking switching networks," Technical Report 2, Bell Labs (1953).

Cole, R. and O. Zajicek, "The expected advantage of asynchrony," *Journal of Computer and System Sciences*, 51, no. 2 (October 1995), 286–300, ISSN 0022-0000.

Cole, Richard, "Parallel merge sort," *SIAM Journal on Computing*, 17, no. 4 (August 1988), 770–85, ISSN 0097-5397.

Cormen, Thomas H., Charles E. Leiserson, Ronald L. Rivest and Clifford Stein, *Introduction to Algorithms* (Cambridge, MA: MIT Press, 1990).

CUDA Development Team, "CUDA toolkit documentation" (2020), URL https://docs.nvidia.com/cuda/.

Culler, David, Richard Karp, David Patterson, Abhijit Sahay, Klaus Erik Schauser, Eunice Santos, Ramesh Subramonian and Thorsten von Eicken, "Logp: Towards a realistic model of parallel computation," in *Proceedings of the Fourth ACM SIGPLAN Symposium on Principles and Practice of Parallel Programming*, PPOPP '93 (New York, NY: Association for Computing Machinery, 1993), pp. 1–12, ISBN 0-897915-89-5.

Dehne, Frank, Andreas Fabri and Andrew Rau-Chaplin, "Scalable parallel geometric algorithms for coarse grained multicomputers," in *Proceedings of the Ninth Annual Symposium on Computational Geometry*, SCG '93 (New York, NY: Association for Computing Machinery, 1993), pp. 298–307, ISBN 0-897915-82-8.

Dijkstra, E. W., "A note on two problems in connexion with graphs," *Numerische Mathematik*, 1 (1959), 269–271.

Driscoll, James R., Harold N. Gabow, Ruth Shrairman, and Robert E. Tarjan, "Relaxed heaps: An alternative to fibonacci heaps with applications to parallel computation," *Communications of the ACM*, 31, no. 11 (November 1988), 1343–54.

Duato, José, Sudhakar Yalamanchili and Lionel Ni, *Interconnection Networks: An Engineering Approach* (San Francisco, CA: Morgan Kaufmann, 2003).

Eager, D. L., J. Zahorjan and E. D. Lozowska, "Speedup versus efficiency in parallel systems," *IEEE Transactions on Computers*, 38, no. 3 (March 1989), 408–23, ISSN 0018-9340.

Egwutuoha, Ifeanyi P., David Levy, Bran Selic and Shiping Chen, "A survey of fault tolerance mechanisms and checkpoint/restart implementations for high performance computing systems," *Journal of Supercomputing*, 65, no. 3 (2013), 1302–26.

El-Ghazawi, Tarek and Lauren Smith, "UPC: Unified parallel C," in *Proceedings of the 2006 ACM/IEEE Conference on Supercomputing*, SC '06 (New York, NY: Association for Computing Machinery, 2006), p. 27–es, ISBN 0-769527-00-0.

El-Rewini, Hesham, Theodore G. Lewis and Hesham H. Ali, *Task Scheduling in Parallel and Distributed Systems* (Prentice-Hall, Inc., 1994), ISBN 0-130992-35-6.

Elnozahy, E. N. (Mootaz), L. Alvisi, Y. M. Wang and D. B. Johnson, "A survey of rollback – recovery protocols in message-passing systems," *ACM Computing Surveys*, 34, no. 3 (2002), 375–408.

Fischer, Michael J., Nancy A. Lynch and Michael S. Paterson, "Impossibility of distributed consensus with one faulty process," *Journal of ACM*, 32, no. 2 (April 1985), 374–82, ISSN 0004-5411.

Flatt, Horace P. and Ken Kennedy, "Performance of parallel processors," *Parallel Computing*, 12, no. 1 (1989), 1–20, ISSN 0167-8191.

Flynn, M. J., "Some computer organizations and their effectiveness," *IEEE Transactions on Computers*, C-21, no. 9 (1972), 948–60.

Fortune, Steven and James Wyllie, "Parallelism in random access machines," in *Proceedings of the Tenth Annual ACM Symposium on Theory of Computing*, STOC '78 (New York, NY: Association for Computing Machinery, 1978), pp. 114–8, ISBN 978-1-450374-37-8.

Foster, Ian, *Designing and Building Parallel Programs: Concepts and Tools for Parallel Software Engineering* (Reading, MA: Addison-Wesley, 1995), ISBN 0-201575-94-9 URL https://www.mcs.anl.gov/~itf/dbpp/text/book.html.

Fredman, Michael L. and Robert Endre Tarjan, "Fibonacci heaps and their uses in improved network optimization algorithms," *Journal of ACM*, 34, no. 3 (July 1987), 596–615.

Gibbons, P. B., "A more practical pram model," in *Proceedings of the First Annual ACM Symposium on Parallel Algorithms and Architectures*, SPAA '89 (New York, NY: Association for Computing Machinery, 1989), pp. 158–68, ISBN 0-897913-23-X.

Gropp, William, Ewing Lusk and Anthony Skjellum, *Using MPI: Portable Parallel Programming with the Message-Passing Interface* (Cambridge, MA: MIT Press, 2014), ISBN 978-0-262256-28-5.

Gropp, William, Ewing Lusk, Nathan Doss and Anthony Skjellum, "A high-performance, portable implementation of the mpi message passing interface standard," *Parallel Computing*, 22, no. 6 (1996), 789–828, ISSN 0167-8191, DOI: https://doi.org/10.1016/0167-8191(96)00024-5.

Gustafson, John L., "Reevaluating amdahl's law," *Communication of the ACM*, 31, no. 5 (May 1988), 532–3, ISSN 0001-0782.

Gustafson, John L., Gary R. Montry and Robert E. Benner, "Development of parallel methods for a $1024$-processor hypercube," *SIAM Journal on Scientific and Statistical Computing*, 9, no. 4 (1988), 609–38.

Hall, L. A. and D. B. Shmoys, "Approximation schemes for constrained scheduling problems," in *30th Annual Symposium on Foundations of Computer Science* (October 1989), pp. 134–9.

Hayashi, T., K. Nakano and S. Olariu, "Work-time optimal k-merge algorithms on the pram," *IEEE Transactions on Parallel and Distributed Systems*, 9, no. 3 (1998), 275–82.

Hennessy, John L. and David A. Patterson, *Computer Architecture: A Quantitative Approach* (Waltham, MA: Morgan Kaufman, 2017).

Herlihy, Maurice, "Wait-free synchronization," *ACM Transactions on Programming Languages and Systems*, 13 (1993), 124–49.

Herlihy, Maurice and Nir Shavit, *The Art of Multiprocessor Programming, Revised Reprint*, 1st ed. (San Francisco, CA: Morgan Kaufmann Publishers Inc., 2012), ISBN 978-0-123973-37-5.

Hoare, C. A. R., "Communicating sequential processes," *Communications of the ACM*, 21, no. 8 (1978), 666–77.

Hwang, Kai, *Computer Architecture and Parallel Processing* (New York, NY: McGraw Hill Education, 2017).

Jájá, Joseph, *Introduction to Parallel Algorithms* (Reading, MA: Pearson, 1992).

Jiang, Yichuan, "A survey of task allocation and load balancing in distributed systems," *IEEE Transactions on Parallel and Distributed Systems*, 27, no. 2 (2016), 585–99, DOI: https://doi.org/10.1109/TPDS.2015.2407900.

Johnson, Theodore, Timothy A. Davis and Steven M. Hadfield, "A concurrent dynamic task graph," *Parallel Computing*, 22, no. 2 (1996), 327–33, ISSN 0167-8191.

Karp, Alan H. and Horace P. Flatt, "Measuring parallel processor performance," *Communication of the ACM*, 33, no. 5 (May 1990), 539–43, ISSN 0001-0782.

Karypis, George and Vipin Kumar, "A fast and high quality multilevel scheme for partitioning irregular graphs," *SIAM Journal on Scientific Computing*, 20, no. 1 (December 1998), 359–92, ISSN 1064-8275.

Kirk, David B. and Wen mei W. Hwu, *Programming Massively Parallel Processors: A Hands-on Approach* (Waltham, MA: Morgan Kaufmann, 2010).

Kruskal, Joseph B., "On the shortest spanning subtree of a graph and the traveling salesman problem," *Proceedings of the American Mathematical Society*, 7, no. 1 (1956), 48–50.

Kuck, David J., "Parallel processing of ordinary programs," in Morris Rubinoff and Marshall C. Yovits (eds.), *Advances in Computers*, vol. 15 (New York, NY: Elsevier, 1976), pp. 119–79.

Kučera, Luděk, "Parallel computation and conflicts in memory access," *Information Processing Letters*, 14, no. 2 (1982), 93–6, ISSN 0020-0190.

Lam, Monica S. and Martin C. Rinard, "Coarse-grain parallel programming in jade," in *Proceedings of the Third ACM SIGPLAN Symposium on Principles and Practice of Parallel Programming*, PPOPP '91 (New York, NY: Association for Computing Machinery, 1991), pp. 94–105, ISBN 0-897913-90-6.

Lamport, L., "How to make a multiprocessor computer that correctly executes multiprocess programs," *IEEE Transactions on Computers*, 28, no. 9 (September 1979), 690–1, ISSN 0018-9340.

LeBlanc, Thomas J., Michael L. Scott and Christopher M. Brown, "Large-scale parallel programming: experience with bbn butterfly parallel processor," in *ACM SIGPLAN Symposium on Principles and Practice of Parallel Programming*, 1988.

Leighton, F. Thomson, *Introduction to Parallel Algorithms and Architectures: Arrays Trees Hypercubes* (San Mateo, CA: Morgan Kaufmann, 1992).

Ma, K., X. Li, W. Chen, C. Zhang and X. Wang, "GreenGPU: A holistic approach to energy efficiency in GPU-CPU heterogeneous architectures," in *2012 41st International Conference on Parallel Processing* (2012), pp. 48–57.

Mehlhorn, Kurt and Uzi Vishkin, "Randomized and deterministic simulations of PRAMS by parallel machines with restricted granularity of parallel memories," *Acta Informatica*, 21, no. 4 (November 1984), 339–74, ISSN 0001-5903.

Mittal, Sparsh, "A survey of architectural techniques for near-threshold computing," *ACM Journal on Emerging Technologies in Computing Systems*, 12, no. 4 (2015), 1–26.

Mosberger, David, "Memory consistency models," *SIGOPS Operating Systems Review*, 27, no. 1 (January 1993), 18–26, ISSN 0163-5980, DOI: https://doi.org/10.1145/160551.160553.

Nakamoto, S., "Bitcoin: A peer-to-peer electronic cash system" (2008), URL https://bitcoin.org/bitcoin.pdf.

Nieplocha, J., R. J. Harrison and R. J. Littlefield, "Global arrays: A portable 'shared-memory' programming model for distributed memory computers," in *Supercomputing '94: Proceedings of the 1994 ACM/IEEE Conference on Supercomputing* (1994), pp. 340–9.

O'brien, Kenneth, Ilia Pietri, Ravi Thouti Reddy, Alexey L. Lastovetsky and Rizos Sakellariou, "A survey of power and energy predictive models in hpc systems and applications," *ACM Computing Surveys*, 50, no. 3 (2017), 1–38.

OpenMP Architecture Review Board, "OpenMP Application Program Interface, Version 5.0" (July 2018), URL http://www.openmp.org.

Papadimitriou, Christos and Mihalis Yannakakis, "Towards an architecture-independent analysis of parallel algorithms," in *Proceedings of the Twentieth Annual ACM Symposium on Theory of Computing*, STOC '88 (New York, NY: Association for Computing Machinery, 1988), pp. 510–3, ISBN 0-897912-64-0.

Prim, R. C., "Shortest connection networks and some generalizations," *The Bell System Technical Journal*, 36, no. 6 (1957), 1389–401, DOI: https://doi.org/10.1002/j.1538-7305.1957.tb01515.x.

Prvulovic, M., Z. Zhang and J. Torrellas, "Revive: Cost-effective architectural support for rollback recovery in shared-memory multiprocessors," in *Proceedings 29th Annual International Symposium on Computer Architecture* (2002), pp. 111–22.

Radetzki, Martin, Chaochao Feng, Xueqian Zhao and Axel Jantsch, "Methods for fault tolerance in networks-on-chip," *ACM Computing Surveys*, 46, no. 1 (2013), 1–38.

Rocklin, Matthew, "Dask: Parallel computation with blocked algorithms and task scheduling," in Kathryn Huff and James Bergstra (eds.), *Proceedings of the 14th Python in Science Conference* (2015), pp. 130–6.

Sarangi, Smruti R., *Computer Organisation and Architecture* (McGraw Hill India, 2017).

Shiloach, Yossi and Uzi Vishkin, "An O(logn) parallel connectivity algorithm," *Journal of Algorithms*, 3, no. 1 (1982), 57–67, ISSN 0196-6774.

Squire, Jon S. and Sandra M. Palais, "Programming and design considerations of a highly parallel computer," in *Proceedings of the AFIPS Spring Joint Computer Conference* (May 1963).

Stone, H. S., "Parallel processing with the perfect shuffle," *IEEE Transactions on Computers*, C-20, no. 2 (1971), 153–61.

Stone, John E., David Gohara and Guochun Shi, "OpenCL: A parallel programming standard for heterogeneous computing systems," *Computing in Science Engineering*, 12, no. 3 (2010), 66–73, DOI: https://doi.org/10.1109/MCSE.2010.69.

Sun, X. H. and L. M. Ni, "Scalable problems and memory-bounded speedup," *Journal of Parallel and Distributed Computing*, 19, no. 1 (1993), 27–37, ISSN 0743-7315.

Tiskin, Alexandre, "The bulk-synchronous parallel random access machine," *Theoretical Computer Science*, 196, no. 1 (1998), 109–30, ISSN 0304-3975.

Ullman, J. and C. Papadimitriou, "A communication-time tradeoff," in *2013 IEEE 54th Annual Symposium on Foundations of Computer Science* (Los Alamitos, CA: IEEE Computer Society, october 1984), pp. 84–8.

Ullman, J. D., "NP-complete scheduling problems," *Journal of Computer and System Sciences*, 10, no. 3 (June 1975), 384–93, ISSN 0022-0000.

Valiant, Leslie G., "A bridging model for parallel computation," *Communications of the ACM*, 33, no. 8 (August 1990), 103–11.

Voss, Michael, Rafael Asenjo and James Reinders, *Pro TBB* (Apress, 2019), ISBN 978-1-484243-97-8.

White, Tom, *Hadoop: The Definitive Guide* (O'Reilly Media, Inc., 2009), ISBN 0-596521-97-9, 978-0-596521-97-4.

Wilt, Nicholas, *The CUDA Handbook: A Comprehensive Guide to GPU Programming* (Upper Saddle River, NJ: Addison-Wesley Professional, 2013).

Woodall, Tim, Galen Shipman, George Bosilca, Richard Graham, and Arthur Maccabe, "High performance RDMA protocols in HPC," *Proceedings of EuroPVM-MPI*, 9, (2006), 76–85.

Worley, Patrick H., "The effect of time constraints on scaled speedup," *SIAM Journal on Scientific and Statistical Computing*, 11, no. 5 (1990), 838–58.

Xu, Chengzhong and Francis C. Lau, *Load Balancing in Parallel Computers: Theory and Practice* (Boston, MA: Springer, 1997), ISBN 0-792398-19-X.

Yalamanchili, Sudhakar, "Interconnection networks," in David Padua (ed.), *Encyclopedia of Parallel Computing* (Boston, MA: Springer US, 2011), pp. 964–75, ISBN 978-0-387097-66-4.

# Index

Printed in the United States
by Baker & Taylor Publisher Services